THE STUDENT'S HANDBOOK

OF MODERN ENGLISH

W. A. GATHERER

Holmes McDougall   Edinburgh

© Holmes McDougall Ltd. 1985

Published by Holmes McDougall Ltd.,
Allander House, 137-141 Leith Walk, Edinburgh EH6 8NS

Printed by Clark Constable, Edinburgh, London, Melbourne

Cover design by Jim Cairns
Text illustration by Robert Britton

British Library Cataloguing in Publication Data

Gatherer, W. A.
    The Student's Handbook of Modern English. —
    (Self study series; 1)
    1. English language — Text-books
    for foreign speakers
    I. Title   II. Series
    428.2'4   PE1128

ISBN 0-7157-2352-9

CONTENTS

Contents

PREFACE

English is spoken throughout the world, and in most multilingual societies it has been adopted as the official language for law, administration, commerce and education. In nearly every country in the world, English is taught in schools as the major second language.

Although it is relatively easy to master the basics of English, it is difficult to learn how to speak and write it well. The grammar and syntax are both subtle and complicated, and there is an enormous vocabulary of more than half a million words. English contains a vast store of idioms, and because it is the native language of many large nations, its vocabulary is always increasing and changing.

This book offers the student an up-to-date guide to many aspects of English. It shows how words are built from their component parts, how words have come into English from other languages, and how new words are invented. It provides vocabularies of modern English used in computing, technology, science and in international business and law. It gives the most recent lists of abbreviations, colloquialisms, slang terms and idioms. It contains guidance on grammar, spelling and punctuation, on how modern English is pronounced, and on common errors made by students. The sections on general knowledge are intended to help students understand the content of books, journals and newspapers of the English-speaking world.

I hope that the book proves valuable to the students who use it, and that it provides them with much interest and with something of the love of the English language which I have felt throughout my life.

W. A. GATHERER

ACKNOWLEDGEMENTS

I wish to record my sincere thanks to the following:
My wife, Mrs Maimie Gatherer, for her help in preparing the text and manuscript;
Dick Shepherd for his invaluable assistance and advice during the compilation of the book; and Caroline Lawrence for her editorial guidance. W.A.G.

1 VOCABULARY

WORD PARTS

English words are made from **morphemes**, which are the smallest units of speech with any meaning or grammatical function. There are two kinds of morphemes: **roots** and **affixes**. Affixes which occur at the beginning of words are called **prefixes**, and affixes which occur at the end of words are called **suffixes**. The root of a word is the part which is left when you remove the affixes:

PREFIX	ROOT	SUFFIX
un	eat	able
dis	grace	ful
com	plain	
	small	est
ex	tend	

PREFIXES

Prefixes have come into modern English from Old English, French, Greek or Latin. Here are the common English prefixes:

PREFIX	ORIGIN	MEANING	EXAMPLES
a-	Greek	not	amoral, amorphous, atheist
a-, ad-	Latin	to	add, advance, affix
aer-	Greek	air	aerogram, aeroplane, aerosol
ambi-	Latin	both, two	ambidextrous, ambiguous, ambivalent
ante-	Latin	before	antecedent, antenatal, anteroom
anti-	Greek	against	anti-Communist, antidote, antiseptic
arch-	Greek	principal	archangel, archbishop, archenemy
auto-	Greek	self	autobiography, automatic, automobile
be- + verb	Old English	around, all over, thoroughly	bedeck, befriend, beside
bene-	Latin	well	benediction, benefactor, beneficial
bi-	Latin	twice	bicycle, bilateral, binary
bio-	Greek	life	biology, bionic, biosphere

PREFIX	ORIGIN	MEANING	EXAMPLES
cent-, centi-	Latin	hundred	centenary, centipede, century
co-, com-	Latin	with	coauthor, combine, cooperative
contra-, counter-	Latin	against	contradict, counteract, counter-productive
de-	Latin	reversal of something	decompose, decompression, defrost
dia-	Greek	through, across	diabetes, diagonal, dialogue
dis-	Latin	not	disable, disadvantage, dislike
em-, en-	Greek	to cover, surround with	embroil, encircle, encourage
equi-	Latin	equal	equidistant, equilateral, equinox
ex-	Latin	out, formerly	exhale, ex-president, extract
extra-	Latin	outside	extracurricular, extraordinary, extraterrestrial
fore-	Old English	before	forearm, forefather, foretell
geo-	Greek	earth	geography, geomorphology, geopolitics
hydro-	Greek	water	hydroelectric, hydrogen, hydrology
hyper-	Greek	above, excessive	hyperactive, hyperbole, hypertension
il-, im-, in-, ir-	Latin	not, in	illogical, immigrant, include, irresponsible
infra-	Latin	below	infra-red, infrasonic, infrastructure
inter-	Latin	between	intercede, intercom, interlude
intra-	Latin	within	intracollegiate, intramural, intravenous
macro-	Greek	large	macroclimate, macrocosm, macroeconomics
micro-	Greek	small	microbe, microcosm, microscope
mal-	Latin	bad	malefactor, malignant, malnutrition
mid-	Old English	middle	mid-career, middling, midterm
mis-	Old English	wrong	miscalculate, misinform, misplace
mono-	Greek	one	monocle, monopoly, monotone
multi-	Latin	much	multimillionaire, multiple, multiracial

PREFIX	ORIGIN	MEANING	EXAMPLES
neo-	Greek	new	neolithic, neologism, neophyte
non-	Latin	not	noncombatant, nonconformist, nonsense
ortho-	Greek	straight, correct	orthodox, orthography, orthopaedic
out-	English	surpassing	outdo, outdrive, outpace
over-	English	too much	overactive, overcrowded, overpaid
pan-	Greek	all	Pan-African, panchromatic, panorama
para-	Greek	along with	parable, paradox, parallel
peri-	Greek	around	perimeter, peripatetic, peritonitis
poly-	Greek	many	polygamy, polygon, polytechnic
post-	Latin	after	postgraduate, post-mortem, postscript
pre-	Latin	before	preamble, preconceived, prefix
pro-	Latin	forward, for	proceed, pro-government, pronoun
pseudo-	Greek	false	pseudo-classical, pseudo-Gothic, pseudonym
quasi-	Latin	half, almost	quasi-liberal, quasi-official, quasi-scientific
re-	Latin	back, again	realign, reconfirm, rekindle
retro-	Latin	backward	retroactive, retrograde, retrospect
semi-	Latin	partially, half	semicolon, semi-conscious, semi-invalid
sub-	Latin	under	subconscious, submarine, subway
super-	Latin	above, extra	superman, superpowers, supervisor
sym-, syn-	Greek	with	sympathy, synchronise, synonymous
tele-	Greek	at a distance	telepathy, telephone, telescope
trans-	Latin	across	transatlantic, trans-continental, transcribe
tri-	Latin	three	triangle, triennial, tripartite
ultra-	Latin	beyond	ultramarine, ultra-modern, ultrasonic
un-	Old English	not	unable, unattractive, unborn
uni-	Latin	one	uniform, unilateral, universe
vice-	Latin	instead of	vice-captain, vice-chairman, vice-president

SUFFIXES

A root may be followed by more than one **suffix**, each contributing to and extending the meaning:

accept + able + ness   fiction + al + ise

Suffixes clearly contribute to the meaning of words and it is worthwhile to know their origin and meaning:

SUFFIX	FUNCTION AND MEANING	EXAMPLES
-able, -ible	makes adjectives meaning able to, likely to, etc.	accountable, adaptable, eligible
-acy	makes nouns of quality or condition from adjectives	aristocracy, diplomacy, privacy
-age	makes nouns meaning collection or service	acreage, coinage, storage
-al	makes nouns and adjectives meaning of, pertaining to, connected with	accidental, appraisal, conjectural
-an, -ian	makes adjectives and nouns meaning of or from a country, group, doctrine	African, Indonesian, Utopian
-ance, -ence	makes nouns from adjectives and adverbs meaning state or condition	abundance, brilliance, dependence
-ant, -ent	makes nouns and adjectives meaning process or one who	absorbent, applicant, stimulant
-arian	makes adjectives and nouns meaning occupation, sect or one who believes in	antiquarian, authoritarian, grammarian
-ary	makes nouns meaning related to	dignitary, granary, monetary
-ate	makes adjectives from nouns meaning possessing or denotes a function	affectionate, foliate, magistrate
-ation	makes nouns meaning action, process of or the result of	accusation, authorisation, damnation
-cide	makes nouns meaning an act of killing	genocide, homicide, suicide
-dom	makes nouns meaning state of or rank	earldom, freedom, officialdom

SUFFIX	FUNCTION AND MEANING	EXAMPLES
-ed	makes adjectives meaning *having, resembling*, etc.	bare-legged, hard-headed, spectacled
-ee	makes nouns meaning *one who*	divorcee, escapee, trustee
-eer	makes nouns and verbs meaning *one who works with* or *one who makes*	auctioneer, electioneer, profiteer
-en	makes verbs from adjectives and nouns meaning *to make*	ashen, blacken, deafen
-er	makes nouns meaning *one who practises* or *one who lives in*	adviser, Berliner, commander
-ery, -ory, -ry	makes nouns meaning *a business, place, behaviour, art, trade*	brewery, discriminatory, lavatory, masonry, tapestry
-ese	makes nouns and adjectives meaning *inhabitant, language*, or *the style of a group or people*	Chinese, journalese, Portuguese
-esque	makes adjectives meaning *having the style of*	arabesque, picturesque, statuesque
-ess	makes nouns *feminine*	countess, goddess, heiress
-ette	makes nouns into *diminutives*	cigarette, launderette, novelette
-fold	makes adjectives meaning *having x parts*	hundredfold, manifold, tenfold
-ful	makes adjectives meaning *full of* or *having the character of*	awful, cupful, tearful
-hood	makes nouns meaning *the state of being*	boyhood, brotherhood, manhood
-ic	makes adjectives meaning *connected with*	alcoholic, Byronic, heroic
-ical	makes adjectives meaning *connected with*	biological, comical, historical
-ician	makes nouns meaning *one who is skilled in* or *engaged in*	beautician, musician, statistician
-ics	makes nouns denoting *an art, science* or *activity*	acoustics, athletics, mathematics
-ie, -y	makes nouns denoting *familiarity*, or forming *nicknames, diminutives*	Daddy, Geordie, piggy

SUFFIX	FUNCTION AND MEANING	EXAMPLES
-ify, -fy	makes verbs meaning *to cause, to be* or *become*	amplify, deify, intensify
-ine	makes adjectives meaning *like*	alpine, equine, feline
-ing	makes nouns and participles denoting *activity* or *state*	cooking, fishing, living
-ise, ize	makes verbs meaning *to make*	criticise, dramatise, fertilise
-ish	makes adjectives meaning *like* or *tending towards*	biggish, fortyish, girlish
-ism	makes nouns denoting *beliefs, act, process* or *characteristic*	criticism, fanaticism, fascism
-ist	makes nouns meaning *one who works with* or *one who practises*	botanist, psychiatrist, racist
-ite	makes nouns meaning *native of*, or *follower of*, and makes adjectives from *names*	dynamite, Hitlerite, Israelite
-ition	makes nouns meaning *doing something, ability* or *state*	abolition, demolition, position
-itious	makes adjectives meaning *state* or *quality*	ambitious, repetitious, surreptitious
-ity	makes nouns meaning *state* or *quality*	ability, charity, sanity
-ive	makes adjectives meaning *quality of*	attractive, creative, demonstrative
-less	makes adjectives meaning *free from, without*	colourless, lawless, senseless
-let	makes nouns meaning *little*, or *an ornament*	booklet, bracelet, piglet
-like	makes adjectives meaning *resembling*	gentlemanlike, lifelike, warlike
-ling	makes nouns meaning *young, little* or *a person from*	earthling, seedling, yearling
-logy	makes nouns meaning *a branch of science*	biology, geology, zoology
-ly	makes adverbs and adjectives meaning *state* or *quality*	cautiously, correctly, lovely
-ment	makes nouns meaning *the product of* or *the state of*	achievement, assessment, retirement

SUFFIX	FUNCTION AND MEANING	EXAMPLES
-most	makes adjectives *superlative*	furthermost, innermost, northernmost
-ness	makes nouns meaning *state* or *quality*	carelessness, coolness, happiness
-ous	makes adjectives denoting *quality*	adventurous, nervous, suspicious
-ship	makes nouns meaning *the quality of*	championship, kinship, membership
-some	makes adjectives meaning *tending to be,* and makes nouns meaning *a group consisting of*	handsome, quarrelsome, threesome
-ster	makes nouns meaning *one who makes* or *belongs to*	gangster, jokester, teamster
-ward, *-wards*	makes adverbs meaning *toward*	homeward, onward, upwards
-wise	makes adverbs meaning *in relation to*	clockwise, moneywise, otherwise

INFLECTIONS

The grammatical inflections of English **nouns** change words from:

1 **singular** to **plural**

		INFLECTION
book	books	*-s*
wolf	wolves	*-es*
baby	babies	*-ies*
child	children	*-en*
man	men	*-e-*
foot	feet	*-ee-*
stimulus	stimuli	*-i*
genus	genera	*-era*
larva	larvae	*-ae*
stratum	strata	*-a*
crisis	crises	*-es*
matrix	matrices	*-ces*
seraph	seraphim	*-im*

2 **common case** to **possessive case**

		INFLECTION
John	John's	*-'s*
boys	boys'	*-s'*
children	children's	*-'s*

The grammatical inflections of English **verbs** change words from:

1	**present tense**	**to**	**past tense**	INFLECTION
	act		acted	*-ed*
	live		lived	*-d*
	cry		cried	*-ied*

2	**root**	**to**	**participle**	INFLECTION
	rain		raining	*-ing*
	rain		(has) rained	*-ed*
	fall		(has) fallen	*-en*
	know		(has) known	*-n*
	build		(has) built	*-t*

3	**root**	**to**	**3rd person singular**	INFLECTION
	live		lives	*-s*
	cry		cries	*-ies*
	go		goes	*-es*

COMPOUNDS

A **compound** is a word formed by combining two or more words together to make a new meaning. Compounds can be written as:

solid (one word) – *motorway*
hyphenated – *double-decker*
open (two words) – *deep freeze.*

There are no safe rules for the choice between these three ways, and the same word may sometimes be written in different ways:

1   **noun + noun** (solid):
  airplane, airport, airspace, bedclothes, cliffhanger, flowchart, fibreglass, footman, grassroots, handbook, headline, leeway, motorway, oilrig, paperback, parkway, playgroup, viewpoint
  noun + noun (hyphenated)
  air-brake, anchor-man, armour-plate, ball-point, bed-sitter, box-office, catch-phrase, clock-face, flag-day, guinea-pig, half-term, head-room, jack-knife, life-style, number-plate, self-esteem, self-service, space-suit, table-napkin, test-tube, top-level
  noun + noun (open)
  air commodore, bank account, belly landing, booking office, card sharper, colour bar, colour code, contact lens, credit card, disc jockey, fly spray, fruit machine, ginger group, log book, spot check

possessive noun + noun
bridesmaid, tradesman, yachtsman

2 **adjective + noun** (solid)
*blacklist, blacksmith, clearway, greenhouse, hardware, lightweight,
redbrick, software*
adjective + noun (hyphenated)
*blue-collar, dead-end, double-decker, free-range, hard-cover,
hard-shoulder, high-level, high-rise, left-wing, long-term, right-wing,
second-class, white-collar*

3 **noun + adjective** (solid)
airtight, roadworthy, threadbare, timeworn
noun + adjective (hyphenated)
brand-new, duty-free, God-forsaken, jet-black, snow-white

4 **adverb + noun** (solid)
*afterthought, outsider, overdraft, overdrive, overkill, overnight, overseer,
overspill, overtime, underhand*
adverb + noun (hyphenated)
*after-life, in-law, in-tray, off-colour, off-the-cuff, off-the-peg,
off-the-record, out-tray, up-market*

5 **verb + adverb** (solid)
blowout, breakdown, breakthrough, dugout, feedback, kickoff, washout
verb + adverb (hyphenated)
*blast-off, check-in, check-out, count-down, cut-off, drop-out, fall-out,
go-ahead, lift-off, lock-out, print-out, rip-off, sit-in, slow-down, spin-off,
take-over, toss-up, walk-over, write-off, write-up*

6 **noun + verb** (solid)
brainwash, handpicked, lifesaving, manhunt
noun + verb (hyphenated)
*baby-sit, bottle-feed, head-count, man-made, money-saving,
self-coloured, self-control, sleep-walk, tape-record*

7 **verb + noun**
grindstone, keepsake, playmate, takehome, telltale, turntable, viewdata

8 **verb + adjective**
drip-dry

9 **adjective + verb**
deep freeze, highflown, short-cut, whitewash

10   adverb + verb
> bypass, early-closing, input, ongoing, open-ended, outbreak, outfit, output, overturn, through-put, underdevelop

11   noun + adverb
> break-out, head-on, knock-out, leg-up

12   adverb + adjective
> evergreen, overripe

13   pronoun + noun
> he-man, she-devil

BLENDS

A **blend** is a word composed of parts of other words combined to form a new word, for example:

BLEND	SOURCE
Amerind	Amer(ican) + Ind(ian)
bedsit	bed(room) + sit(ting room)
bit	bi(nary) + (digi)t
breathalyser	breath + (an)alyser
brunch	br(eakfast) + (l)unch
electrocute	electro + (exe)cute
Eurovision	Euro(pean) + (tele)vision
guesstimate	guess + (es)timate
heliport	heli(copter) + (air)port
hi-fi	hi(gh) + fi(delity)
Interpol	Inter(national) + Pol(ice)
moped	mo(tor bike) + ped(al bike)
motel	mo(tor) + (ho)tel
newscast	news + (broad)cast
paratroops	para(chute) + troops
positron	posi(tive) + (elec)tron
quasar	quas(i) + (st)ar
sima	si(licon) + ma(gnesium)
sitcom	sit(uation) + com(edy)
smog	sm(oke) + (f)og
telecast	tele(vision) + (broad)cast
telecom	tele(phone) + com(munications)
telethon	tele(vision) + (mara)thon
transistor	trans(fer) + (res)istor
travelogue	travel + (catal)ogue

INVENTIONS

The English language contains many words which have been specially invented. Some derive from a proper name, e.g. *sandwich, wellington*. Some originate from a product marketed by a company, e.g. *biro, hoover*. Others are invented for commercial purposes, e.g. *acrilan, aerosol*.

CLIPPING

New words can be formed by omitting part of a word. The omission is normally at the end of a word: *photo(graph)*. More unusually, the omission is at the beginning: *(aero)plane*. See Chapter 2 (Abbreviations) for a full list.

ACRONYMS

An **acronym** is made up from some or all of the initial letters of an organisation, title, institution, political party, etc. The abbreviation is normally pronounced as one word, e.g. UNESCO (United Nations Educational, Scientific and Cultural Organisation), KANU (Kenya African National Union). See Chapter 2 for a full list.

LOAN WORDS

Certain words, now accepted as English words, have been borrowed freely from other languages. The following are brief lists of common foreign imports to English vocabulary, with indications of when they first appeared:

ORIGIN	CENTURY	EXAMPLES
African	13th-17th	banana, guinea, yam, zebra
	17th-18th	tote
	18th-19th	canary, chimpanzee, cola, ebony, gorilla, raffia, voodoo
Amerindian	18th-20th	chipmunk, gourd, hickory, hooch, moose, poke, raccoon, skunk, squash, squaw, tomahawk, wigwam
Arabic	13th-17th	alchemy, algebra, alkali, almanac, camphor, cotton, lute, mattress, nadir, salt, syrup
	17th-18th	alcove, candy, carafe, harem, sequin, sofa
	18th-19th	alfalfa, ghoul, safari
Australian	18th-20th	barrack, billabong, boomerang, budgerigar, corroboree, dingo, kangaroo, wombat

ORIGIN	CENTURY	EXAMPLES
Celtic	5th-10th	coracle, crag, dun, tor
	13th-17th	banshee, bog, gull, inch, slogan
Chinese/	13th-17th	sampan, tea, typhoon
Tibetan	17th-18th	lama
	18th-19th	kaolin, ketchup, kowtow, polo, yak
Dutch	13th-17th	boor, groat, ravel, spool
	18th-19th	kraal, laager, trek (via South Africa)
East Indian	17th-18th	bungalow, pundit
	18th-19th	bangle, cheetah
French	10th-12th	baron, barrister, beef, crown, duke, lance, mutton, rabbit, realm, venison
	13th-17th	colonel, gauze, grotesque, machine, pioneer, unique, vase
	17th-18th	crayon, detour, glacier, rouge
	18th-19th	coupon, restaurant
	20th	garage, discotheque
German	13th-17th	buoy, deck, hose, rack, snap
	17th-18th	sauerkraut
	18th-19th	cobalt, kindergarten, poodle, seminar, yodel
	20th	blitz
Greek	13th-17th	alphabet, dilemma, drama, elegy, enigma
	17th-18th	hyphen, orchestra, tonic
	18th-19th	agnostic, camera, phase
Italian	17th-18th	balloon, ditto, gazette, intrigue, opera, parasol, serenade, umbrella
Japanese	17th-18th	soy
	18th-19th	geisha, hara-kiri or hari-kari, judo, kimono, samurai, tycoon
	20th	ju-jitsu, karate
Latin	5th-10th	altar, bishop, camp, church, pound
	13th-17th	album, cadaver, cornea, focus, genius, junior, pollen, virus
	17th-18th	alibi, antenna, bonus, lens
	18th-19th	bacillus, duplex
Malaysian/	13th-17th	bamboo
Polynesian	17th-18th	gingham, gong, junk, launch, taboo, tattoo
	18th-19th	bantam, caddy, kapok, orang-utan, sarong
	20th	ukelele

ORIGIN	CENTURY	EXAMPLES
New Zealand	18th-19th	kauri, kiwi, moa, tiki
Persian	13th-17th	arsenic, azure, check, chess, salamander, scarlet, spinach, taffeta, tiara, tiger
	17th-18th	jackal, julep, lilac, shawl
	18th-19th	khaki, seersucker
Portuguese	17th-18th	caste, pagoda, tank
	18th-19th	veranda
Scandinavian	5th-10th	link, keg, oaf, rug, scrub, snag
	10th-12th	egg, fellow, husband, kid, skip, sky
Slavonic	18th-19th	mammoth, polka, vodka
	20th	pogrom, robot, soviet
Spanish	13th-17th	alligator, armada, cask, negro, renegade
	17th-18th	cargo, cockroach, desperado, guitar, parade, plaza, turtle, vanilla
	18th-19th	bonanza, cigarette, mustang, picaresque, rodeo
South African	18th-20th	aardvark, apartheid, commando, kraal, laager, spoor, trek
South Indian	13th-17th	calico, coolie, curry
	17th-18th	atoll, teak
	18th-19th	pyjamas, sari, shampoo, thug
Turkish	13th-17th	caftan, caviar, coffee, horde, tulip, turban
	17th-18th	kiosk, yoghurt
	18th-19th	bosh, fez

WORDS FROM SCIENCE & TECHNOLOGY

absolute zero   lowest temperature possible
accelerator   machine for increasing the kinetic energy of charged particles
acceleration   rate of change of speed
accumulator   device for storing electricity
acetic acid   acid contained in vinegar
acetylene   inflammable gas used in welding
acoustic   pertaining to sound
activation   producing radioactivity
additive   substance that is added to another
adhesives   glues, cements, etc. for sticking things together
adrenaline   hormone produced by adrenal glands
aerial   (also called *antenna*) device for picking up or transmitting radio energy

aerodynamics	scientific study of the movement of bodies in air
aerosol	dispersion of solid particles in a gas
aerospace	atmosphere and space beyond earth
alpha particles	particles emitted from the nuclei of certain radioactive elements
alpha rays	streams of alpha particles
amino acids	acids which link to form proteins
ampere	SI unit of electric current
amplifier	electronic device for increasing the strength of a signal
aneroid	without liquid
anhydrous	without water
antibiotics	chemicals which act against bacteria
antiseptic	substance which prevents bacteria growing
apogee	most distant point in the orbit of a satellite round the earth
armature	coils of a dynamo
aseptic	free from bacteria
astronautics	study of travel in space
astronomical unit	92.9×10^6 miles = mean distance between the centre of the earth and the centre of the sun
astrophysics	study of the physics of celestial bodies
atom smasher	colloquial term for an accelerator
atomic clock	clock regulated by atomic or molecular vibrations
atto-	prefix meaning one million million millionth in metric units (10^{-18})
audiometer	device for measuring hearing
automation	elimination or reduction of human effort in mechanical or electronic processes
bacillus	kind of bacteria
bactericide	substance that destroys bacteria
bacteriology	study of bacteria
ballistic missile	ground-to-ground rocket-bomb
ballistics	study of projectiles and their flight
barbiturates	sleep-inducing chemicals
barometer	device for measuring atmospheric pressure
beam	stream of radiation
Beaufort Scale	scale for measuring wind force
bel	ten decibels (units of sound intensity)
beta ray	stream of beta particles, which are emitted by a radioactive nucleus
big-bang theory	theory that the universe originated in one huge explosion
billion	**1** in Britain, one million million: (10^{12}) **2** in USA, one thousand million: (10^9)

biochemistry	study of the composition of living matter
biology	science of organic life
breeder reactor	nuclear reactor that can produce as much material as it uses
by-product	something produced incidentally in the process of producing something else

calcinate	to heat a metal and convert it to its oxide
calculus	mathematical process of analysis used to solve problems
calibration	dividing into a scale for measuring
calorie	measured unit of heat
candlepower	luminous intensity of a source of light: measured in *candela* (SI unit)
capacitance	ability to store electric charge
capacitor	device for storing electric charge
capillarity	(or *capillary action*) rise or depression of liquids in narrow tubes
capillary	small blood vessel
carbohydrates	organic compounds such as sugars, starches, or cellulose
carburettor	device in an internal combustion engine for mixing air with fuel
carcinogen	substance capable of producing cancer in an organism
cardiac	pertaining to the heart
casein	main protein in milk
catalysis	causing (or speeding up) a chemical reaction by means of a catalyst, a substance that remains unchanged at the end of the process
cell	**1** unit of protoplasm **2** device for producing electricity by chemical action
cellulose	fibrous substance obtained from pulped wood, cotton, etc.
centi-	prefix meaning one hundredth in metric units (10^{-2})
centrifuge	machine used to separate substances by spinning around an axis
chain reaction	reaction which produces substances which contribute to further action
channel	waveband used by a transmitter
channel capacity	number of signals per second that can be transmitted through a particular channel
chemotherapy	treatment of disease by chemicals
chlorination	treatment of water by introducing chlorine
chlorophyll	green pigment found in plants
cholesterol	fatty alcohol present in the tissues of the human body

chromatography	method of chemical analysis of a liquid mixture by moving it along an absorbent material, during which process the components of the mixture become separated
chromosomes	thread-like bodies in the nuclei of living cells which carry the genetic material
coaxial	having a common axis: e.g. *coaxial cable* has two conductors, one inside the other
colloid	substance suspended in a liquid
compound	substance composed of chemically combined elements
condenser	1 optics — device for concentrating light 2 electricity — same as *capacitor*
conductor	body which will allow energy to flow through it
continuum	continuous series of parts
cosmic dust	particles of matter in space
cosmic rays	radiation from outer space
coulomb	SI unit of electric charge
critical mass	minimum amount of fissile material needed for a chain reaction to occur in a nuclear reactor
cryogenics	study of phenomena at extremely low temperatures
crystal	substance that has solidified in a form with a certain arrangement of atoms
culture	nutrient preparation for growing living cells, viruses, etc.
curie	measure of radioactivity
cybernetics	study of automatic control systems
cyclotron	particle accelerator
cytochemistry	chemistry of cells
deca-	prefix meaning ten in metric units (10^1)
deci-	prefix meaning one tenth in metric units (10^{-1})
decibel	unit of sound intensity (one tenth of a bel)
degradation	breakdown of molecules into fragments
dehydration	loss of water
density	mass of a substance
depilatory	substance for removing hair
derivative	chemical derived from another
detergent	cleaning agent
dialysis	separation of substances in solution
diffraction	causing patterns of light and dark or coloured bands when a beam of light passes through a narrow aperture or past an opaque body
diffusion	scattering of gases, liquids or solids as the result of spontaneous movement

digitalis	mixture used for treating certain heart diseases, derived from the foxglove plant
distillation	conversion of a liquid into vapour, and collection of the liquid yielded by the condensing of the vapour
Doppler effect	change in the apparent frequency of sound or light waves or electromagnetic radiation when there is relative motion between the source and the observer
dynamics	branch of mechanics which deals with the behaviour of bodies in motion
dynamo	machine for converting mechanical energy into electrical energy
ecology	study of the relationship of plants and animals and their environment
ectoplasm	outer layer
ecosystem	a community and its environment as a self-sustaining unit
effervescence	escape of gas bubbles from a liquid
electro-cardiograph	known as *ECG*: an instrument for recording the waveforms associated with the beating of the heart
electrolysis	passing of an electric current through substances (called *electrolytes*) to generate a gas or deposit a metal on an object serving as an electrode
electro-magnetism	magnetism produced by an electric current
electron	elementary particle
electronics	science or technology dealing with the behaviour and effects of electrons in thermionic valves, etc.
electrostatic	pertaining to static electricity
elementary particles	basic units of matter: protons, electrons, neutrons, etc.
empirical	based entirely on evidence gained from observation and experimentation
emollient	something which makes a substance soft
emulsion	one liquid dispersed in droplets throughout another
energy	capacity for doing work
epicentre	point on the earth's surface that lies directly over the focus of an earthquake
epoxy resin	substance used in adhesives or coatings
equilibrium	state of balance between opposing forces
erg	measure of energy or work
ergonomics	study of the relation between workers and their work environment

ester	fragrant liquid
ethers	volatile inflammable liquids
eugenics	science dealing with the improvement of a race or breed by genetic control
exa-	prefix meaning one million million million in metric units (10^{18})
fall-out	polluting radioactive particles from a nuclear explosion
farad	SI unit of electric capacitance
femto-	prefix meaning one thousand millionth in metric units (10^{-15})
field	region over which an electrically-charged body exerts its influence
filament	thin thread, such as that in an electric light bulb
film	thin layer of one substance on another
filtration	separation of solids from liquid by passing through a filter
fissile material	isotopes capable of undergoing nuclear fission
fluorescence	emitting of light of one wavelength by a substance which has absorbed light of another wavelength
fluoridation	adding of fluorides (salts) to water supplies
focus	meeting point of light rays
foot-candle	unit of illumination
foot-pound	unit of work
freeze-drying	drying a substance such as food or blood plasma by freezing it and then removing water by volatilisation (i.e. causing it to evaporate)
frequency	1 number of cycles, oscillations, etc. per second of a wave 2 number of sound waves per second
galvanometer	instrument for identifying small electric currents
gas-cooled reactor	nuclear reactor in which the coolant is a gas
gauss	unit of magnetic induction
Geiger counter	instrument for detecting the presence and indicating the intensity of ionising radiations
gel	colloidal solution in the form of a jelly
gene	unit of inheritance which is carried on a chromosome
genetic code	code which transmits inherited characteristics
genetics	study of heredity
geocentric	measured from the earth's centre
giga-	prefix meaning one thousand million in metric units (10^9)
gillion	one thousand million (USA equivalent, *billion*)
glass fibre	fine fibres of glass woven into a cloth
glucose	sugar that occurs in natural foods such as honey and fruits

gravity	gravitational force between the earth and a body on its surface or within its gravitational field, responsible for a body's weight
gyroscope	spinning wheel which is free to turn in any direction and which can thus maintain rigidity in space
half-life	time taken for half the atoms of an isotope to decay
heat exchanger	device for transferring heat from one fluid to another without the fluids being in contact
heat pump	device for extracting the heat from a fluid that is slightly warmer than its surroundings
heavy water	water in which the hydrogen is replaced by deuterium; used in some nuclear reactors
hecto-	prefix meaning one hundred in metric units (10^2)
henry	SI unit of electric inductance
hertz	SI unit of frequency
heterogeneous	of unlike parts; not of uniform composition
heuristic	problem-solving by reasoning on the basis of past experience
histogram	graph using rectangles to show frequency distributions
hologram	three-dimensional image
homogeneous	of uniform composition
hormones	substances produced by living cells, which circulate in body liquids and produce effects on the activity of cells elsewhere in the body
hydraulic	operated by a liquid
hydrodynamics	study of liquids in motion
hydroelectric power	electrical energy produced from water power
hydrogenation	action of hydrogen on a substance
hydroponics	cultivation of plants in solutions
impact	collision of bodies
impermeable	preventing the passage of fluids
implosion	collapsing inwards of a vessel which has been evacuated
impulse	force acting for a very short time
incandescence	light caused by great heat
inert	not easily changed by chemical reaction
inertia	**1** tendency for a body to remain in uniform motion in a straight line **2** tendency for a body to remain at rest
information theory	branch of cybernetics that deals statistically with the efficiency of communication processes
infrared radiation	**1** invisible heat **2** radiant heat

infrasonic	having a frequency below the lower threshold of human hearing
inorganic	of mineral origin
interface	surface that separates bodies, regions or phases
Interferon	substance produced by viruses in animal cells, which can inhibit the development of viruses
in vitro	(*in glass*) term used of biochemical experiments on cells or tissues which have been removed from an organism
ion	atom or group of atoms carrying an electric charge
ionisation	forming of ions
ionosphere	outer layer of the earth's atmosphere in which free ions can exist
isotopes	species of atoms of an element with the same atomic number but which differ in mass number
joule	SI unit of work or energy
kelvin	SI unit of thermodynamic temperature
kilo-	prefix meaning one thousand in metric units (10^3)
kilogram	SI unit of mass
lactose	milk sugar
lamina	thin sheet
laser	(*Light Amplification by Stimulated Emission of Radiation*) device that produces a powerful coherent beam of light
latent	present but not apparent
lens	device that causes rays of light to converge or diverge as they pass through it
lumen	SI unit of luminous flux
luminescence	emission of light
lux	SI unit of illuminance
Mach number	ratio of the speed of a body to the speed of sound
macro-	prefix meaning large, the opposite of *micro* (small)
magnetic field	space around a magnetised or electrically charged body in which magnetic forces can be detected
magnetic force	force of attraction or repulsion exerted by a magnetic field
magnetic storm	disturbance in the earth's magnetic field
magneto	small dynamo formerly used to ignite petrol vapour in an internal combustion engine
magneton	unit of measurement of the magnetic moment of a particle
malleable	able to be hammered out into thin sheets

maser	*(Microwave Amplification by Stimulated Emission of Radiation)* device like a laser, which amplifies microwave radiation
mass	measure of a body's inertia (the property which causes a body to have weight)
matrix	**1** mould for shaping a cast **2** substance between the cells of a tissue which holds them together **3** in computing, array of numbers that enables translation from one code to another **4** rock in which gems are embedded
mechanics	branch of physics dealing with the behaviour of matter under the influence of energy and forces
mega-	prefix meaning one million in metric units (10^6)
megaton bomb	nuclear weapon with an explosive power equivalent to that of a million tons of TNT
metabolism	chemical processes associated with the building up and destruction of living tissue
metallurgy	science and technology of metals
metre	SI unit of length
micro-	prefix meaning one millionth in metric units (10^{-6})
microelectronics	science and technology dealing with miniaturised electronic circuits and components
micron	one millionth of a metre
mil	one thousandth of an inch
milli-	prefix meaning one thousandth in metric units (10^{-3})
modulation	varying the amplitude frequency or phase of a wave by combining with a wave of a different frequency
module	**1** unit used as a standard **2** detachable section **3** detachable unit in a computer system
mole	SI unit of amount of substance
molecule	smallest particle of a substance capable of existing independently and retaining its characteristic properties, consisting of one or more atoms
momentum	product of a body's mass and its velocity
mono-	prefix meaning one single
mutation	change in an organism's hereditary material
nadir	lowest point
nano-	prefix meaning one thousand millionth in metric units (10^{-9})
neuron	nerve cell

newton	SI unit of force
nodule	small round mass
noise	unwanted signals in an electrical circuit
nuclear fission	nuclear reaction in which a heavy atomic nucleus splits into two parts, releasing large amounts of nuclear energy
nuclear fusion	nuclear reaction between light atomic nuclei which releases a large amount of nuclear energy
ohm	SI unit of electric resistance
optics	science of light
orbital	area round an atom or molecule
organic chemistry	chemistry of organic compounds
ortho-	prefix meaning correct, or straight
osmosis	movement of a solvent through a semi-permeable membrane into a solution: the solutions thus separated tend to become equal in concentration
oxidation	combining oxygen with a substance
para-	prefix meaning beside, irregular or beyond
parallax	shift in the apparent direction of a body due to a shift of the observer's position
parameter	variable that can be kept constant while the effects of other variables are examined
pascal	SI unit of pressure
penumbra	shadow created when an object cuts off light
per-	in chemistry, prefix meaning excess
peri-	prefix meaning around or about
perigee	least distant point in the orbit of a satellite round the earth
permeable	allowing a substance to pass through
peta-	prefix meaning one thousand million million in metric units (10^{15})
petrology	science of rocks
phase	homogeneous, separable part of a body or system
phon	unit of loudness
phot	unit of illumination
photochemistry	chemistry dealing with the effects of radiation on chemical changes
photoelectric cell	cell with properties that are affected by the action of light
photosynthesis	process by which green plants form carbohydrates under the influence of sunlight

pico-	prefix meaning one million millionth in metric units (10^{-12})
plastics	polymers that can be moulded and extruded when hot but which are stable when normal
poly-	prefix meaning many
polymer	chemical compound formed by the combination of many small molecules
positron	positive electron
potential energy	energy a body (such as a coiled spring) possesses because of its position
precipitate	substance formed in a solution by chemical change
pressure	force acting on a surface
propellant	substance used to propel bodies, vehicles, etc. by exploding
proteins	organic compounds that are constituents of living cells and essential to the diet of humans and animals
pulse	short-lived variation of electrical current, voltage, etc.
pyro-	prefix meaning fire or very hot
quantum	unit of energy
quarks	hypothetical particles
radian	SI unit of plane angle
radiation	emission of rays or particles or wave motion
radio	use of electromagnetic radiation for sending signals
radioactivity	spontaneous disintegration of unstable nuclei and the consequent emission of particles or rays
radiology	science of radioactivity and X-rays
refraction of light	bending of a ray of light when passing from one medium to another (e.g. from glass to air)
saline	containing salt
satellite	body that rotates in orbit around another body
second	SI unit of time
serum	part of a body liquid that remains after blood-clotting
SI	(*Système International d'Unités*) a system of basic units of measurement
siemens	SI unit of electric conductance
slide rule	scaled ruler used for mathematical calculations
solar	pertaining to the sun
soluble	capable of being dissolved
solvent	liquid which can dissolve substances
sonic boom	loud noise following the shock wave caused by an aircraft travelling above the speed of sound
space probe	missile travelling fast enough to escape the earth's atmosphere

specific	term meaning divided by mass
spectrum	1 product of resolving electromagnetic radiations into their wavelengths or frequencies 2 coloured bands of light resulting from passing light through a prism
stable	not susceptible to decomposition
steady state theory	theory that the universe was always in a steady state
steradian	SI unit of solid angle
synthesis	formation of a compound by putting together its elements
tachometer	instrument for measuring a revolving shaft's revolutions
telecommunications	transmission of signals by radio or by line
tensile strength	force that has to be applied to pulling a material to break it
tera-	prefix meaning one million million in metric units (10^{12})
terminal	1 the point where an electrical connection occurs 2 an input or output point of a computer
tesla	SI unit of magnetic flux density
tetra-	prefix meaning four
therm	measure of heat
thermal neutrons	very slow and consequently low-energy neutrons
thermodynamics	science of heat changes and energy conservation
thio-	prefix meaning sulphur
tissues	clusters of cells and intercellular material
transformer	device for changing an alternating current of one voltage to another voltage without altering the frequency
transistor	semiconductor that makes use of a small current to control a larger one
trillion	1 in Britain, one million million million: (10^{18}) 2 in USA, one million million: (10^{12})
turbogenerator	steam turbine connected to an electric generator for producing power
ultrasonics	study of sound waves with frequencies above the limit of audibility
vaccine	preparation containing killed micro-organisms which can be introduced into the body to produce immunity to infection
vacuum	space in which there are no molecules or atoms
valence	degree of combining power of an atom
vapour density	measure of the density of a gas, usually in relation to oxygen or hydrogen

variable	symbol with different numerical values
velocity	speed in a given direction
Vernier Scale	graduated scale for measuring subdivisions of another scale
virology	study of viruses
virus	disease-inducing particle
viscosity	resistance to flowing in a liquid
vitamins	substances in foods which are necessary for diet
volt	SI unit of electric potential
voltage	potential of a supply of electricity, measured in volts
watt	SI unit of electric power
wave	**1** periodic disturbance of air or of a surface **2** periodic variation of pressure, or of electrical or magnetic intensity
wavelength	distance between points of a wave, e.g. from crest to crest of waves in the sea
weber	SI unit of magnetic flux
xerography	method of photographic copying of documents, etc.
X-rays	(*Röntgen rays*) electromagnetic radiations like light but of much shorter wavelength, used to photograph bones, etc.
zenith	highest point
zoology	study of animals

WORDS FROM COMPUTING

access	obtaining data from storage (the computer's 'memory')
access time	time taken to obtain data
acoustic coupler	device enabling a signal to be transmitted by telephone
adder	device for adding digital signals
ALGOL	(*Algorithmic Language*) programming language used for scientific and mathematical projects
algorithm	sequence of instructions for solving a particular problem
analog computer	(or *analogue*) computer which performs calculations by means of numbers represented by some physical quantity, such as voltage, angular positions of levers, etc.
archived	stored on tape and not in the main store
artificial intelligence	use of computers to represent the working of the human brain
autocode	basic language; a computer language near to human language
automatic coding	using a computer to do the mechanical work in writing a program
available time	time when a computer is ready and available for use

BASIC	*(Beginner's All-purpose Symbolic Instruction Code)* programming language
batch	set of records processed in a single unit
binary digit	(or *bit*) unit in the binary scale, i.e. either 1 or 0
bit	binary digit
Boolean algebra	form of algebra that provides rules for making logical statements, just as ordinary algebra makes mathematical statements
branch	(or *jump*) to depart from the normal sequence of program steps to another instruction as a result of an instruction
bug	1 error in a program 2 some malfunction in a system
bus	(or *highway*) route shared by signals from various components of the computer
byte	(or *bite*) set of eight bits
cell	smallest unit of a computer store, capable of holding a single bit
central processing unit	*(CPU* or *central processor)* main part of a computer, which provides the arithmetical and logical processors
channel	any path along which data flows
chip	integrated circuit
clock	electronic unit which synchronises other units in a system
COBOL	*(Common Business Oriented Language)* computer programming language used for commerce
code	set of instructions for a program
COM	*(Computer Output on Microfilm)* technique for putting output directly on film
compiler	program for translating a high-level language program into machine code
computer	electronic machine for processing data
cursor	point or line on a video terminal
data	information coded in a form suitable to be fed into a computer
data bank	files of data
database	collection of data
data dictionary	index of data
data processing	complete procedure of collecting and processing data and presenting the results
debugging	finding the faults in a program or computer, and correcting them
denary notation	notation system using the numbers from 0 to 9

digital computer	computer using data represented by discrete numbers
direct access	(or *random access*) storing or retrieving data items without first having to read any other stored data
disk	flat circular plate used as a storage device
DMA	direct memory access
down	faulty, not working — a term used of computers
down time	(or *fault time*) time in which a computer is not working because of a fault
dry run	checking the paths through a program without using the computer
dump	**1** whole content of memory **2** to print out the content of a memory
dynamic stop	use of a branch instruction to make a program loop which suspends execution of a program until the operator intervenes
effective time	time during which a computer is working to produce useful results
execution	carrying out a program's instructions
fault time	same as *down time*
feedback	information about an operation returned to the processor
field	section of a record (which is a collection of related data)
file	collection of related records
floppy disk	light flexible disk
flowchart	diagram of the operations involved in a system
FORTRAN	*For(mula) Tran(slation)*: high-level programming language used for scientific and mathematical purposes
function	(or *procedure, routine, subprogram*) set of instructions which forms part of a program
gate	**1** device that controls the pulse flow **2** electronic switch
graph plotter	output device that draws lines on paper
hardware	machinery and equipment of a computer system
high-level languages	computer languages which allow users to write notation resembling 'natural' language: e.g. *FORTRAN* uses mathematical notation, *COBOL* uses English, etc.
highway	same as *bus*
immediate access store	store in the central processor
information	meaning given to data
input	data put into a system
interpreter	program which translates and executes a source program

jump	same as *branch*
key	record identifier
language	artificial language created for programming computers
light pen	device like a thin torch used to input data with a graphical display unit
liveware	people who work with a computer system
low-level language	machine-oriented language
machine code	basic programming language in which operations are represented by numeric functions
media	tapes, cards, etc. which hold information
memory	part of a computer which holds data and instructions
micro-	prefix meaning one millionth
microfiche	microfilm sheets which can be accessed by an optical reader
multi-access	(or *time sharing*) simultaneous use of a computer by several users
nano-	prefix meaning one thousand millionth
network	linked set of computer systems
off-line processing	processing by devices not connected with the central processor
on-line processing	processing by devices operating under the control of the central processor
output	results produced by a computer
peripheral	any hardware which provides input to or receives output from a computer system
procedure	same as *function*
process	operation on data in the computer
program	set of instructions to the computer
random access	same as *direct access*
raw data	data that has not been processed
real-time system	system capable of dealing with data during the time an event is happening and able to respond to rapidly changing data, e.g. air-traffic control, assembly-line operations, etc.
record	collection of related data
routine	same as *function*
run	executing a program
search	to examine data methodically for specific items
software	packages, programs and other materials for use in a computer system

source program	program as produced by a programmer, before it is compiled or interpreted for execution
storage	equipment used to store data and programs
subprogram	same as *function*
systems analysis and design	analysis of what a job requires and design of a suitable system to do it
teletypewriter	keyboard, tape punch, reader etc. used for communicating with the computer
terminal	any device used for communicating with the computer from a distance
time sharing	same as *multi-access*
track	path on a tape, disk, etc. on which data can be stored
visual display unit	*(VDU)* terminal device on which text can be displayed
word	set of bits
zone	area on a printed output or punched card

WORDS FROM ADMINISTRATION, BUSINESS & LAW

action research	research aiming at improving the situation being examined as well as merely describing it
advance	loan
advice note	letter from a seller to a buyer specifying the goods sent
advocate	lawyer who pleads a client's case in a court of law
annuity	sum of money paid regularly to someone for a fixed period or until death
antitrust	in USA, legislation against monopolies
appraisal review	interview in which an employee's job and work are discussed with a senior colleague
arbitration	impartial hearing and judgement of a dispute
arrears	unpaid debt
articles of association	constitutional rules for a registered company
asset	1 something owned 2 an economic benefit
asset stripping	taking over a company in order to sell off its assets
audit	examination of accounts, carried out by an *auditor*
authorised capital	value of all the shares a company is entitled to issue

backshift	afternoon shift in a three-shift order of working
balance of payments	difference between what a country pays out and what it earns
balance of trade	difference between a country's exports and its imports
balance sheet	statement of financial position at any one time
bank rate	official rate at which the Bank of England will discount bills of exchange
bankrupt	insolvent person declared by law to be unable to pay his debts
bar	the legal profession
barrister	lawyer who is qualified to plead in higher courts
bear	**1** dealer who sells securities he does not own and hopes to buy them at a lower price before they have to be delivered **2** someone who expects that prices will fall
bear market	time in a stock market when people are selling in the expectation that prices will fall
bearer bond	bond whose ownership is not recorded, which can therefore be freely exchanged
bench, the	judge or magistrate sitting in court in a judicial capacity
blacklist	**1** list of persons who are to be excluded from given jobs, or from selection for a team, etc. **2** list of individuals or firms who are to be denied credit
block release	release of employees for training for a period of weeks rather than one day per week (which is called *day release*)
blue book	government publication: a blue cover usually denotes an annual report
blue chip	limited company thought highly of by investors
blue-collar	pertaining to manual workers
blueprint	detailed plan
board	group of directors who administer a company
bond	security which can earn interest
bonded goods	goods on which customs duty must be paid
bonus	payment made at the discretion of management
boom	period when trade is good, employment level high, etc.
brand	label; a symbol which gives goods a special identity
brand leader	branded product which sells better than any other similar product
break-even point	when sales revenue is sufficiently greater than costs to allow a firm to survive
break-up value	amount of money realisable when a firm's assets are sold off
broker	dealer who arranges transactions for a commission
bucket shop	firm which trades without being a member of an organised or official market

budget	written plan of expenditure and revenue
building society	non-profit-making society which raises money from investors and pays money to borrowers, mainly to assist in the buying of houses
bull	dealer who buys securities in the expectation that the price will rise
bull market	time in a stock market when prices are expected to rise
buyer's market	market that favours the buyers; that is, there is an ample supply of goods and the sellers cannot command a good price
by-law	**1** in Britain, law made by local government under authority granted by national government **2** in USA, rule made by a corporation, dealing with stockholders' rights, directors' responsibilities, etc.
capital	wealth (money or saleable goods) owned by a person or firm
capital gains tax	tax levied on profits gained by an individual from selling capital assets
capital goods	objects such as machines, tools, etc. which are used in the production of other goods
capital transfer tax	tax levied on gifts of money or goods made by a person to another during his lifetime or by his will
cash-flow	**1** amount of money taken in and paid out by a firm weekly, monthly or annually **2** supply of money needed to meet a firm's weekly or monthly business
caveat emptor	Latin for 'let the buyer beware', which means that you must buy goods at your own risk
central bank	bank set up by a government to regulate currency, obtain loans, etc.
certificate of origin	certificate stating that goods were manufactured in a particular country
chamber of commerce	local association of business persons
charter	record of property owned, rights, power, etc.
chartered accountant	in Britain, an accountant who has passed the professional examinations of the Institute of Chartered Accountants (in USA, *certified public accountant*)
cheap money	money current when bank rates are low — when rates are high money is said to be *dear*
clawback	money that is returned to the payer for some reason
clearing house	institution set up by a group of banks where they can settle accounts with each other by exchanging cheques, credit transfers, etc. and pay off outstanding balances

closed shop	firm or occupation in which all employees must be members of recognised unions
collateral	securities offered by a borrower as assurance that a debt will be covered
commission	payment for services rendered, usually a percentage of the cash value realised by the transaction
commodity	exchangeable unit of economic wealth
Consolidated Fund	money in an account into which all British Government revenues must be paid
consortium	association of companies, especially an international one
consumer durables	goods, such as land and buildings, which are long-lasting
contingency	liability which cannot be budgeted for because it cannot be anticipated
conveyancing	formal process of transferring property between persons
cooling-off period	in USA, period in which a strike is legally prohibited to allow for negotiation
co-operative	arrangement whereby all personnel in a firm share in management and profits
copyright	right to control the use of a work of art, its publication, etc.
corporation	organisation, e.g. a limited company, which has a legal identity separate from those of the individual members
corporation tax	tax levied on a corporation
cost benefit analysis	study of the value that would accrue from various options
cost of living index	comparative analysis of the prices of all goods and services deemed to be essential for ordinary life in a country
credit squeeze	restriction by government of the ease of access to bank loans, hire purchase, etc.
dawn raid	sudden and unexpected buying of shares to gain control of a company
dawn shift	early morning group of workers
dear money	money current when bank rates are high
death duty	duties paid when property is transferred on a person's death
debenture	certificate of debt or security for a loan
default	failure to pay a debt
deferred payments	payments for a hire purchase agreement; that is, regular payments made for a period after goods have been received
deflation	general decrease in costs, prices, money supply, etc.
demarcation dispute	conflict over which union members should do a particular job

depreciation	fall in value of a currency
depression	period of high unemployment and low investment and trade
devaluation	decrease in the international value of a currency
direct taxes	taxes levied on individuals' income or wealth rather than on goods and services, etc.
discount	deduction from the normal price
discount house	firm that lends money to business and public organisations
discretionary	in accordance with one's own judgement
distrain	to seize goods on the non-payment of a debt
district attorney	in USA, state prosecuting officer in a judicial district
diversify	to invest in a variety of securities or manufactures
dividend	profits paid out to shareholders
double-entry book-keeping	accounting system which records each transaction in accordance with both its credit aspect and its debit aspect
dumping	selling off products at a specially low price
Dutch auction	sale at which the price asked is steadily lowered until someone makes a bid
duty	any tax other than income tax
econometrics	application of mathematical techniques to the study of economic problems
economic man	ideal or model consumer, worker, etc. used in theoretical economics
embezzlement	dishonest use of someone else's money for which you are responsible
endorse a cheque	to write on a cheque transferring to someone else the right to its value
endowment insurance policy	insurance contract guaranteeing payment of a fixed sum after an agreed period or on the death of the insured person
equity	1 body of law that is not included in statutes or common law 2 ownership of a firm's assets after payment of all debts
estate duty	tax levied on a person's estate
exchange rate	number of units of a particular currency that can be bought or sold for a unit of another currency
excise duty	tax on certain goods (e.g. whisky, beer, petrol), licences (e.g. for cars) and services (e.g. betting)
executor	representative named in a will
ex officio	Latin term for 'by virtue of his official position'
face value	value of a currency note, security, etc. printed on the document

family allowance social security payments to people with children
feather-bedding   assistance by government to industry, which is considered excessive
fiduciary issue   paper money not covered by gold reserves
financial year   the twelve months ending on 31 March
fiscal   pertaining to governmental taxation or spending policies
float   small sum of money for everyday use
floating assets   assets that can easily be converted to cash for use when required
foreign exchange procedures for buying and selling foreign currencies
  market
franchise   the right to sell certain goods in a particular district
freetrade area   group of countries where there are no custom duties at the frontiers
fringe benefits   rewards other than wages, e.g. a free car, meal vouchers

gazumphing   increasing a price after an agreement has been reached but before papers are signed
general strike   strike by all or most unions at one time
gilt-edged   extremely safe — a term used of government stocks
giro   system of transferring money between persons
gnomes of   term used for international money dealers
  Zurich
gold standard   arrangement whereby a government guarantees to cover the value of paper money with gold
goodwill   value of customers' loyalty to a firm
grievance   formal process allowing an employee to seek redress for
  procedure   allegedly unfair treatment
Gross National   (GNP) total value of all the goods and services produced in a
  Product   country over a year, but subtracting goods and services used only to produce further goods
guesstimate   colloquial term for an estimate based solely on guesswork

hedge   to protect oneself against loss
holding   company whose business consists of holding the securities
  company   and shares of other companies
hyperinflation   very great inflation

import duty   tax on goods brought into a country
income tax   personal tax levied on annual income
incomes policy   government plan for controlling people's earnings
indent   to place an order for goods
indirect tax   tax on goods and services rather than on incomes

industrial dispute	dispute between workers and management
industrial tribunal	panel set up to settle cases of workers' grievances, etc.
inflation	continuing increase in prices and decrease in the value of money
in loco parentis	Latin phrase meaning 'in place of the parent'; that is, when an adult is responsible for a child
insolvent	unable to pay one's debts
intangible asset	something of value which is abstract, e.g. a firm's goodwill
interest	payment made for the use of someone else's money
internal audit	audit of accounts made by an employee of the firm
International Monetary Fund	(IMF) global lending agency to help member nations with temporary budget deficits
intestate	without leaving a will
inventory	detailed list of articles
investment	using money to gain income by lending it or purchasing securities
investment income	money gained from investments, not earned from employment
invoice	statement describing goods supplied and their price
jobber	dealer who acts between buyers and sellers
Jobcentre	employment office
job description	statement of the duties and responsibilities of an employee
job sharing	arrangement allowing two persons to share one job and share the pay
Keynesian economics	(Keynesianism) economic policy to maintain full employment without inflation
kind	goods rather than money; as in 'payment in kind'
late shift	the afternoon or evening group of workers
lawyer	a member of the legal profession
lay off	to dismiss (staff) temporarily
lease	to grant possession (of property) for payment
legal tender	money whose value is backed by law
liabilities	a firm's debt
liability	obligation to pay
limited company	company whose shareholders would be liable for limited sums in case of bankruptcy
liquidation	the selling off of a firm's assets so that it can be dissolved
liquidity	ability to produce cash
loan shark	person who lends money at excessive rates of interest

lockout	prevention, by an employer, of employees' freedom to do their jobs, in the course of an industrial dispute
loss leader	something sold without profit in order to attract custom
management consultant	someone who advises firms on how to solve problems, increase efficiency, etc.
manpower planning	estimating the number of employees required over a period, and deciding how they can be obtained
market research	study of the potential sales of a product
market value	amount a product can be expected to fetch
mark up	difference between the cost of a product to the seller and its selling price
merchant bank	bank which provides finance to industrial and commercial firms
merger	the bringing together of firms under common ownership
middle management	managers who are subordinate to first-tier management
mixed economy	mixture of state-owned enterprises and independent companies
monetarism	theory that inflation and depression can be cured by controlling the supply of money
monopoly	virtual control of the production and sale of certain goods by a single firm
moonlighting	doing an extra job, usually after the day's work in the main job
mortgage	loan obtained by putting up property as security
mothballed	(of a factory, etc.) kept in operating condition, but not producing
multinational	firm that has business in various countries
nationalise	to take a business into public ownership
net	term meaning 'after all deductions have been made'
nightshift	group of workers who work during the night
official receiver	person appointed to oversee the liquidation of a company
Old Bailey	central criminal court of England
ordinary shareholder	shareholder who is entitled to dividends, votes at meetings and receives a share of the assets if the company is liquidated
overdraft	amount of money drawn from a bank in excess of the amount actually owned
overtime	time worked beyond normal hours
patent	licence guaranteeing sole right to make or sell a certain product
payroll	a firm's total payments in salaries and wages

personal allowance	(or *personal relief*) amount deducted from an individual's income before tax is deducted
petty cash	small fund used for meeting minor items of expenditure
picket	striking worker posted outside a firm's premises to tell workers about the strike and encourage them to join it
piece work	kind of job in which one is paid a certain amount for each item produced
policy holder	someone who has an insurance contract
portfolio	set of securities
premium	sum paid out, e.g. for an insurance policy
premium savings bond	bond which can be cashed in at face value but which also entitles the owner to a chance to gain a prize in a national lottery
price fixing	agreement among sellers as to the price each will ask for a product
price war	competition among sellers which results in the lowering of prices by one seller, so that others will be forced to charge less than they can afford
proceeds	amount of money gained from selling goods
productivity	measured output of a firm or manufacturing process
protectionism	government action against imports to protect domestic producers
quid pro quo	Latin term meaning 'something in return'
quotation	statement of what a firm will charge for goods or services
redeem	to buy back (a security, etc.)
redundancy	being no longer required: a term used of surplus staff
reserve	money retained which has not been set aside for any particular purpose
restrictive practices	actions by employees to restrict output during an industrial dispute
revenue account	statement of income
security	financial asset, such as shares or bonds
seller's market	market in which demand exceeds supply
shares	equal parts into which the capital stock of a company is divided
shop steward	unpaid union official representing the workers of a particular section of a firm
solicitor	lawyer who advises on legal matters
solvent	able to pay one's debts
spin-off	outcome not planned for

stagflation	mixture of stagnation and inflation; that is, output is not growing yet prices are rising
standby pay	pay given to employees who are on call but not actually working
statutory audit	audit carried out because it is required by law
stock	capital raised by a company through the issue of shares
stockbroker	dealer in securities, etc. on behalf of clients
stock exchange	market for buying and selling securities
sympathy striking	going on strike in support of a strike in another industry, firm, etc.
takeover	acquisition of one firm by another firm
tariff	1 list of charges 2 list of import duties
tax haven	country where taxes are very low
tender	offer to perform a piece of work and a statement of the costs
tort	wrong imposed on someone for which he can claim damages in court
trade association	society of firms set up to protect their interests
trademark	symbol used to identify a product
trade price	price charged by a firm to other firms in the same trade
trade union	association of workers to protect their interests
traveller's cheque	cheque form issued for use in another country, which can be cashed when signed by the user
trust	legal arrangement vesting ownership of property in 'trustees', who are responsible for using the income for certain objectives
trustee savings bank	non-profit-making bank run in the interests of its customers
underwriter	person who insures property, etc.
Value Added Tax	(*VAT*) tax on all goods and services charged when they are supplied
voucher	document which can be used to pay for something
warrant	document carrying authority for an action or payment
warranty	guarantee — of quality, delivery, etc.
white-collar	pertaining to workers in offices, etc.
work-to-rule	restrictive practice which entails workers applying all rules rigidly and thus slowing up production
yield	money an investment earns
zero-rated	incurring no tax

2   ABBREVIATIONS

Abbreviations are shortened versions of words or phrases omitting some of the letters, or using the initials of words, e.g. abbr. (abbreviation); AA (Automobile Association). **Acronyms** are formed by using the initial letters or parts of words to make up titles, proper names or descriptive phrases, e.g. Oxfam (Oxford Committee for Famine Relief); awol (absent without leave). **Clipped words** omit some of the letters of a word, e.g. intro — intro(duction); pub — pub(lic house).

A1	first class
AA	Alcoholics Anonymous; Automobile Association
AAA	Amateur Athletic Association; American Automobile Association; Australian Automobile Association
AAEC	Australian Atomic Energy Commission
AAM	Anti-Apartheid Movement
A & N	Army and Navy
AAPC	All African Peoples' Conference
AAPO	All African Peoples' Organisation
AATUF	All-African Trade Union Federation
AB	able-bodied seaman
ABA	Amateur Boxing Association
abbr., abbrev.	abbreviated; abbreviation
ABC	American Broadcasting Company; Associated British Cinemas; Australian Broadcasting Commission
ab. init.	*(ab initio)* Latin for 'from the beginning'
ABM	anti-ballistic missile
abr.	abridged
abs., abstr.	abstract
AC	Air Commodore; alternating current
A/C	account
acad.	academy
acct.	account
ACER	Australian Council for Educational Research
ack.	acknowledged
act.	active
ACTU	Australian Council of Trade Unions
AD	*(Anno Domini)* Latin for 'in the year of our Lord'
ad.	adverb; advertisement
ADC	aide-de-camp
add.	*(addendum)* Latin for 'addition'; address
adj.	adjective; adjunct

ad lib	*(ad libitum)* Latin for 'as you will'
admin.	administration
adv.	adverb/adverbial
advt.	advertisement
ae., aet.	*(aetatis)* Latin for 'aged'
AEA	Atomic Energy Authority; American Economic Association
AERA	American Educational Research Association
AFC	Air Force Cross
AFD	accelerated freeze drying
AFG	Afghanistan (vehicle registration)
AFM	Air Force Medal
Afrik.	Afrikaans
AG	Attorney General
Ag	chemical formula for silver
AGM	Annual General Meeting
agric.	agricultural
AI	Amnesty International
AIBS	American Institute of Biological Sciences
AID	Artificial Insemination by Donor
AIDS	Acquired Immune Deficiency Syndrome
AIM	African Inland Mission
AIR	All-India Radio
AL	Albania (vehicle registration)
Al	chemical formula for aluminium
al.	alcohol
Ala., AL	Alabama
Alas., AK	Alaska
Alb.	Albania
Alta.	Alberta
ALCAN	Aluminium Company of Canada
ALBM	air-launched ballistic missile
A Level	Advanced Level (GCE examination)
Alg.	Algeria
alg.	algebra
ALGOL	Algorithmic Language
alk.	alkali
ALO	Asian Labour Organisation
ALP	American Labour Party; Australian Labour Party
alt.	alternative; altitude
alum.	aluminium
AM	Air Marshal; Master of Arts
Am	chemical formula for americium

a.m.	*(ante meridiem)* Latin for 'before noon'
amal.	amalgamated
Amb.	Ambassador
Amer.	American
AMM	anti-missile missile
amn., ammo	ammunition
amp.	ampere
amu	atomic mass unit
An	chemical formula for actinon
anag.	anagram
anal.	analogy
ANC	African National Congress
AND	Andorra (vehicle registration)
Angl.	Anglican
annot.	annotation
anon.	anonymous
ans.	answer
ant.	antonym
anthol.	anthology
ANZAC	Australian and New Zealand Army Corps
a/o	on account of
AOB	any other business
AOCB	any other competent business
AOC-in-C	Air Officer Commanding-in-Chief
AOK	excellent
AP	atmospheric pressure; Associated Press
APC	automatic pitch control
APEX	Advance Purchase Excursion
apo.	apogee
apos.	apostrophe
app.	appendix
appro	approval
approx.	approximately
apptd.	appointed
APT	Advanced Passenger Train
apt.	apartment
aq.	*(aqua)* Latin for 'water'
Ar	chemical formula for argon
a.r.	*(anno regni)* Latin for 'in the year of the reign (of)'
Arab.	Arabian
Aram.	Aramaic
ARAMCO	Arabian-American Oil Company

ARC	Agricultural Research Council
Arch.	Archbishop
arch.	archaic
archaeol.	archaeology
archit.	architecture
Arg.	Argentina; chemical formula for silver
arith.	arithmetical
AZ	Arizona
AR	Arkansas
ARM	anti-radar missile
ARP	air raid precautions
arr.	arrival
art.	article
AS	Anglo-Saxon
As	chemical formula for arsenic
As.	Asian
ASA	Amateur Swimming Association
a.s.a.p.	as soon as possible
ASBU	Arab States Broadcasting Union
a.s.e.	air standard efficiency
ASEAN	Association of South East Asian Nations
ASH	Action on Smoking and Health
ASI	air speed indicator
ASM	air to surface missile
Ass.	Assembly; Association
Assn.	Association
Assoc.	Associate
asst.	assistant
Assyr.	Assyrian
astr., astron.	astronomy
ASW	Anti-Submarine Warfare
at.	atomic
ATC	Air Training Corps
at. no.	atomic number
ATS	Auxiliary Territorial Service (for women)
Att.	Attorney
att.	attached
attrib.	attributed
ATUC	African Trade Union Confederation
Au	chemical formula for gold
a.u.c.	*(ab urbe condita)* Latin for 'from the founding of the city (of Rome)'

Aug.	August
AUM	air to underwater missile
AUS	Australia (vehicle registration)
auth.	author
auto	automobile
aux.	auxiliary
AV	audio-visual; Authorised Version
Av., Ave.	Avenue
av.	average
a.w.	atomic weight
awol	absent without leave
awu	atomic weight unit
B	Belgium (vehicle registration)
BA	Bachelor of Arts; British Academy; British Airways
Ba	chemical formula for barium
BAA	British Airports Authority
BAAB	British Amateur Athletic Board
Bab.	Babylonian
BACIE	British Association for Commercial and Industrial Education
BACO	British Aluminium Company
bact.	bacteria
bacteriol.	bacteriology
BAdmin.	Bachelor of Administration
BAgr.	Bachelor of Agriculture
Bah.	Bahamas
bal.	balance
BALPA	British Air Line Pilots' Association
Balt.	Baltimore
B. & B.	bed and breakfast
bap.	baptised
bar.	barometric
Bart.	Baronet
BASIC	Beginner's All-purpose Symbolic Instruction Code
Bav.	Bavaria
BB	Boys' Brigade
BBC	British Broadcasting Corporation
BC	Before Christ
BCG	vaccine against tuberculosis (*Bacillus Calmette-Guérin*)
BCom.	Bachelor of Commerce
BD	Bachelor of Divinity
b/d	brought down

BDU	Bomb Disposal Unit
BE	bill of exchange
Be	chemical formula for beryllium
bec.	because
BEd.	Bachelor of Education
bef.	before
beg.	begin
Belg.	Belgium
BEM	British Empire Medal
Benelux	customs union of Belgium, the Netherlands and Luxembourg
Beng.	Bengal
bet.	between
b/f	brought forward
BFI	British Film Institute
BG	Bulgaria (vehicle registration)
b.h.p.	brake horse power
Bi	chemical formula for bismuth
Bib.	Biblical
bibliog.	bibliographer, bibliography
bicarb	bicarbonate of soda
biog.	biographical
biol.	biological
Bk	chemical formula for berkelium
bk.	book
BL	Bachelor of Law
bldg.	building
BLitt.	Bachelor of Literature (or Letters)
blitz	blitzkrieg
blvd.	boulevard
BM	Bachelor of Medicine
BMA	British Medical Association
BMech.E	Bachelor of Mechanical Engineering
BMJ	British Medical Journal
BMus.	Bachelor of Music
Bn.	Battalion
B.O.	box office
b.o.	body odour
b/o	brought over
Boh.	Bohemia
Bol.	Bolivia
BOT	Board of Trade
bot.	botanical; bottle

BP	British Petroleum; British Pharmacopoeia
bp, bpl	birthplace
b.p.	below proof
BPhil.	Bachelor of Philosophy
BR	Brazil; British Rail
Br.	branch
br.	brown
bra	brassiere
Braz.	Brazil
Brig.	Brigadier
Brig. Gen.	Brigadier General
Brit.	British
BRN	Bahrain (vehicle registration)
Bros.	brothers
BRU	Brunei (vehicle registration)
BS	Bahamas (vehicle registration)
b.s.	bill of sale
BSc.	Bachelor of Science
BST	British Standard Time (or British Summer Time)
Bt.	Baronet
BTA	British Travel Association
BThU, Btu	British Thermal Unit
Bulg.	Bulgaria
Bur.	Burma
bus.	business
bus	omnibus
b/w, b & w	black and white
Byz.	Byzantine
Bz	chemical formula for benzene
C	chemical formula for carbon; Celsius; Centigrade; common time in music; coulomb; Cuba (vehicle registration)
c	carat; cent; centimetre; century; *(circa)* Latin for 'about (the time)'
CA	Chartered Accountant; chronological age
C/A	capital account; credit account; current account
Ca	chemical formula for calcium
CAA	Civil Aviation Authority
CAB	Citizens' Advice Bureau
cab	taxi cab
CAD	cash against documents
CAF, c & f	cost and freight

Cal.	Calcutta
Cal., CA	California
cal.	calendar; calorie
CALPA	Canadian Air Line Pilots' Association
Can.	Canberra
Canad.	Canadian
c. & b.	caught and bowled (in cricket)
Cant.	Canterbury; Cantonese
Cantab.	Cambridge (from Latin *Cantabrigiensis*)
CAP	Common Agricultural Policy
cap.	capital
caps.	capital letters
Capt.	Captain
car.	carat
CARD	Campaign Against Racial Discrimination
carr.	carriage
cartog.	cartography
cat.	catalogue
Cath.	Catholic
cath.	cathode
CB	Citizens' Band (radio)
CBA	Council for British Archaeology
Cb	chemical formula for columbium
CBC	Canadian Broadcasting Corporation
c.b.d.	cash before delivery
CBE	Commander of the British Empire
CBI	Confederation of British Industry; Central Bureau of Investigation (USA)
CBS	Columbia Broadcasting System
cc	carbon copy; closed circuit; cubic centimetres
CCC	County Cricket Club
CCP	Chinese Communist Party
CCTV	closed circuit television
c.c.w.	counter clockwise
CD	Corps Diplomatique
C/D	customs declaration
Cd	chemical formula for cadmium
cd	candela
c.d.	cash discount
CDN	Canada
Cdr.	Commander
Cdt.	Cadet

Ce	chemical formula for cerium
Cel.	Celsius
Celt.	Celtic
cent.	century
CEO	Chief Executive Officer; Chief Education Officer
cert.	certificate
cet. par.	(*ceteris paribus*) Latin for 'other things being equal'
Cf	chemical formula for californium
cf	compare
c/f	carried forward
CFI	cost, freight and insurance
cfm	cubic feet per minute
cfs	cubic feet per second
cft	cubic feet
cg	centigram
c.g.	centre of gravity
cgs	centimetre-gram-second
CH	Switzerland (vehicle registration)
chap.	chapter
char.	character
Chas	Charles
ChB	Bachelor of Surgery (Latin, *Chirurgiae Baccalaureus*)
chem.	chemistry
Chr.	Christ
chron.	chronological
chs.	chapters
CI	Commonwealth Institute; Ivory Coast (vehicle registration)
Ci	curie
CIA	Central Intelligence Agency (USA)
CID	Criminal Investigation Department
CIF	cost, insurance and freight
cig	cigarette
C-in-C	Commander-in-Chief
Cinn.	Cincinnati
cit.	citizen
civ.	civilian
ckw.	clockwise
CL	Sri Lanka (vehicle registration)
cl	centilitre
c.l.	centre line
class.	classical
CND	Campaign for Nuclear Disarmament

Co., Coy.	Company
c/o	care of
COBOL	Common Business Oriented Language
COD, c.o.d.	cash on delivery
coef.	coefficient
C of E	Church of England
c.o.g.	centre of gravity
Col.	Colonel
coll.	colloquial
Col., CO	Colorado
Comecon	Council for Mutual Economic Assistance, founded in 1949 by Soviet Russia to assist countries within Communist bloc
Cominform	Communist Information Bureau
Comintern	International Organisation of Communist Parties
compl.	complement
con	confidence trick
conf.	conference
confab	confabulation
conj.	conjunction
Cons.	Conservative
consols	Consolidated Annuities (British government securities)
contd.	continued
contemp.	contemporary
contr.	contraction
co-op	co-operative (store, farm or society)
Corp.	Corporation
corr.	correction
cox	coxswain
CP	Communist Party
CPA	Certified Public Accountant
CPF	Central Provident Fund (Singapore)
cpd.	compound
Cpl.	Corporal
CPR	Canadian Pacific Railway
CR	Costa Rica (vehicle registration)
Cr	chemical formula for chromium
cr.	credit
CRAC	Careers Research and Advisory Centre
Cres.	Crescent
crit.	criticism
croc	crocodile
CS	Czechoslovakia (vehicle registration)

Cs	chemical formula for caesium
CSE	Certificate of Secondary Education
CST	Central Standard Time
Conn., CT	Connecticut
Cu	chemical formula for copper
cu.	cubic
CV	*(Curriculum Vitae)* Latin for 'account of (one's) life'
CWO, c.w.o.	cash with order
CY	Cyprus (vehicle registration)
cyc.	cycle
cyl.	cylinder
CYO	Catholic Youth Organisation
D	Germany (vehicle registration)
d., dec.	deceased
d	(old) penny
DA	District Attorney
D/A	deposit account
DAK	Dakota
Dan.	Danish
D. & D.	drunk and disorderly
DAR	Daughters of the American Revolution
dB	decibel
DC	direct current; District Commissioner
DD	Doctor of Divinity
D-day	a date assigned for an important event, as in Allied invasion of Europe, 1944 (D: military symbol for day)
DDR	*(Deutsche Demokratische Republik)* East Germany
DDT	insecticide (dichlorodiphenyltrichlorethane)
d.e.	double entry
deb	debutante
deb.	debit
Dec.	December
def.	deficit
deg.	degree
dept.	department
deriv.	derivation
DES	Department of Education and Science
Det.	Detective
Det. Con.	Detective Constable
Det. Insp.	Detective Inspector
Det. Sgt.	Detective Sergeant

Deut.	Deuteronomy
DFC	Distinguished Flying Cross
di.	diameter
diag.	diagonal
dial.	dialect
dict.	dictionary
diff.	difference
DIG	Disablement Income Group
dil.	dilute
Dip.	Diploma
Dir.	Director
disc.	discount
diss.	dissertation
div.	dividend
DIY	do-it-yourself
DJ	disc jockey
DK	Denmark (vehicle registration)
DLit., DLitt.	Doctor of Literature; Letters
DM	Deutsche Mark
DMA	direct memory access
DNA	deoxyribonucleic acid
DNB	Dictionary of National Biography
DO	District Officer; delivery order
DOA	dead on arrival
doc	doctor
DOE	Department of the Environment
DOM	Dominican Republic (vehicle registration)
doz.	dozen
DP	displaced person
DPhil., DPh.	Doctor of Philosophy
DPP	Director of Public Prosecutions
DR	dead reckoning
Dr	Doctor
DSc.	Doctor of Science
DSC	Distinguished Service Cross
DSM	Distinguished Service Medal
DSO	Distinguished Service Order
DTs	delirium tremens
DV	*(Deo volente)* Latin for 'God willing'.
DY	Dahomey (vehicle registration)
DZ	Algeria (vehicle registration)
E	East; Spain (vehicle registration)

ea.	each
EAAC	East African Airways Corporation
EAC	East African Community
EAIRO	East African Industrial Research Organisation
EAK	Kenya (vehicle registration)
EAT	Tanzania (vehicle registration)
EAU	Uganda (vehicle registration)
EB	Encyclopedia Britannica
E-boat	enemy boat (motorboat for naval warfare)
EC	Ecuador (vehicle registration)
Eccl.	Ecclesiastical
ECG	electrocardiogram/electrocardiograph
econ.	economics
ed.	edited
educ.	educated
EE	Early English
EEG	electroencephalogram
EFL	English as a foreign language
EFTA	European Free Trade Association
e.g.	*(exempli gratia)* Latin for 'for example'
EHF	extremely high frequency
elect.	electric
Eliz.	Elizabethan
ELT	English language teaching
Emp.	Empire
enc.	enclosed
ENE	East North East
Eng.	English
engr.	engraved
env.	envelope
EO	Executive Officer
EOC	Equal Opportunities Commission
Episc.	Episcopalian
EPNS	electroplated nickel silver
eq.	equal
equiv.	equivalent
Er	chemical formula for erbium
Ernie	Electronic Random Number Indicator Equipment: computer used for British national lottery for Premium Bonds
Es	chemical formula for einsteinium
ESE	East South East
ESL	English as a second language

ESN	educationally subnormal
ESP	extra-sensory perception
esp.	especially
Esq.	Esquire
ESRO	European Space Research Organisation
ESSO	Standard Oil Company (SO)
EST	Eastern Standard Time
Est., estab.	established
est.	estimated
ET	Egypt (vehicle registration); extra-terrestrial
Et	chemical formula for ethyl
ETA	estimated time of arrival
et al.	*(et alii)* Latin for 'and others'
etc.	*(et cetera)* Latin for 'and so on'
ETD	estimated time of departure
ETV	educational television
etym.	etymological
Eu	chemical formula for europium
Eur.	European
Euratom	European Atomic Energy Community
Eurodollars	American money held in European banks
Europort	international airport at Rotterdam
Eurospace	association of space equipment makers in Europe
e.w.	each way
ex.	excluding
exam	examination
exec.	executive
ex lib.	*(ex libris)* Latin for 'from the library of'
ex off.	*(ex officio)* Latin for 'from/because of an official position'
expat	expatriate
F	Fahrenheit; chemical formula for fluorine; France (vehicle registration)
f	feet; franc
FA	Football Association
fac.	facsimile
fam.	familiar
FAR	Federation of Arab Republics
FBI	Federal Bureau of Investigation (USA)
FC	Football Club
fscap	foolscap
FD, Fid. Def.	*(Fidei Defensor)* Latin for 'Defender of the Faith'

Fd	forward
Fe	chemical formula for iron
Feb.	February
fed	federal
fem.	feminine
ff.	following
FFI	free from infection
FH	fire hydrant; field hospital
FI	Falkland Islands
fict.	fiction
FIFA	Fédération Internationale de Football Associations
fig.	figuratively
Fin.	Finland
fin.	finish
FJI	Fiji (vehicle registration)
F.Lt.	Flight Lieutenant
FL	Liechtenstein (vehicle registration)
Fl	Flanders
fl.	fluid; flourished (around that time)
Fla	Florida
fld.	field
fl. dr.	fluid dram
Flem.	Flemish
Flor.	Florida
fl. oz.	fluid ounce
flu	influenza
FM	frequency modulation
Fm	chemical formula for fermium
fm	fathom
FMD	foot and mouth disease
fn	footnote
FO	Flying Officer
fo.	folio
FOB	free on board
foll.	following
Four-H	youth club movement in USA (Head, Heart, Hands, Health)
FP	fireplug; former pupil
f.p.	foot-pound; freezing point
FPA	Family Planning Association
f.p.m.	feet per minute
FPO	Fire Prevention Officer
Fr	chemical formula for francium

Fr.	Father
Fr.	French
fr.	franc
Fri.	Friday
fridge	refrigerator
f.s.	foot-second
ft.	feet/foot
ft.-lb	foot-pound
fwd.	forward
G	German
g	gram
Ga	chemical formula for gallium
Ga., GA	Georgia
Gael.	Gaelic
gal.	gallons
galv.	galvanic
GATT	General Agreement on Tariffs and Trade
gaz.	gazette
GB	Great Britain (vehicle registration)
GBA	Alderney (vehicle registration)
GBG	Guernsey (vehicle registration)
g.b.h.	grievous bodily harm
GBJ	Jersey (vehicle registration)
GBM	Isle of Man (vehicle registration)
GBZ	Gibraltar (vehicle registration)
GC	George Cross
GCA	Guatemala (vehicle registration)
GCE	General Certificate of Education
GCF	greatest common factor
Gd	chemical formula for gadalinium
gd.	good
Gdns.	Gardens
GDR	German Democratic Republic (East Germany)
Ge	chemical formula for germanium
Gen.	General
gen.	gender
genit.	genitive
gent	gentleman
Geo.	Georgia
geog.	geography
geol.	geology

geom.	geometry
Ger.	Germany
Gestapo	*(Geheime Staatspolizei)* Hitler's secret police
GFR	Federal Republic of Germany (West Germany)
GH	Ghana (vehicle registration)
GI	Government Issue (GI = a private in the US army, from the initials on army equipment)
Gib.	Gibraltar
Gk.	Greek
g/l	grams per litre
Glas.	Glasgow
GLC	Greater London Council
GM	General Manager; George Medal
G-man	Government man: federal government agent in the USA
g	gram
GMC	General Medical Council
GMT	Greenwich Mean Time
GNP	Gross National Product
GOP	Grand Old Party (USA)
goth.	gothic
govt.	government
GP	general practitioner; general purpose
Gp. Capt.	Group Captain
gpm	gallons per minute
GPO	General Post Office
gps	gallons per second
gr.	grade
gram.	grammar
gr. wt.	gross weight
GS	groundspeed
gtd.	guaranteed
Guat.	Guatemala
GUY	Guyana (vehicle registration)
gym	gymnasium
gyro	gyroscope
H	Hungary (vehicle registration); chemical formula for hydrogen
h	hour
ha	hectare
hab.	habitat
h. & c.	hot and cold (water)

Haw.	Hawaii
HC	House of Commons
HCF	highest common factor
HD	heavy duty
HDB	Housing Development Board (Singapore)
hdbk.	handbook
HE	His Excellency
He	chemical formula for helium
Heb.	Hebrews
helio	heliograph
HF	high frequency
Hf	chemical formula for hafnium
Hg	chemical formula for mercury
HGV	Heavy Goods Vehicle
HI	Hawaiian Islands
Hind.	Hindi
hippo	hippopotamus
hist.	historical
HK	Hong Kong (vehicle registration)
HKJ	Jordan (vehicle registration)
HM	head master/mistress; Her Majesty; His Majesty
HMI	His/Her Majesty's Inspector
HMSO	His/Her Majesty's Stationery Office
HMV	His Master's Voice
HNC	Higher National Certificate
HND	Higher National Diploma
Ho	chemical formula for holmium
Hon.	Honourable
Hond.	Honduras
Hons.	Honours
Hon. Sec.	Honorary Secretary
hort.	horticulture
hosp.	hospital
HP	hire purchase; Houses of Parliament
hp	horse-power; high pressure
HQ	headquarters
HR	House of Representatives
HRH	Her/His Royal Highness
Ht.	height
HV	high voltage
hwy	highway
Hz	hertz

I	chemical formula for iodine; Italy (vehicle registration)
Ia	Iowa
IATA	International Air Transport Association
IBA	Independent Broadcasting Authority
ibid.	*(ibidem)* Latin for 'in the same place'
IBM	International Business Machines
IC	integrated circuit
i/c	in charge
ICBM	inter-continental ballistic missile
Ice.	Iceland
ICU	intensive care unit
ID	identification
Id., Ida.	Idaho
id.	*(idem)* Latin for 'the same'
i.e.	*(id est)* Latin for 'that is'
IF	intermediate frequency
IHP	indicated horse power
ILC	irrevocable letter of credit
ILEA	Inner London Education Authority
Ill.	Illinois
ILO	International Labour Organisation
ILP	Independent Labour Party
ILR	Independent Local Radio
ILTF	International Lawn Tennis Federation
IMF	International Monetary Fund
Imp.	*(Imperator)* Latin for 'Emperor'
imper.	imperative
imperf.	imperfect
imp. gall.	imperial gallon
In	chemical formula for indium
in.	inch
Inc.	Incorporated
incl.	including
incog.	incognito
incr.	increased/increasing
IND	India (vehicle registration)
Ind.	independent; Indiana
indef.	indefinite
individ.	individual
Inf.	Infantry
inf.	infinitive
info	information

init.	initial
in loc. cit.	*(in loco citato)* Latin for 'in the place cited'
INRI	*(Iesus Nazarenus Rex Iudaeorum)* Latin for 'Jesus of Nazareth, King of the Jews'
ins.	inches
insp.	inspected
Inst.	Institute
inst.	instant
Intelsat	International Consortium for Satellite Telecommunications
inter.	intermediate
intercom	intercommunication
interj.	interjection
Interpol	International Criminal Police Commission
intl.	international
intrans.	intransitive
intro	introduction
Io	chemical formula for ionium
Io.	Iowa
IOC	International Olympic Committee
IOU	I owe you
IPA	International Phonetic Alphabet
ips	inches per second
IQ	intelligence quotient
IR	Iran (vehicle registration)
Ir	chemical formula for iridium
IRA	Irish Republican Army
IRL	Republic of Ireland (vehicle registration)
IRQ	Iraq (vehicle registration)
IS	Iceland (vehicle registration)
Is.	island
isth.	isthmus
It., Ital.	Italian
ITA	Independent Television Authority
ITN	Independent Television News
ITV	Independent Television
IU	international unit
i.v.	initial velocity
IVR	International Vehicle Registration
J	Japan (vehicle registration); joule
JA	Jamaica (vehicle registration)
Jan.	January

Jas.	James
JC	Jesus Christ
JCR	Junior Common Room
jct.	junction
JCWI	Joint Council for the Welfare of Immigrants
jeep	army vehicle: from G(eneral) P(urpose)
Jnr.	junior
JP	Justice of the Peace
jt.	joint
K	kelvin
k	kilogram
Kan.	Kansas
KANU	Kenya African National Union
kc	kilocycle
KCB	Knight Commander of the Order of the Bath
kCi.	kilocurie
Ken., KY	Kentucky
kg	kilogram
KGB	*(Komitet Gosudarstvennoi Bezopasnosti)* State Security Police, USSR
kHz	kilohertz
kilo	kilogram
KKK	Ku Klux Klan (USA)
kl	kilolitre
km	kilometre
kn	knot (nautical mile)
KO	knock out
Kosbies	King's Own Scottish Borderers
Kr	chemical formula for krypton
K-ration	US army emergency food pack
Kt	Knight
kW	kilowatt
L	Latin; Luxembourg (vehicle registration); Roman numeral 50
l	litre
l.	pound (money); lire
LA	Los Angeles
La	chemical formula for lanthanum
La., LA	Louisiana
Lab.	Labrador
lab	laboratory
LAFTA	Latin American Free Trade Association

LAMDA	London Academy of Music and Dramatic Art
lang.	language
LAO	Laos (vehicle registration)
LAR	Libya (vehicle registration)
laser	lightwave amplification by stimulated emission of radiation
Lat.	Latin
lat.	latitude
LB	Liberia (vehicle registration)
lb.	pound (weight)
l.b.w.	leg before wicket (in cricket)
L/C	letter of credit
l.c.	lower case (in print)
LCC	London County Council
LCD	lowest common denominator
LCM	lowest common multiple
L/Cpl	Lance-Corporal
Ld.	Lord
LEA	Local Education Authority
LEPRA	Leprosy Relief Association
lexicog.	lexicographer
LF	low frequency
l.h.d.	left hand drive
Li	chemical formula for lithium
linac	linear accelerator
lit	literature
Litt.D.	Doctor of Letters
ll.	lines (verse, etc.)
LL.B.	Bachelor of Laws
LL.D.	Doctor of Laws
LMT	Local Mean Time
LOA	leave of absence
loc. cit.	*(loco citato)* Latin for 'in the place cited'
log	logarithm
logo	logotype (company emblem)
LP	long playing (record)
LPG	liquified petroleum gas
Lr	chemical formula for lawrencium
LRBM	long range ballistic missile
LS	Lesotho (vehicle registration)
LSD	pounds, shillings and pence; lysergic acid dicthylamide (drug)
LSE	London School of Economics

LSO	London Symphony Orchestra
Lt.	Lieutenant
LTA	Lawn Tennis Association
Lt. Col.	Lieutenant Colonel
Lt. Comdr.	Lieutenant Commander
Ltd.	Limited
Lt. Gov.	Lieutenant Governor
Lu	chemical formula for lutetium
Lux.	Luxembourg
LW	long wave
M	mach; Malta (vehicle registration); Monday
m	metre
m.	male; masculine; mile; minute; month
MA	Master of Arts; Morocco (vehicle registration)
mag.	magazine; magnitude
Maj.	Major
Maj. Gen.	Major General
MAL	Malaysia (vehicle registration)
manuf.	manufacture
MAO	chemical formula for monoamine oxidase
Mar.	March
MAS	Monetary Authority of Singapore
masc.	masculine
maser	microwave amplification by stimulated emission of radiation
MASH	Mobile Army Surgical Hospital (USA)
Mass., MS	Massachusetts
maths, math.	mathematics
max.	maximum
MB	Bachelor of Medicine
MBE	Member of the Order of the British Empire
MC	Master of Ceremonies; Military Cross; Monaco (vehicle registration)
MCh	Master of Surgery
MCS	missile control system
MD	Doctor of Medicine; Managing Director
Md	chemical formula for mendelivium
Md., MD	Maryland
Mdlle, Mlle	Mademoiselle
Mdme, Mme	Madame
ME	Medical Examiner
Me	chemical formula for methyl

MEd.	Master of Education
med.	medical; medieval
mem., memo	memorandum
merc.	mercury
Messrs	Messieurs
met.	metaphor
MEX	Mexico (vehicle registration)
MF	medium frequency
Mg	chemical formula for magnesium
mg	milligram
Mig	(*Mikoyan-Gurevich*) Russian aircraft
mike	microphone
Min.	Ministry
min.	minute
mini	mini car, mini skirt
Minn., MN	Minnesota
Mintech	Ministry of Technology
misc.	miscellaneous
Miss.	Mississippi
MIT	Massachusetts Institute of Technology
mk.	mark
ml	millilitre
Mlle	Mademoiselle
MLR	Minimum Lending Rate
Mme	Madame
Mmes	Mesdames
Mn	chemical formula for manganese
MO	Medical Officer; (*modus operandi*) Latin for 'mode of operation'
Mo	chemical formula for molybdenum
Mo., MO	Missouri
MOD	Ministry of Defence
mod	modern
MOH	Medical Officer of Health
Mons., M	Monsieur
Mont., MT	Montana
MP	Member of Parliament; Military Police
mpg	miles per gallon
mph	miles per hour
Mr	Mister
MRA	Moral Rearmament
MRBM	medium range ballistic missile

MS	manuscript
ms	millisecond
m/s	metres per second
MSC	Manpower Services Commission
MSG	chemical formula for monosodium glutamate
msl	mean sea level
Mt.	mountain
MTB	motor torpedo boat
MW	Malawi (vehicle registration); medium wave
N	chemical formula for nitrogen; North; Norway (vehicle registration); November
n.	noon; noun
NA	Netherlands Antilles (vehicle registration)
N/A	not applicable
Na	chemical formula for sodium
NAACP	National Association for the Advancement of Colored Peoples (USA)
NAAFI	Navy, Army and Air Force Institutes
NASA	National Aeronautics and Space Administration
Nat.	National
NATO	North Atlantic Treaty Organisation
Nats	Nationalists
NB	*(nota bene)* Latin for 'note well'
Nb	chemical formula for niobium
NBC	National Broadcasting Corporation (USA)
NBL	National Book League
NC	North Carolina
NCB	National Coal Board
NCCL	National Council for Civil Liberties
N. Dak., ND	North Dakota
Nd	chemical formula for neodymium
NE	New England; North East
Ne	chemical formula for neon
NEB	New English Bible
Neb., NB	Nebraska
Neddy	National Economic Development Council
nem. con.	*(nemine contradicente)* Latin for 'no one against'
NEPA	National Electric Power Authority (Nigeria)
NERC	Nigerian Educational Research Council
neut.	neuter
Nev., NV	Nevada

NF	National Front
NFER	National Foundation for Educational Research
NFS	National Fire Service
NFT	National Film Theatre
NFU	National Farmers' Union
NG	New Guinea; nitro-glycerine
NH	New Hampshire
NHS	National Health Service
Ni	chemical formula for nickel
NIC	Nicaragua (vehicle registration)
NIG	Niger (vehicle registration)
NJ	New Jersey
NL	Netherlands (vehicle registration)
NLF	National Liberation Front
NNE	North North East
NNN	New Nigerian Newspapers
NNSC	Nigerian National Supply Company
NNW	North North West
No	chemical formula for nobelium
no.	number
n.o.	not out (in cricket)
nom.	nominative
noncom.	noncommissioned
non seq.	*(non sequitur)* Latin for 'not logically following'
nos.	numbers
Nov.	November
NP	noun phrase
Np	chemical formula for neptunium
n.p.	new paragraph
NPA	Newspaper Publishers' Association; Nigerian Publishers' Association
NPC	National People's Congress
nr.	near
NS	Nova Scotia
NSPCC	National Society for the Prevention of Cruelty to Children
NSW	New South Wales
NT	National Trust
NTUC	National Trade Union Congress (Singapore)
NUM	National Union of Mineworkers
NUT	National Union of Teachers
NUS	National Union of Seamen; National Union of Students; National University of Singapore

NW	North West
NY	New York
NZ	New Zealand (vehicle registration)
NZBS	New Zealand Broadcasting Service
O	chemical formula for oxygen
o/a	on account
O & M	organisation and method
OAP	old age pensioner
OAS	Organisation of American States
OAU	Organisation of African Unity
OB	outside broadcast
OBE	Officer of the Order of the British Empire
obj.	object; objective
obs.	obscure
Oct.	October
ODA	Overseas Development Administration
OE	Old English
OED	Oxford English Dictionary
OF	Old French
OH	Ohio
OHMS	On Her/His Majesty's Service
Okla., OK	Oklahoma
O Level	Ordinary Level (GCE examination)
OM	Order of Merit
ONC	Ordinary National Certificate
OND	Ordinary National Diploma
o.n.o.	or nearest offer
Ont.	Ontario
007	code number for James Bond (in the Ian Fleming novels and films)
op.	operation
op. cit.	*(opere citato)* Latin for 'in the work cited'
OPEC	Organisation of Petroleum Exporting Countries
OR	operational research
Ore., OR	Oregon
orig.	original; originally
Os	chemical formula for osmium
OSS	Office of Strategic Services
OTC	Officers' Training Corps
OU	Open University
OXFAM	Oxford (Committee for) Famine Relief

oz.	ounce
P	chemical formula for phosphorus; Portugal (vehicle registration)
p.	page
PA	Panama (vehicle registration); personal assistant
Pa	chemical formula for protactinium
Pa., PA, Penn.	Pennsylvania
p.a.	*(per annum)* Latin for 'each year'
PAK	Pakistan (vehicle registration)
Pal	Phase Alternation Line (625-line colour TV)
PAP	People's Action Party (Singapore)
P & O	Peninsular and Oriental (Shipping Co.)
para	paratroop
part.	participle
Pat. Off.	Patent Office
PAYE	pay as you earn (tax)
Pb	chemical formula for lead
PBS	Public Broadcasting System (USA)
PC	Police Constable; Provincial Commissioner
p.c.	post card
Pd	chemical formula for palladium
pd.	paid
PDSA	People's Dispensary for Sick Animals
PE	Peru (vehicle registration); physical education
PEN Club	Poets, Playwrights, Essayists, Novelists Club
perm	permanent wave
PERT	Program Evaluation and Review Technique
PF	pro forma (invoice)
PFC	Private First Class (USA)
PG	paying guest
PGA	Professional Golfers' Association
PhD	Doctor of Philosophy
phone	telephone
photo	photograph
phr.	phrase
phys. ed.	physical education
PI	Philippine Islands (vehicle registration)
pkt.	packet
PL	Poland (vehicle registration)
plane	aeroplane
PLC, plc	public limited company

PLO	Palestine Liberation Organisation
plur.	plural
PM	Prime Minister
Pm	chemical formula for promethium
p.m.	*(post meridiem)* Latin for 'after noon'
PMG	Paymaster General
PO	Post Office; Petty Officer
Po	chemical formula for polonium
polio	poliomyelitis
Politburo	Political Bureau (Russia)
poly	polytechnic
pop	popular music
POSB	Post Office Savings Bank (Singapore)
poss.	possessive
POW	prisoner of war
pp	*(per procurationem)* Latin for 'on behalf of'
pp.	pages
PPE	Philosophy, Politics and Economics ('Modern Greats')
PPS	Parliamentary Private Secretary
PR	Proportional Representation; Public Relations
Pr	chemical formula for prosodymium
pram	perambulator
pred.	predicate; predicator
prefab	prefabricated
prep.	preparation; preparatory; preposition
Presb.	Presbyterian
prim.	primary
prin.	principal
PRO	Public Relations Officer
pro.	professional
Prof.	Professor
prom	promenade; promenade concert
pron.	pronoun
prop	stage property
Provo.	Provisional (IRA)
PSA	Port of Singapore Authority
pseud.	pseudonym
psf	pounds per square foot
psi	pounds per square inch
PSV	Public Service Vehicle
PT	physical training
Pt	chemical formula for platinum

pt.	part; point
PTA	Parent Teacher Association
Pte	Private
PTO	please turn over
pts.	pints; points
Pty	proprietary
Pu	chemical formula for plutonium
pub	public house
pub.	published/publisher
PVC	polyvinylchloride
PW	policewoman
PX	Post Exchange (USA)
PY	Paraguay (vehicle registration)
Q	Queen
q.	question
QC	Queen's Counsel
QED	*(quod erat demonstrandum)* Latin for 'which was to be proven'
Qld	Queensland
QM	Quartermaster
qt.	quart
q.t.	quiet
qtr.	quarter
quad	quadrangle; quadruplet
quango	quasi-autonomous nongovernmental organisation
quin	quintuplet
quot.	quotation
q.v.	*(quod vide)* Latin for 'which see'
R	Rumania (vehicle registration)
r.	river
RA	Argentina (vehicle registration); Rear Admiral
Ra	chemical formula for radium
RAAF	Royal Australian Air Force
RAC	Royal Automobile Club
RACA	Royal Automobile Club of Australia
RACP	Royal Australian College of Physicians
RADA	Royal Academy of Dramatic Art
radar	radio detection and ranging
RAF	Royal Air Force
RAMC	Royal Army Medical Corps
RAN	Royal Australian Navy

R & D	research and development
RB	Botswana (vehicle registration)
Rb	chemical formula for rubidium
RC	China (vehicle registration); Roman Catholic
RCA	Central African Republic (vehicle registration)
RCAF	Royal Canadian Air Force
RCB	Congo (vehicle registration)
RCH	Chile (vehicle registration)
RCMP	Royal Canadian Mounted Police
Rd.	road
RE	religious education
re.	rupee
recap	recapitulate
ref	referee
ref.	reference
rel.	relative; related
REME	Royal Electrical and Mechanical Engineers
rep	representative; repertory theatre
repro.	reproduction
resp.	respectively
Rev.	Reverend
rev.	review
revs	revolutions (engine)
RF	radio frequency
RFC	Rugby Football Club
RGS	Royal Geographical Society
Rgt.	Regiment
RH	Haiti (vehicle registration)
Rh	chemical formula for rhodium
rhino	rhinoceros
RI	Indonesia (vehicle registration)
RIBA	Royal Institute of British Architects
RIM	Mauritania (vehicle registration)
RIP	(*requiescat in pace*) Latin for 'rest in peace'
RL	Lebanon (vehicle registration)
RM	Malagasy Republic (vehicle registration)
RMM	Mali (vehicle registration)
RN	Royal Navy
Rn	chemical formula for radon
RNA	ribonucleic acid
rnd.	round
RNLI	Royal National Lifeboat Institution

RNR	Zambia (vehicle registration)
RNVR	Royal Naval Volunteer Reserve
ROK	Korea (vehicle registration)
RP	received pronunciation
rph	revolutions per hour
rpm	revolutions per minute
rps	revolutions per second
rpt	report
RR	Rolls Royce
RSC	Royal Shakespeare Company
RSM	Regimental Sergeant Major; San Marino (vehicle registration)
RSPB	Royal Society for the Protection of Birds
RSPCA	Royal Society for the Prevention of Cruelty to Animals
RSPCC	Royal Society for the Prevention of Cruelty to Children
RSVP	*(repondez s'il vous plaît)* French for 'please reply'
RT	radio telegraphy; radio telephony
Rt.Hon.	Right Honourable
RU	Burundi (vehicle registration)
RUC	Royal Ulster Constabulary
RWA	Rwanda (vehicle registration)
RZS	Royal Zoological Society
S	Saturday; South; Sweden (vehicle registration)
s	second
SA	South Australia
s.a.e.	stamped addressed envelope
SALT	Strategic Arms Limitation Talks
SAM	surface to air missile
SANU	Sudan African National Union
SAT	South Australian Time
Sat.	Saturday
SAYE	save as you earn
sax	saxophone
Sb	chemical formula for antimony
SBC	Singapore Broadcasting Corporation
SBS	Singapore Bus Service
Sc	chemical formula for scandium
SCE	Secondary Certificate of Education
SCM	Student Christian Movement
Scot.	Scotland; Scottish
SCR	Senior Common Room
SD	Swaziland (vehicle registration)

SDP	Social Democratic Party
SE	South East
Se	chemical formula for selenium
SEAC	South-East Asia Command
SEATO	South-East Asia Treaty Organisation
Secy.	Secretary
SEN	State Enrolled Nurse
Sen.	Senator
Sept.	September
SF	Finland (vehicle registration); science fiction
SGP	Singapore (vehicle registration)
Sgt.	Sergeant
Shak.	Shakespeare
SHAPE	Supreme Headquarters, Allied Powers, Europe
Si	chemical formula for silicon
sing.	singular
SJ	Society of Jesus
SME	Surinam (vehicle registration)
SN	Senegal (vehicle registration)
Snr.	senior
SOS	Save Our Souls (distress signal)
sp.	spelling
Spasur	Space Surveillance
SPCK	Society for Promoting Christian Knowledge
SPQR	(*Senatus Populusque Romanus*) Latin inscription meaning 'The Roman Senate and People'
sq.ft.	square foot
sq.in.	square inch
Sr	chemical formula for strontium
SRBM	short range ballistic missile
SRN	State Registered Nurse
SSE	South South East
SSM	surface to surface missile
SSW	South South West
St.	Saint; street
Sta.	station
START	Strategic Arms Reduction Talks
STD	subscriber trunk dialling
STOL	short take-off and landing
Stuka	(*Stutzkampfbomber*) German dive bomber
STV	Scottish Television
SU	USSR (vehicle registration)

Sun.	Sunday
suppl.	supplement
Supt.	Superintendent
SW	South West; short wave
SWAPO	South West Africa People's Organisation
SY	Seychelles (vehicle registration)
syn.	synonym
SYR	Syria (vehicle registration)
T	Thailand (vehicle registration); chemical formula for tritium; Tuesday
TA	Territorial Army
Ta	chemical formula for tantalum
TAM-ratings	Television Audience Measurement
TANU	Tanganyikan African National Union
tarmac	tarmacadam
taxi	taxi cab
TB	torpedo boat; tuberculosis
Tb	chemical formula for terbium
tech.	technical
TEFL	teaching English as a foreign language
temp.	temperature
Tenn., TN	Tennessee
TES	Times Educational Supplement
TESL	teaching English as a second language
Tex., TX	Texas
TG	Togo (vehicle registration)
Th.	Thursday
Thos.	Thomas
Ti	chemical formula for titanium
tkt.	ticket
TLS	Times Literary Supplement
TN	Tunisia (vehicle registration)
TNT	trinitrotoluene (explosive)
TR	Turkey (vehicle registration)
trans.	transitive; translated
tripl.	triplicate
trs.	transpose
TSB	Trustee Savings Bank
TT	teetotaller; Trinidad and Tobago (vehicle registration)
TUC	Trades Union Congress
Tues.	Tuesday

TVEI	Technical and Vocational Education Initiative
TWA	Trans-World Airlines
U	chemical formula for uranium; Uruguay (vehicle registration)
UAE	United Arab Emirates
UAR	United Arab Republic
U-boat	*(Unterseeboot)* German submarine
u.c.	upper case (in print)
UCAR	Union of Central African Republics
UCCA	Universities Central Council on Admissions
UDA	Ulster Defence Association
UDI	Unilateral Declaration of Independence
UDR	Ulster Defence Regiment
UFO	unidentified flying object
UGC	University Grants Committee
UHF	ultra high frequency
UK	United Kingdom (of Great Britain)
ult.	*(ultimo)* Latin for 'last month'
UN	United Nations
UNESCO	United Nations Educational, Scientific and Cultural Organisation
UNICEF	United Nations International Children's Emergency Fund
univ.	university
UNO	United Nations Organisation
US	United States
USA	United States of America (vehicle registration)
USSR	Union of Soviet Socialist Republics
usu.	usually
V	Vatican City (vehicle registration)
v	volt
v.	versus; verb
Va., VA	Virginia
VAT	Value Added Tax
Vat.	Vatican
VC	Victoria Cross
VDU	visual display unit
vet	veterinary surgeon
v.g.	very good
VHF	very high frequency
v.i.	verb intransitive
VIP	Very Important Person
viz.	*(videlicet)* Latin for 'namely'

VJ Day	Victory against Japan Day (14 August 1945)
VLF	very low frequency
VN	Vietnam (vehicle registration)
vocab.	vocabulary
VP	verb phrase
vs.	(versus) Latin for 'against'
VSO	Voluntary Service Overseas
VTOL	vertical take-off and landing (aircraft)
VTR	video tape recorder
W	West
WA	West Africa; Western Australia
WAAF	Women's Auxiliary Air Force
WAG	Gambia (vehicle registration)
WAI	War Against Indiscipline (Nigeria)
WAL	Sierra Leone (vehicle registration)
WAN	Nigeria (vehicle registration)
WASP	White Anglo-Saxon Protestant
WBA	World Boxing Association
WBC	World Boxing Council
w.c.	water closet
WCC	World Council of Churches
W/Cdr	Wing Commander
WD	Dominica (vehicle registration); War Department
WEA	Workers' Educational Association
Wed.	Wednesday
WG	Grenada (vehicle registration)
WHO	World Health Organisation
WI	West Indies; Women's Institute
wkly	weekly
WL	St Lucia (vehicle registration)
WLM	women's liberation movement
WMA	World Medical Association
WNW	West North West
WO	War Office; Warrant Officer
WPC	Woman Police Constable
wpm	words per minute
WRNS (WREN)	Women's Royal Naval Service
WRI	Women's Rural Institute
WS	Western Samoa (vehicle registration)
WSW	West South West
wt.	weight

WV	St Vincent (vehicle registration)
WWF	World Wildlife Fund
WX	women's extra (large size)
WZO	World Zionist Organisation
X	Christ
Xe	chemical formula for xenon
XL	extra large
Xmas	Christmas
Xty	Christianity
Y	chemical formula for yttrium
y, yd.	yard
YB	year book
YHA	Youth Hostels Association
YMCA	Young Men's Christian Association
YOP	Youth Opportunities Project
yr.	year
YTS	Youth Training Scheme
YU	Yugoslavia (vehicle registration)
YV	Venezuela (vehicle registration)
YWCA	Young Women's Christian Association
Z	Zambia (vehicle registration)
ZANU	Zimbabwe African National Union
ZAPU	Zimbabwe African People's Union
ZC	Zionist Congress
Zn	chemical formula for zinc
Zod.	zodiac
zoo	zoological gardens
ZR	Zaire (vehicle registration)
Zr	chemical formula for zirconium

3 USAGE

FORMAL AND INFORMAL USAGE

There are many forms of English in current use in the world. One important distinction is that between **formal English** and **informal English**. Formal English is usually known as 'correct' English. The vocabulary and grammar of formal English are common to the English spoken everywhere by well-educated people and in written English. Informal English is normally used in everyday speech or in the dialogue of novels, plays, etc.

	FORMAL	INFORMAL
GRAMMAR	I am not, he is not I do not have, he does not have She asked me if I would join her.	I'm not, he's not (I ain't, he ain't) I haven't got, he hasn't got She asked me would I join her.
VOCABULARY	food steal puzzle money friend father umbrella	grub swipe bamboozle dough, bread pal dad, daddy, pop brolly

DIALECTS OF ENGLISH

Dialects are varieties of the language used by certain groups of people. A **social dialect** is the variety used by people of similar social habits. A **geographical dialect** is the variety used by people living in a particular district or country. Modern English has many dialects, the principal ones being Southern County English, North Country English, Scots, Irish, Welsh, certain American varieties (such as Kentucky, Bronx), Black American, West Indian, Australian, African, Asian:

STANDARD ENGLISH	DIALECT ENGLISH	SCOTS	AMERICAN
child	youngster	bairn	kid
man	chap	chiel	guy
policemen	bobbies	polis	cops

GEOGRAPHICAL VARIATIONS

Standard English spoken in different countries also contains different words for the same things. The principal variations are those between **British English** and **American English**. Some of the American words are now commonly used in British English:

BRITISH ENGLISH	AMERICAN ENGLISH
aerial	antenna
anywhere	any place
autumn	fall
block of flats	apartment building
bonnet (of car)	hood (of car)
boot (of car)	trunk (of car)
braces	suspenders
caravan	house trailer
caretaker	janitor
carrier bag	shopping bag
chemist (shop)	druggist or drug store
chips (potato)	french fries
cliff	bluff
cooker	stove
corn	wheat
cot	crib
cotton wool	absorbent cotton
crash	wreck
crisps (potato)	potato chips
crossroads	intersection
cuff	turn-up
cul de sac	dead end
cupboard	closet
directory enquiries	(telephone) information
diversion	detour
draughts	checkers
drawing pin	thumbtack
driver (of train)	engineer
dual carriageway	divided highway
dustbin	garbage can
dust cart	garbage truck
dustman	garbage man
dynamo	generator

BRITISH ENGLISH	AMERICAN ENGLISH
engine	motor
essay (assignment)	term paper
estate agent	realtor
film, picture	movie
first floor	second floor
first year student	freshman
flat	apartment
flyover	overpass
gear lever	gear stick
give way	yield
grain	corn
grill	broiler
grilled	broiled
ground floor	first floor
gym-shoes	sneakers
head-master/mistress	principal
hire purchase	instalment buying
hoarding	billboard
holiday	vacation
hood (of car)	top (of car)
housing estate	housing project
ill	sick
interval	intermission
ironmonger	hardware store
jug	pitcher
jumper	sweater
lay-by	roadside parking
lift	elevator
lorry	truck
mackintosh	raincoat
motor car	automobile
motor caravan	camper
motorway	thruway, turnpike, parkway
mudguard	wing or fender
nursing home	private clinic
optician	optometrist
opthalmic surgeon	opthalmologist

BRITISH ENGLISH	AMERICAN ENGLISH
option	elective
oven glove	pot-holder
paraffin	kerosene
part exchange	trade-in
petrol	gasoline
pillar box	mailbox
polo-neck (sweater)	turtle-neck
post	mail
power point	electric outlet
perambulator	baby carriage
public house	bar
public lavatory	rest room
public school	private school
puncture (flat tyre)	flat
push-chair	baby stroller
queue	stand (or wait) in line
railway	railroad
record player	phonograph
reel (of cotton)	spool
return ticket	round trip
reverse charges	call collect
roller blind	window shade
roundabout	traffic circle, rotary
rubbish	garbage or trash
saloon car	sedan
serviette	napkin
shop assistant	sales clerk
silencer	muffler
single (ticket)	one-way (ticket)
solicitor	attorney
spanner	wrench; monkey wrench
standard	regular
sump	oil pan
suspenders	garters
sweet biscuits	cookies
sweets	candy
tap	faucet
taxi	cab
tea towel	dish towel

BRITISH ENGLISH	AMERICAN ENGLISH
ticket office	booking office
timetable	schedule
toilet	lavatory
torch	flashlight
tramcar	streetcar
tramp	hobo
transport	transportation
underground	subway
unit trust	mutual fund
van	truck
verge (of road)	shoulder (of road)
vest	undershirt
waistcoat	vest
waste paper	trash
waste paper basket	trash can
windscreen	windshield
zebra crossing	pedestrian crossing
zip	zipper

COLLOQUIALISMS AND SLANG

Colloquialisms are words and phrases which are not suitable for formal correct English but which are used in everyday speech by all speakers of modern English. **Slang** words and phrases are regarded as being below the standard of 'educated' speech and are used by particular social groups. Here is a list of the most common colloquial and slang expressions in current use:

EXPRESSION	MEANING
abo	aboriginal (Australian)
ace	1 winning serve at tennis 2 anything very successful 3 star at a sport
acid	LSD, a hallucinatory drug
across the board	without exceptions
afters	sweet course at a meal
anchor-man	chairman of a TV panel
appro, on	on approval
argy-bargy	1 argument 2 to argue
bad lot	wicked person

EXPRESSION	MEANING
bag (verb)	to obtain
bag (noun)	trade or specialism
bag *of tricks, the whole*	every object or device
bags *of*	plenty of (usually money)
ball game, a new	changed situation
ball park figure	rough estimate
bally-hoo	fuss
bamboozle	to trick
banger	**1** sausage **2** old car
barmy, balmy	slightly insane
bash, have a	to try
basinful, a	excess
bats	eccentric
bawl out	to give someone a talking-to
beat	**1** popular music with strong rhythm
	2 exhausted
beat it	to leave
beat up	to attack someone brutally
beef	to complain
belly-ache	to complain loudly
belt up	be quiet
belt, to hit below the	to give someone an unfair shock
bevvy	drink, usually of beer
big noise	important person
big shot	important person
big wig	important person
bike, get on your	**1** to hurry **2** to go away
bird	girl
bitch, to	to complain
blink, on the	not working properly
blitz	sudden attack
blow (your) top	to be suddenly angry
blower	telephone
blue-collar	connected with manual work
blue moon, once in a	very seldom
bomb, cost a	to be very expensive
bone up	to study
boot, to get the	to get the sack
boot, put in the	to attack someone cruelly
boozer	public house
bottle	courage
bounce	(of a cheque) to be rejected

EXPRESSION	MEANING
bouncer	someone employed to throw out trouble-makers
box clever	to act cunningly
break	chance
brick, drop a	to make a mistake
brinkmanship	in politics, relying on a crisis
broke	without any money
browned off	1 bored 2 dissatisfied
brunch	breakfast and lunch together
bubbly	champagne
buff	enthusiast (e.g. for a sport or hobby)
bug (verb)	1 to plant a listening device 2 to annoy
bug (noun)	1 germ 2 infection 3 listening device
bull	foolishness
bumf	useless paperwork
bundle	a lot (of money)
bunk, do a	to flee
bus, miss the	to miss an opportunity
bushed	exhausted
busker	street entertainer
busted	arrested
buzz-word	fashionable new term
cackle, cut the	stop speaking and get down to business
cagey	cautious
canned	drunk
carpet, on the	to be in trouble with a superior
carry the can	take the blame
carve up	1 preplanned agreement (to share loot) 2 a swindle
chamber of horrors	collection of hateful people
chancer	1 liar 2 someone who tries to deceive
chat show	TV programme of interviews and discussion
chat up	to flirt
cheesed off	1 bored 2 disgruntled
chicken-feed	very small amount
choke off	to reprimand
chronic	very bad
chuffed	pleased
cliff hanger	film or story full of exciting dangers
clot	fool
clueless	1 ignorant 2 stupid
cock up, to	to spoil

EXPRESSION	MEANING
cock-up	mess
codswallop	nonsense
come across	to yield
come clean	to confess
come-down	disgrace
come off it!	stop pretending!
come-on	trick to gain attention
commie	communist
con	**1** to cheat **2** a deception
cool	**1** good (at jazz) **2** pleasant **3** calm
cop, not much	of little value
corny	old-fashioned; out of fashion
crawler	ingratiating person
crook	criminal
crummy	**1** dirty **2** very bad
crunch	crisis
dandy	very good
dash	bribe (West Africa)
dead beat	exhausted
dead loss	**1** dull **2** useless
deep end, to throw someone in at the	to plunge someone into the most difficult part of an activity
dig	to understand
dim	stupid
disc jockey	someone who conducts a radio or TV show for playing records, or who plays the records at a disco
discotheque, disco	dance at which the music is from records
dish	attractive girl
dishy	pretty
dive	night club
do, to	**1** to cheat **2** to suffice **3** to assault
do	ceremony or party
do gooder	someone intent on charity
do in	to kill
do your stuff	do your best
do time	to be in prison
dodge	trick
dodgy	difficult
dolly bird	attractive young girl
done for	**1** exhausted **2** ruined
dope	**1** drugs **2** stupid person **3** information

EXPRESSION	MEANING
dopey	stupid
dot, the year	long time ago
dough	money
drag	women's clothing (when worn by a man)
drip	silly person
drip-dry	clothing which does not need to be ironed
drop-out	someone who has rejected conventional standards of life, etc.
dud	valueless
dumb	stupid
dummy run	rehearsal
dump	poor place to live
eager beaver	enthusiast
ear, bend someone's	to bore someone
elevenses	midmorning cup of tea or coffee
even Steven	share equally
fab	*(fabulous)* excellent
fall for	to be attracted to
fall through	to fail
far out!	excellent!
fed up	**1** bored **2** disgusted **3** depressed
fiddle	to cheat
fill someone in	to assault someone
fire	to dismiss from a job
fishy	strange
flap, in a	excited and confused
flash	showy
flog	to sell
flop	failure
frame	to falsely put the blame on someone
freak	**1** addict **2** enthusiast
freak out	**1** become faint or unconscious **2** lose control **3** become hysterical
fudge	to confuse deliberately
funk	fear
fuzz	police
gab	to talk foolishly or endlessly
gag	**1** joke **2** stage trick
gate-crasher	uninvited guest
gay	homosexual

EXPRESSION	MEANING
gear	clothing
get *away with*	succeed
get *cracking*	to hurry
get *it in the neck*	to be punished
get *your head down*	work harder
get *weaving*	hurry
gig	single booking for a band
gimmick	**1** trick or device **2** catch-phrase
ginger-group	group formed to persuade others to take some action
give-away	revealing sign
glossy	magazine with many photographs
go-ahead	determined to succeed
go back on	to desert
go by	deliberate snub
go over big	to be a success
goner	**1** dead person **2** unsuccessful person
gong	**1** medal **2** decoration
goon	stupid person
graft	work hard
grass	**1** to inform **2** police informer **3** marijuana
grass roots, at the	among ordinary people
grease *(someone's palm)*	to bribe
grotty	unpleasant
group	band of popular musicians
groupie	follower of a pop group
guff	nonsense
gush	talk foolishly
guts	courage
hair, get in someone's	to annoy someone
hair-do	having your hair set, etc.
hairs, get by the short (and curly)	to have someone at your mercy
hairy	**1** uncertain **2** dangerous
half-baked	badly thought out
ham	old actor
hang-up	neurosis or obsession
hangover	sick feeling after over-indulgence in alcohol
hard case	'tough' person
hard cheese	bad luck
hard-up	lacking money

EXPRESSION	MEANING
hassle	**1** quarrel **2** trouble
have had it	to be defeated
have it in for someone	to bear a grudge
haywire, to go	to go badly wrong
head case	lunatic
head down, get your	to have a sleep
head down, have your	**1** to be tired **2** to be ashamed **3** to be defeated
head down, keep your	to be careful
head, swelled	conceited
head cook and bottle washer	boss
heart, have a	be considerate
heel	bad person
hi-fi	high fidelity (in sound reproduction)
high	intoxicated (usually on drugs)
high-up	important person
high-rise	very tall building
highbrow	intellectual
highjack	to steal by menacing (e.g. an aeroplane or lorry)
hippie	young person who has rejected conventional society
hit	success
hold it!	stop everything!
hold on!	wait a moment!
hold your horses!	wait!
holy terror	badly-behaved person
hooey	nonsense
hoo-ha	fuss
hooked	addicted
hop, keep (someone) on the	to keep (someone) busy
horn in	to interfere
horse-trading	bargaining
hot	**1** stolen **2** (of music) strongly rhythmical
hot, not so	not attractive
hot stuff	to be very skilled or attractive
hot time, have a	to have an enjoyable time
howler	mistake
hunch	intuition
hype	**1** to make something stronger, or more dramatic **2** to promote (with publicity)

EXPRESSION	MEANING
iffy	uncertain
in	popular, fashionable
in on, to be	to be privy to (a secret or a joke)
in the red	in debt
info	information
into (something)	to be interested in (something)
intro	introduction
jackpot	**1** main prize **2** great deal of money
jag	inoculation
Jag	Jaguar car
jam	jazz
jam on it, to want	to want more than your due
jammy	lucky
jinx	bringer of bad luck
jitters	bad nerves
joint	**1** cigarette containing marijuana
	2 place with a disreputable atmosphere
juice	fuel (petrol, gas, electricity)
juicy	attractive
jumbo jet	**1** Boeing 747 aircraft **2** very large aeroplane
jump the queue	to go ahead of your turn
jumped-up	snobbish
jumpy	nervous
just the job	the right thing
keep tabs on	to stay in contact with
keep under your hat	to keep secret
keep your hair on!	calm down!
key man	most important man
kick-off	beginning
kicked upstairs	promoted
kid	to fool someone, to joke
kip; (to)	**1** bed **2** (to) sleep
knackered	**1** exhausted **2** spoiled
knees-up	party
knock	to criticise
knock-about	noisy
knock back	to drink
knock into	to meet
knock off	to steal
knock-out	**1** final blow **2** great success

EXPRESSION	MEANING
know your onions	to be well-informed
know-how	**1** skill **2** knowledge
la-di-da	**1** too smartly dressed **2** snobbish
laid back	relaxed
lambast	to criticise severely
lark	trick
laugh like a drain	laugh heartily
layabout	lazy, idle person
lay about	to attack indiscriminately
lay into	to attack (usually verbally)
leak	to disclose information
lean over backwards	to make an effort (e.g. to conciliate someone)
leg-pull	joke
let-down	disappointment
let on	to admit
let out	to reveal
lifer	someone with a life sentence in prison
lift	to steal
lift your elbow	to drink excessively
like greased lightning	exceedingly fast
like it or lump it	take it or leave it
livid	very angry
lobby	to try to persuade someone to help your cause
local	public house in the area
lock-out	exclusion of workers by an employer
lolly	money
loo	lavatory
lousy	contemptible
lousy with (money)	very rich
lowbrow	not an intellectual
lowdown	information
low profile	not attracting attention
Mackay, the real	the genuine article
make it	succeed
make your pile	to become rich
mark	victim
mash	mashed potatoes
measly	**1** mean **2** contemptible
menace	nuisance
mess about	to waste time

EXPRESSION	MEANING
Mickey Mouse	**1** artificial **2** oddly constructed
mind-bending	astounding
mind-blowing	very exciting
mini	small
mob	gang
month of Sundays	very long time
mooch	to beg
moonlight	to have a spare-time job
mouldy	of no value
muck about	to waste time
muck in	to join in, to share
muck up	to spoil
muff	to play a poor shot (in a game)
mug	**1** to attack and rob **2** a fool
mugs away	losers begin the next game
off-the-cuff	without forethought or preparation
off the peg	ready-made (of clothing)
off the record	unofficial
oiled	drunk
oldie	**1** old record or song **2** older person
on the ball	**1** efficient **2** alert
on the spot	immediately
open-ended	without conclusion in mind
out of the wood	out of danger
out of this world	very good
over the moon	very happy
packet	large amount of money
paddy	fit of temper
pain in the neck	boring person
panic	flurry of excitement
paralytic	very drunk
pass the buck	put the blame on someone else
pay-off	bribe, settlement
payola	practice of bribery in advertising
pay-rise	increase in pay
peg out	to die
phony	false
pie in the sky	dreamed-of prosperity
pig	policeman
pile-up	multiple car accident

EXPRESSION	MEANING
pin-up	picture of an attractive girl
pinch	1 to arrest 2 to steal
pink, in the	to be fit
pitch in	join in
plant	to hide something
plastered	drunk
plonk	cheap wine
plug	to advertise
polish off	to complete
pong	smell
pooped	exhausted
pop	popular music
pops, the	the current favourite songs
porridge	time spent in jail
posh	1 upper-class 2 very smart
pot	marijuana
pot, to go to	to go towards ruin
potty	crazy
pre-fab	prefabricated house
private eye	private detective
pro	professional
pro, old	old actor or performer
psychedelic	1 brilliantly colourful 2 hallucinatory
puff	to give publicity to a song, record, etc.
pukka	genuine
pull your punches	to be moderate
punk	1 inferior 2 particular lifestyle in 1980s, characterised by style of dressing, etc.
push the boat out	1 to be adventurous 2 to take a chance
put a sock in it!	be quiet!
put down	to disparage
quack	originally a fraudulent doctor, now any doctor
queer	1 unwell 2 slightly mad 3 homosexual
quicky	short question (in a quiz)
quid	£1 note
quit	1 to give in 2 concede defeat
rabbit	beginner (at a sport)
racket	illegal or unsavoury business
rake-off	share of dishonest gains
rampage, on the	showing fury
rap, take the	take the blame

EXPRESSION	MEANING
raspberry	rude noise
rat	**1** to inform **2** to betray
rave-up	great enjoyment
recap	(*recapitulate*) run through the main points again
red, in the	to be in debt
ref	referee
rep	**1** repertory (theatre) **2** travelling salesman
re-think	to reconsider
rib	to tease
ride, take (someone) for a	to cheat (someone)
rig	to arrange matters for a purpose
right on	well done
rings a bell	reminds you of something
rip off	to steal from or cheat
rock	type of popular music
rough up	to beat someone up
round the bend	crazy
row	quarrel
rub in	to emphasise
rumble	to detect
rumpus	uproar
run the show	to be the boss
sabre-rattling	threatening
sack	dismiss
sauce	impudence
sausage, not have a	to be without money
scab	worker who refuses to go on strike
scarce, make yourself	**1** to go into hiding **2** to go away
scarper	to run away
scoff	**1** to eat **2** to be scornful
scoot	to run away
screwball	crazy person
scrounge	to beg
scrubby	untidy
scuppered	**1** spoiled **2** damaged beyond repair
send up	to make fun of
send-up	satire
shiner	black eye
shirt, lose your	lose all your money (in gambling)
shoot!	begin!
shoot your mouth off	to boast

EXPRESSION	MEANING
shop, to	to inform on someone
shove, the	dismissal
show	1 affair 2 event 3 operation
show-biz	business of the theatre, films, TV, etc.
show-down	confrontation
show, steal the	to gain the credit
shut-eye	sleep
side-kick	partner
sing	confess
sissy, cissy	effeminate
sit-in	occupation of a building in order to protest
sitter	easy target
sitting pretty	to be successful
skates on, put your	hurry
skint	to have no money
skip it!	pay no attention!
skive	to evade responsibility
skunk	contemptible person
slam	to criticise severely
slip up	to make a mistake
slob	lazy or overweight, untidy person
slog	hard work
slug	to strike savagely
smarmy	ingratiating
smashing	excellent
sneezed at, not to be	not to be despised
snide	1 sarcastic 2 sneering
snifter	drink
snip	bargain
snoop	to investigate
snooper	detective
snooty	snobbish
snort	drink
snuff it	to die
soak	drunkard
soap opera	popular serial on radio or TV
soft option	choice which is easier than others
soft soap	flattery
spare	mad
spec, on	1 as a gamble 2 unplanned
spiel	sales talk

EXPRESSION	MEANING
spin-off	related benefit
split	to run away
spoof	1 trick 2 hoax
spot check	unexpected inspection
square	someone old-fashioned or conventional
squatter	illicit occupant of an empty house
stacks	many
stall	to delay
stand-off	impasse
starkers	naked
stewed	drunk
stick	dull person
sticks, the	the provinces (country as opposed to town)
sting	swindle
stooge	1 scapegoat 2 assistant
straight	honest
streaker	someone who runs naked in public
stuck up	conceited
stuffy	1 dull 2 strait-laced
stunning	1 excellent 2 beautiful
stunt	contrived publicity event or entertainment
suck up to someone	to ingratiate yourself with someone
super	excellent
swan around	to go about aimlessly
swanky	conceited
swap, swop	exchange
swell	important person
swinger	modern, lively person
swinging	lively, cheerful
swiz	cheat
tail	to follow
take off	go away
take-over	purchase of one company by another
take the can (back)	take the blame
taped, have someone	to understand or see through someone
tarmac	tarred surface of a road
tatty	cheap
telly	television
tenner	£10 note
tested	very drunk
thick	stupid

EXPRESSION	MEANING
think tank	group of experts
tick	credit
tin	money
toff	well-dressed person
toffee-nosed	snobbish
ton, do a	drive at 100 miles per hour
top, go over the	to take a chance
tops, the	the best
tosh	nonsense
trad	traditional (music)
trap!, shut your	be quiet!
trendy	fashionable
trick cyclist	psychiatrist
trip	effect of a drug session
tripe	rubbish
twee	too sweet or sentimental
twist	cheat
undies	underwear
unisex	clothing which can be worn by both sexes
unstuck, come	to fail
uptight	**1** nervous **2** anxious
u/s	useless
vamoose	to go away
VIP	Very Important Person
wacky	crazy
waffle	to speak nonsense
wallop	**1** to strike violently **2** beer
wangle	to contrive
warts and all	with all (one's) faults
wash-out	failure
wasted	**1** spoilt **2** drunk
way-out	fantastic
weed	cigarette
weird	**1** strange **2** unusual **3** wonderful
wet	**1** weak **2** moderate (in politics)
wet blanket	someone who spoils the fun
whack at, have a	to attempt
whale of a time	very enjoyable time
wheeze	trick
white-collar	connected with office or desk work

EXPRESSION	MEANING
whopper	something big
windy	fearful
wow	**1** success **2** enjoyable event
write-off	**1** ruined **2** declared useless
yen	passion
yobbo	lout
zap	to destroy (by death ray, etc.)

JARGON

Jargon is vocabulary which appears to be part of an occupation's special terminology but which in fact may be unnecessary. It is sometimes unintelligible to ordinary people, and one of its main characteristics is the use of clichés, i.e. expressions which are so commonly used as to be almost nonsensical:

He was seen in a recumbent position   *Take due cognisance*
His age was in the region of 40   *We are in a negative situation*
Housing-wise the situation is serious   *Yours to hand*

SYNONYMS AND ANTONYMS

Synonyms

Synonyms are words whose meanings are equivalent. No two words in English have precisely the same meaning, since almost all words carry different connotations or associations. The term synonym is therefore used to signify words having **the same or nearly the same** essential meaning. Many words have distinct sets of synonyms because they have distinct essential (or **core**) meanings. The verb *build*, for example, has two distinct core meanings, and each has its set of synonyms:

WORD	CORE MEANING	SYNONYMS
build	**1** to form or fashion a structure	assemble, construct, erect, fashion, forge, form, mould, produce, put up, shape, raise
	2 to make or become greater	aggrandise, augment, boost, compound, enlarge, expand, heighten, magnify, mount, multiply, wax

Antonyms

Antonyms are words which negate one another's meanings. Thus the antonym of a word has an **opposing meaning** to one of its meanings:

WORD	CORE MEANING	ANTONYM
crooked	1 departing from a straight line	straight
	2 (informal) deviating from rectitude	honest

Related words

Related words are **near-synonyms**. They cannot strictly be defined as synonyms, but their meanings are closely related:

WORD	SYNONYM	RELATED WORDS
clever	intelligent	erudite, learned, sage, wise

Contrasted words

Contrasted words are **near-antonyms**:

WORD	ANTONYM	CONTRASTED WORDS
light	heavy	bulky, burdensome, cumbersome, huge, massive, overweight, ponderous

IDIOMATIC EXPRESSIONS

Clichés

Clichés are expressions which have been used so often that they are avoided by good writers:

a foregone conclusion	easier said than done
all work and no play	filthy lucre
beat a hasty retreat	grass roots
beauty sleep	leaps and bounds
bitter end	sell like hot cakes
blushing bride	stony silence
budding genius	this day and age
depth of despair	to all intents and purposes
each and every one	top-notch

Idioms

An idiom is a word or phrase whose meaning is not readily seen from the meaning of its word parts. Idiomatic expressions have their own essential meanings. Modern English contains a very large number of idioms. Here is a list of the most common of them:

about time: when someone/something delayed actually comes
above all: the most important thing
accounts, by all: according to what everyone says
ace in the hole: an advantage
across the board: everywhere
act your age: behave according to your age
afraid, I'm: I regret
air, clear the: remove doubts and suspicions
air, in the: imminent; rumoured
alive and kicking: healthy
all along: from the start
all in: exhausted
all, not at: no need to thank me
all the best: good luck to you
all the same: nevertheless
all told: in total
also ran: an unsuccessful contestant
anything but: just the opposite
apron strings: mother's influence
around the clock: all day
Aunt Sally: something/someone to mock at
axe to grind, have an: be biased

babes in the woods: innocents
back of beyond: remote (place)
back number: out of date
back to square one: start again
backbone: courage
backroom boy: research scientist
badly off: having little money
ball's in (someone's) court: (someone's) turn to act
balloon goes up, when the: when the catastrophe happens
bandwagon, jump on the: join a successful movement/party
bargain, into the: in addition to
bargain, it's a: I accept; I agree
bark up the wrong tree: be on the wrong track; make a mistake in choice
base, reach first: reach the first stage

bat, off your own: independently
bean, not have a: have no money
beans, full of: having plenty of energy
bear with a sore head, be like a: be in a very bad mood
beauty of it: the best part
bedrock, down to: reach the fundamental point
bed-sitter: living/sleeping room
bee in (your) bonnet: preoccupation; obsession
beg the question: miss the point
behind the times: out of date
belt, below the: unfair
bend over backwards: take trouble to help/please
between you and me; between ourselves: in confidence
big fish in a little pond: important person in a small community
big guns: important people
bird in the hand: available opportunity (PROVERB: A bird in the hand is better than
    two in the bush.)
birds of a feather: similar people (PROVERB: Birds of a feather flock together.)
bit by bit: gradually
bite off more than (you) can chew: be too ambitious
bites of the cherry, two: two opportunities
bitten by the bug: become an enthusiast
bitter pill to swallow: (something) difficult to accept
black books, to be in someone's: to be disapproved of by someone
black list: list of unwanted persons
blank cheque, to be given a: to be allowed to do anything
blanket, wet: a gloomy person in company
blaze a trail: pioneer
blessing in disguise: an apparent misfortune which turns out well
blind alley: wrong direction
blood and thunder: violence in a play, novel or film
blot (your) copybook: make a mistake
blow hot and cold: be in favour of something and then against it
blow (your) own trumpet: boast
blow the gaff: give away a secret
blue blood: royal descent
blue moon, once in a: very rarely
blue, out of the: very unexpectedly
bluff, call (someone's): make (someone) reveal the truth
bolt from the blue: very unexpected
born yesterday: naive; innocent
bow and scrape: be humble

breadline, on the: poverty
breath of fresh air, like a: very welcome
bring down a peg or two: to humble
bury the hatchet: make peace
busman's holiday: a holiday like work
butter would not melt in (someone's) mouth: (someone) looked innocent/honest
butterflies in (one's) stomach: very nervous
buy a pig in a poke: buy something without knowing exactly what it is

calf love: love as experienced by a very young person
call a spade a spade: speak frankly
cannon fodder: expendable troops
cap in hand: humbly
carbon copy: identical
carpet, on the: summoned to be rebuked
cast pearls before swine: waste effort or favours
castles in the air: dreams, ambitions
catch (someone's) eye: be noticed by (someone)
catch 22: a situation in which any decision will lead to trouble
change horses in midstream: suddenly switch to a different policy/plan
chapter and verse: the complete version; all the details
charmed life, lead a: to be lucky
chase after rainbows: to be idealistic
cheek by jowl: close together; side by side
chew the cud: meditate
chew the fat: gossip
chew the rag: complain
chill the blood: horrify
chink in (someone's) armour: a weakness in someone strong
chip off the old block: a son/daughter like his/her father
chip on (your) shoulder: bear a grudge; be resentful
chop, get the: be sacked; be killed
clear as mud: confusing
climb down: apologise
cloak-and-dagger: secret; mysterious
clockwork, like: efficiently
closed book: a mystery
clover, in: prosperous
cold comfort: false sympathy
cold shoulder, give (someone) the: ignore (someone)
Colonel Blimp: old-fashioned, pompous person
concrete jungle: large city

cooked to a turn: very well cooked
cool as a cucumber: very calm
cost the earth: very expensive
count one's blessings: be thankful
country cousin: someone who lives quietly and is unused to city life
Coventry, send to: to punish someone by refusing to speak to him/her
cover up your tracks: conceal some action
crack of dawn: very early in the morning
creature comforts: luxuries
crest of the wave: the height of success
crocodile tears: hypocritical sympathy
cross the Rubicon: take a decision that cannot be reversed
cross (your) bridges before you come to them: to do something sooner
    than is wise
cross (your) fingers: hope for good luck
crunch, when it comes to the: when a decision is unavoidable
cry over spilt milk: to be distressed when it is too late
cry wolf: raise a false alarm
cupboard love: to like someone because you want something from him/her
curate's egg: something good in parts
cut and dried: complete and settled
cut corners: act more quickly than necessary, at the risk of acting wrongly
cut out for: suitable

daggers drawn: hostile
damp squib: failure
Darby and Joan: a loving, older married couple
daylight robbery: charging far too much
dead end: a situation leading to nothing
dead to the world: unconscious
deaf as a post: very deaf
dear to (your) heart: most attractive; much loved
deliver the goods: do something which has been promised
devil-may-care: careless; reckless
devil's advocate: someone who argues against a case for the sake of examining its
    merits or demerits
different as chalk and cheese: completely dissimilar
digs: lodgings
do or die: be brave to the point of foolishness
do's and don'ts: rules
dodge the column: evade one's duty
dog eat dog: fierce conflict

dose of (your) own medicine: treatment (you have) given others
double Dutch: incomprehensible language
down at heel: shabby; poor
down in the dumps: sad; depressed
down in the mouth: sad; sulky
down the drain: lost; wasted
down to earth: realistic
down under: Australia or New Zealand
draw a blank: be unsuccessful
draw a veil over: say nothing about (something)
drawing board, back to the: go back to the beginning of a plan
dribs and drabs: piece by piece; item by item
drive (something) home: impress (something) upon (someone)
drop of a hat, at the: casually; without hesitation
drop in the ocean: a tiny amount
dry as dust: very dull
Dutch courage: courage gained from drink or drugs

early bird: someone who rises early in the morning; or gets somewhere first
easy come, easy go: money earned without effort will be easily spent
eat one's words: apologise
elbow grease: hard work
eleventh hour: the last minute; almost too late
end of one's tether: the limit of endurance
end of the tunnel: the end of a difficult period
eternal triangle: the common situation of a married couple and a third person intervening in the relationship
everything but the kitchen sink: all the furniture or goods in the house
evil eye: a look that conveys hatred
eyeball to eyeball: face to face; in confrontation

face the music: be prepared to be punished
fairweather friend: a friend only in prosperity
fall between two stools: suffer from either of two options
fall from grace: become unpopular
fall over backwards: take trouble to help (someone)
fasten your safety belt: be prepared for trouble
fat is in the fire, the: the damage has been done
feather (your) nest: make money for (yourself)
fetch and carry: be like a servant
fight shy of: avoid
fine kettle of fish: an unwelcome situation

fish in troubled waters: to take advantage of other people's troubles
fits and starts, by: spasmodically
flash in the pan: a sudden show of talent; an unusual success
flog a dead horse: persist in a useless cause
flotsam and jetsam: useless things
fly high: to be ambitious
fly in the ointment: something that spoils something
fly off the handle: to lose one's temper
foam at the mouth: to be excessively angry
follow the crowd: to conform with others
fool's paradise: something (or place) mistakenly believed to be perfect
foot the bill: pay for something
footloose and fancy free: to be independent
forbidden fruit: something desired but not allowed
forewarned is forearmed: if you know what to expect you can prepare for it
forty winks: a short sleep
free and easy: very friendly

get in (someone's) hair: annoy (someone)
ghost of a chance: slender opportunity
gift of the gab: ability to talk well
gild the lily: try to improve something already perfect
give a dog a bad name: blame someone unjustly
give and take: be cooperative
give (yourself) airs: be pretentious
give the green light: allow to begin; encourage
give (someone) the slip: escape from (someone)
give up the ghost: die; admit defeat; surrender
glutton for punishment: be recklessly brave; extremely hard-working
go Dutch: pay for yourself
go halves: take an equal share
go haywire: become confused; out of order
go it alone: do something by oneself
go overboard for (someone): to fall in love with (someone)
go round in circles: be confused; exert effort without success
go through the roof: explode with anger
go to seed: become a failure; become shabby
go to the dogs: become a failure
go wrong: to fail
good for nothing: useless
good old days: the past
Gordon Bennett!: good heavens!

grasp the nettle: tackle a dangerous task
grass roots: ordinary people or where they live
grass widow: woman whose husband is absent
greased lightning, like: very fast
grey matter: brains
grind (your) teeth: be very angry
grist to the mill, (it's all): (it's all) useful
Grundy, Mrs: disapproving woman
gum up the works: spoil a plan or process

hair of the dog: drink supposed to cure the effects of drinking too much alcohol
happy as a lark: very happy
hard as nails: ruthless
hard lines: bad luck
hard put to it: finding it difficult
hard time, give (someone) a: treat (someone) unpleasantly
hard up: poor
harden (your) heart: resolve to be firm
have a down on: bear a grudge towards
have a head for: be clever at
have (your) head in the clouds: be a dreamer
have (your) head screwed on: be wise; be sensible
have a heart of gold: be kind
have (your) heart in (your) boots: feel melancholy
have (your) heart in (your) mouth: be nervous; afraid
have (your) heart in the right place: be a sympathetic person
have the heart for: feel able to
have it in for (someone): bear (someone) a grudge
have it out with (someone): settle a quarrel with (someone)
hewers of wood and drawers of water: ordinary workers
hiding to nothing, on a: to be in a hopeless situation
high and dry: deserted; helpless
high and mighty: proud and powerful
high dudgeon: indignation
hit or miss: haphazardly
hit (your) head against a brick wall: have no success despite all (your) efforts
hit the nail on the head: get the right answer
hitch (your) wagon to a star: be idealistic
Hobson's choice: a choice between something offered or nothing at all
hold a pistol to (someone's) head: threaten (someone)
hold all the aces: have all the advantages
hold (someone's) hand: sympathise with (someone)

hold (your) head high: be proud
holier-than-thou: falsely superior; hypocritical
home and dry: safe; successful
home truth: something true but not easy to accept
hornets' nest: sudden trouble
horns of a dilemma, on the: facing two difficult choices
horses for courses: matching people with tasks
hostages to fortune: loved persons whose safety may be at risk
hot line: direct telephone contact between heads of state
hot potato: a delicate or awkward matter
hot seat: a position of responsibility or danger
house of cards: a plan or organisation that can be easily ruined
household name: someone very famous
hue and cry: loud public protest

I'm all right, Jack: I'm well placed and I don't care about anyone else
ins and outs: details
iron hand in a velvet glove: a harmless appearance masking a rigorous nature
irons in the fire: interests; tasks

Jack of all trades: someone with various jobs; a versatile person
jackpot: unexpected good fortune
Jekyll and Hyde: a person with two personalities; someone who leads a
    double life
Jeremiah: a person who predicts a disastrous future
jet set: rich people who travel world-wide
jitters: a feeling of anxiety
jobs for the boys: jobs given to friends or influential people
Job's comforter: one who aggravates the distress of the one being comforted
Joe Bloggs: the ordinary man
Jonah: someone who brings bad luck
Joneses: the neighbours
Judas: a betrayer
jump down (someone's) throat: be very angry with someone
jump in at the deep end: tackle the most difficult or dangerous task first
jump out of (your) skin: be very alarmed
jump the gun: do something before the proper time
jump to it: hurry

keen as mustard: very enthusiastic
keep a level head: keep calm
keep a low profile: behave quietly

keep a tight rein on (someone): be strict with (someone)
keep a weather eye open: keep vigilant
keep at arm's length: avoid being close to someone
keep at it: keep on working/doing something
keep mum: keep quiet
keep (someone) posted: inform (someone) regularly
keep (something) dark: keep (something) confidential
keep (something) under (your) hat: keep (something) secret
keep the ball rolling: carry on the work/game/conversation
keep the wolf from the door: earn enough to live on
keep to the beaten track: remain on familiar ground
keep up with the Joneses: do as well as (your) neighbours
keep (your) chin up: keep being brave
keep (your) end up: do your duty; do your own part of a job
keep (your) fingers crossed: hope for good luck
keep (your) head: keep calm
keep (your) head down: keep out of trouble; concentrate
keep (your) nose clean: behave (yourself)
keep (your) nose to the grindstone: work hard and steadily
keep (your) shirt on: don't get annoyed
kick (yourself): regret (some action)
kick (your) heels: wait impatiently
kick over the traces: rebel
kick up a dust: make trouble
kick up (your) heels: behave extravagantly
kick (someone) when he is down: add to someone's suffering
kid's stuff: childish; easy to understand
kill (yourself) laughing: be very amused
kill or cure: solve a problem or make it much worse
kill the goose that lays the golden eggs: spoil/damage some very
    valuable/profitable thing
kill two birds with one stone: accomplish two objectives with one action
kill with kindness: be excessively generous
kingdom come: a very long time; never
kiss of death: a gesture that signals the end of something
knees knocking: afraid
knight in shining armour: a heroic rescuer
knock: criticise
knock for six: defeat heavily
knock holes in (something): criticise (something)
knock (someone) off his pedestal: bring about the downfall of someone
    important/highly respected

knock (your) head against a brick wall: try something that is sure to fail
know on which side (your) bread is buttered: be aware of (your) own
   best interests
know one's onions: know one's subject
know (something) backwards: know (something) very well
know (something/someone) inside out: know (something/someone) very well
know (something/somewhere) like the back of (your) hand: know
   something/somewhere very well
know the ropes: be familiar with (a place/subject/process)
know (your) own mind: be confident

labour of love: duty (you) are happy to undertake
la-di-da: effeminate; pretentious; snobbish
lap of luxury: wealthy life
lap of the gods: chance
larger than life: exaggerated
last gasp: near death
last straw: final blow; final provocation
laughing stock: object of ridicule
law of the jungle: fierce competition
lay down the law: insistently state what (you) wish to be done
lay odds: bet
lead a dog's life: live in misery
lead (someone) up the garden path: deceive (someone)
leading light: important person
leading question: a question that suggests the answer wanted
lean over backwards: try hard to please
leap in the dark: an act whose consequences are unknown
leaps and bounds, by: extremely quickly
learn the hard way: learn by suffering
leave a nasty taste in the mouth: make an unpleasant impression
leave (someone) to it: let (someone) do (something) alone
left; left-wing: having socialist political views
left, right and centre: everywhere
let bygones be bygones: forgive
let (someone) have his head: give (someone) responsibility/freedom to act
let off steam: release energy
let sleeping dogs lie: do not cause unnecessary provocation
let the cat out of the bag: reveal a secret
lick (your) wounds: recover from damage/injuries
lift the lid off: reveal the facts about (something)
limelight: fame

little by little: gradually
live beyond (your) means: be unable to pay (your) debts
live from hand to mouth: live poorly
live off (your) fat: rely on your own resources
live off the fat of the land: live prosperously
live rough: live like a tramp
lock, stock and barrel: everything; totally
long in the tooth: old
look like thunder: look very angry
look lively/sharp: hurry
look on the bright side: be optimistic
lose face: be humiliated
lose ground: lose advantage; suffer a setback
lose (your) bearings: be confused
lose (your) grip: lose control
lose (your) head: become agitated
lose (your) heart: fall in love
lose (your) touch: become less skilful
lower (your) sights: be less ambitious
lunatic fringe: people with foolish/odd ideas

mad as a hatter/March hare: very eccentric
made of money: very rich
make a bomb/packet: make a fortune
make a killing: make a large profit
make a mountain out of a molehill: exaggerate the importance of (something)
make a name for (yourself): become famous
make a noise in the world: become important
make a splash: draw attention to (yourself)
make good: succeed in life
make hay: take advantage of (something)
make headway: make progress
make it: be successful
make (someone's) day: please (someone) very much
man to man: frank
man Friday: servant
man in the street: the ordinary man
manna from heaven: unexpected good fortune
McCoy, the real: genuine
Mecca: a place that everyone would like to visit
middle-of-the-road: average
mind your Ps and Qs: be vigilant

mint condition: very new
mixed blessing: an event that is partly good, partly bad
moment of truth: the most important/revealing time

neck and neck: level; even
neck or nothing: at any risk
next to nothing: very little
nine days' wonder: a short-lived, marvellous thing
nobody's fool: a smart person
nodding acquaintance: slight acquaintance
null and void: invalid

odd man out: the exception
old hand: veteran
old school tie: advantage from having been at a public school; having
    important connections
old woman: effeminate man
olive branch: gesture of peace
on and off: irregularly
on the wagon: abstaining from alcohol
once in a blue moon: very seldom
once or twice: a few times
one by one: singly
one or two: a few
open and shut: certain; clear
open book: very obvious
open sesame: the secret of getting into a place/project
openhanded: generous
out and about: going around
out-and-out: complete
out of bounds: prohibited
out of (your) depth: in a situation which (you) cannot control
out of sorts: unwell
out of the blue: sudden; unexpected
over and above: in addition
over and done with: finished
over (your) head: beyond (your) understanding
overstep the mark: go too far

paddle (your) own canoe: do something for/by yourself
paint in glowing colours: describe with praise
parrot fashion: imitating; repeating
part and parcel of: integral to

party line: the strict policy of a party/organisation
pass muster: be adequate
pass the buck: give someone else the responsibility or blame
pat on the back: praise
pave the way: help (someone's/something's) progress
pay lipservice: to agree/praise without sincerity
pay through the nose: pay too much
pay (your) way: meet all debts
pennies from heaven: unexpected receipt of money not earned
penny wise, pound foolish: careful in unimportant matters, careless with
    important matters
pick and choose: choose with caution/hesitation
pick holes in: criticise
pick (someone's) brains: seek advice/information from (someone)
pick up the pieces: rescue (a project)
pick up the threads: renew; begin again
pig in a poke: an unknown quantity
pinch and scrape: economise strictly
pipeline, in the: being made/completed/prepared
plain as a pikestaff: very clear
plain sailing: smooth progress
play a part: pretend
play ball: be fair (with someone); cooperate
play for time: delay
play into (someone's) hands: allow someone to take advantage
play (your) cards close to (your) chest: behave secretively
play (your) cards right: act in a way that will bring success
play to the gallery: act so as to attract people's attention and approval
play with fire: take risks
played out: spoiled; exhausted
plough a lonely furrow: live/act alone
plough the sands: waste effort
pomp and circumstance: empty show; ceremonial
pour cold water over: disparage
pour oil on troubled waters: make peace; settle a quarrel
pour out (your) heart: confide; confess
power to (your) elbow: (I wish you) success
powers that be: the authorities
practise what (you) preach: behave as (you) advise others to
preach to the converted: use persuasion on people who are already convinced
pride of place: priority
pros and cons: the advantages and disadvantages; for and against

pull a fast one: cheat
pull in (your) belt: economise
pull in (your) horns: be less determined/forceful/reckless
pull (your) punches: be less aggressive
pull (your) socks up: improve (yourself)
pull (your) weight: make (your) contribution
pull (someone's) leg: play a trick/joke on (someone); tease (someone)
pull strings: use influence
pull the chestnuts out of the fire for someone: accomplish something
    unpleasant/dangerous for someone
pull the wool over (someone's) eyes: deceive (someone)
put a foot wrong: make a mistake
put all (your) eggs in one basket: risk all (your) assets
put (someone) off his stroke: disconcert (someone)
put on airs: be pretentious; act proudly
put on an act: make a pretence
put (your) best foot forward: do your best
put (your) feet up: rest
put (your) foot down: insist
put (your) foot in it: blunder
put (your) oar in: interfere
put (your) shoulder to the wheel: work/try hard
put paid to: destroy

Queer Street: poverty
quick off the mark: prompt
quick on the uptake: smart
quits: even; equal
Quixote, Don: excessively idealistic; prone to take up causes

Rs, the three: Reading, (W)riting and (A)rithmetic
rags to riches, from: from poverty to wealth; becoming a very rich person after a
    humble beginning
rainy day: a time in the future when (you) will need help
raise an eyebrow: question (something)
raise Cain: cause trouble
raise (your) hand against (someone): attack (someone)
raise (your) hat to: pay respect to
raise (your) sights: be more ambitious
raise (someone's) hackles: make (someone) angry
raise the ante: make a higher bid
raise the roof: cause great laughter; cause a sensation

raise the stakes: take a riskier course of action
raise the wind: raise money
ram (something) down (someone's) throat: insist excessively that (something) is true/necessary
rank and file: the ordinary members of society
rant and rave: shout passionately but irrationally
rap on the knuckles: a rebuke
rare bird: an unusual person
rat race: the highly competitive society we live in today
rattle (your) sabre: threaten to attack
razor's edge: very near danger
reach first base: achieve the first stage
reach rock bottom: come to the end; reach the lowest point
read between the lines: perceive meaning implied but not openly stated
read (someone) like a book: understand someone completely
read the riot act: threaten or announce punishment
ready to drop: exhausted
ready to hand: easily available
red as a beetroot: embarrassed
red carpet: a welcome
red-handed, caught: caught in the course of a crime
red herring: a distraction; a false direction
red-letter day: an important day; a day of good fortune
red rag to a bull: a provocation
red tape: bureaucracy
regular as clockwork: very regular
rest on (your) laurels: be satisfied with your achievements
rest on (your) oars: take a well deserved rest; pause for a time
return to the fold: come home
rhyme or reason: meaning; reason
rich as Croesus: very rich
ride high: to be successful; triumphant
ride roughshod over (someone): treat (someone) harshly
right end of the stick, get hold of the: understand
right, right-wing: having conservative political views
ring the changes: have variety
rise from the ashes: be renewed
risk (your) neck: take a great risk
rock the boat: endanger the project/group
roll in the aisles: laugh heartily (as an audience)
rose-tinted spectacles: a particularly optimistic outlook
rough and ready: imperfect; made hastily but not thoroughly

rough diamond: a good/admirable person who seems unattractive
rough ride: unpleasant experience
round the clock: all day; 24 hours
rub salt in (someone's) wounds: make an injury worse
rub shoulders: mix/make contact (with people)
rub (someone) up the wrong way: irritate/provoke (someone)
rubber stamp: automatic approval
ruffle (someone's) feathers: annoy/offend someone
rule of thumb: a rule/guide which is not exact/detailed
rule out of court: declare (something) to be inadmissible
rule the roost: to dominate
run an eye over: examine quickly
run foul of (someone): earn (someone's) disapproval/dislike
run-of-the-mill: ordinary
run out of steam: lose energy/willpower
run rings round (someone): to be much superior to (someone) at something
run to seed: deteriorate
rut: a dull way of life

sack: dismissal from a job
sackcloth and ashes: repentance
sacred cow: something/someone specially respected/revered
safe and sound: unharmed
safe as houses: very safe/secure
sail close to the wind: take risks
salad days: days of youth
salt of the earth: the best people
Samaritan: generous/kind/charitable person, who helps less fortunate people
save face: avoid humiliation; avoid loss of status
Scrooge: a mean person
see eye to eye: agree
see red: be angry
see the light: become converted
send in one's papers: resign from a post/committee, etc.
send the hat round: collect contributions
set in (your) ways: conservative; unused to change
set little store by (something): have a poor opinion of (something)
set (your) face against (something): oppose (something)
set (your) heart on (something): desire (something) strongly
set (your) jaw: be determined
set (your) shoulder to the wheel: make a great effort
set (someone's) mind at rest: reassure (someone)

set the ball rolling: begin (something)
set the record straight: provide the correct information
set the wheels in motion: begin the process
set tongues wagging: cause gossip/rumours
settle a score: get revenge
shoestring, on a: very cheaply
shoot (your) bolt: make a last effort
short cut: a quicker way of doing something
shoulder to shoulder: together; in cooperation
show of hands: a casual vote
show (your) cards: reveal (your) plans
show (your) face: appear
show the flag: make an appearance in order to be seen
shrug (your) shoulders: deny responsibility; show lack of interest
sing (someone's) praises: praise (someone) to others
sink or swim: succeed or fail at all costs
sit at (someone's) feet: study under (someone's) supervision; work under
    (someone's) leadership
sit in judgement: pronounce an opinion about
sit on (your) hands: do nothing
sit on the fence: be neutral; non-committal
sit tight: take no action; wait; remain silent
sitting pretty: satisfied; comfortable
six of one and half a dozen of the other: equal
sixes and sevens: confusion
sixth sense: intuition; premonition
sixty-four thousand dollar question: the most important question
skate on thin ice: take risks; be in danger
slap in the face: insult; blow
slap on the back: praise
slip of the tongue: verbal mistake
Sloane Ranger: upper-class socialite in the 1980s
smack in the eye: unpleasant surprise
smell a rat: be suspicious
smooth (someone's) ruffled feathers: calm (someone) down
stand firm: be resolute
stand head and shoulders above (someone): be much superior to (someone)
stand on ceremony: insist on things being done formally
stand (your) ground: be firm
stand on the sidelines: be neutral; observe but not participate in a project
stand/stick out a mile: be conspicuous
stand up and be counted: vote openly; take sides openly

steal a march on (someone): get something/do something before (someone)
steal (someone's) thunder: take credit due to (someone)
steal the show: be the most successful person (of a group)
step by step: gradually
step into the breach: take (someone's) place; take over a job
step on (someone's) toes: interfere with (someone); offend (someone)
step out of line: depart from (one's) duty
stick it out: endure; persevere
stick (your) neck out: take a risk; venture
stick (your) oar in: interfere
stick out like a sore thumb: be conspicuous
stick to (your) guns: persevere
sticky wicket: risky/difficult situation
straight from the shoulder: frankly; honestly
straw in the wind: a sign of something due to happen; indication
streets ahead of someone/something: much superior to (someone/something)
strength to (your) elbow: may (your) work be successful
strengthen (someone's) hand: reinforce (someone's) efforts
strike a blow for: do something in support of
strike a chord: to remind (someone) of (something)
strike it rich: make a large amount of money quickly
strike oil: be successful
strike while the iron is hot: take advantage of an opportunity
strings attached: conditions
suffer fools gladly: be tolerant of other people's 'foolishness'
sugar the pill: make an unwelcome experience bearable
suit (someone) down to the ground: be wholly suitable (to someone)
suit (someone's) book: be to (someone's) advantage
suit the action to the word: do something promptly
supper, sing for (one's): work in exchange for food/hospitality
swallow (your) pride: refuse to take offence
swan song: a last creative act/work
sweep (someone) off his/her feet: make (someone) fall in love with (you)
sword of Damocles: imminent threat

tail wags the dog: the least important part controls the main part
take a back seat: retreat into the background
take a hand in: participate
take a leaf out of (someone's) book: imitate someone
take a sledgehammer to crack a nut: go to great trouble to accomplish
    something trivial
take (something) as gospel: believe something completely

take (something) as read: assume (something) to be so
take (someone) at his/her word: believe (someone) without question
take heart: be encouraged
take issue with (someone): challenge (someone)
take leave of (your) senses: become mad
take (something) lying down: accept (something) without protest
take off the gloves: begin to fight in earnest
take (your) hat off to (someone): pay someone a compliment
take (your) medicine: accept punishment/suffering
take pains: go to considerable effort
take (someone's) breath away: astound (someone)
take (someone's) measure: be sure of (someone's) strength/ability
take stock: appraise the situation
take the bit between (your) teeth: make a determined effort
take the bull by the horns: tackle a difficult/dangerous problem boldly/directly
take the long view: look ahead to the future
take the plunge: enter a project boldly
take (someone) to task: rebuke (someone)
take up the gauntlet: accept the challenge
take (something) with a pinch of salt: accept (something) sceptically
talk nineteen to the dozen: talk fast and at length
talk of the town: a sensation
talk shop: talk about business/one's job
tear (your) hair: be in despair
tell tales out of school: give confidential information to someone who is not
  entitled to have it
tempt providence: take unnecessary risks
think the world of (someone): admire (someone) greatly
think twice: reconsider
throw a spanner in the works: damage a project
throw a veil over: conceal
throw cold water over: discourage
throw dust in (someone's) eyes: deceive (someone)
throw in (your) lot with (someone): join (someone's) side/group
throw (something) in (someone's) teeth: defy (someone); reject (something)
throw in the towel: surrender
throw (yourself) at (someone's) feet: plead for mercy/forgiveness
throw (your) hat in the air: rejoice
throw (someone) to the lions: sacrifice (someone)
tighten (your) belt: economise
tip of the iceberg: evidence that shows the presence of something important
tip the balance: change the situation

tit for tat: revenge; returning like for like
toff: member of high society
touch and go: uncertain
touch (someone) on the raw: offend (someone's) sensibilities
treadmill: dreary routine work
turn a blind eye: pretend not to see
turn a deaf ear: pretend not to hear
turn (one's) coat: be a traitor; change sides
turn (your) nose up at (something): despise (something)
turn on (your) heels: retreat
turn out to grass: retire
turn over a new leaf: repent; resolve to do something different
turn tail: retreat
turn the corner: improve
turn the other cheek: forgive
turn-up for the book: (something) very surprising
twist (someone's) tail: compel (someone) to do something

under the hammer: due to be sold
under (your) hat: secret
under (someone's) nose: in full view
under the weather: unwell
under way: in process; happening
up-and-coming: becoming successful
up to (your) elbows/ears/eyes: extremely busy
up to the minute: fashionable
upper crust: the aristocracy; the rich

variety is the spice of life: changes make life more interesting
vicious circle: something leads to something else and the end result is the same
    as the first cause
villain of the piece: the guilty person

wagging tongues: gossip; rumours
wait in the wings: await (your) turn
walk of life: occupation
walk on air: to be happy
walls have ears: rumours spread easily; secrets tend to be found out
wally: a fool
Walter Mitty: someone ordinary who dreams of being heroic
Waterloo: a defeat
way out: very advanced; ahead of fashion

wear and tear: damage
wear (your) heart on (your) sleeve: show emotion openly
wear the trousers: (of a woman) dominate the household
weather the storm: endure misfortune successfully
weigh (your) words: speak carefully
weigh up a situation: appraise a situation carefully
weight off (your) mind: relief
well off/well-to-do: prosperous
wheel, big: important person
wheels within wheels: hidden influences
white lie: a falsehood which is not very blameworthy
whizz kid: a young, very clever person
whys and wherefores: reasons
wild goose chase: investigation/search doomed to fail
win hands down: win convincingly
win the day: succeed in the end
window dressing: pretence; presenting the best side of things
wipe the slate clean: return to the beginning; forget what has happened
wishful thinking: being optimistic without cause
witch hunt: seeking out victims to persecute
wrong end of the stick, get hold of the: misunderstand

you and yours: you and your wife/husband/family

4 PARTS OF SPEECH

Traditional English grammar recognised eight classes of words called the **parts of speech**. These are: *noun, pronoun, adjective, verb, adverb, preposition, conjunction* and *interjection*. These terms are used in most dictionaries, usually in the abbreviated forms *n., pron., adj., v., adv., prep., conj.* and *interj.*

In modern English grammar we recognise many more classes of words. The first distinction is between **function words** and **content words**.

FUNCTION WORDS AND CONTENT WORDS

Function words
In English there are the following groups of function words. These are so called because they have little meaning in themselves but merely have a function in a sentence:

1 **Pronouns:**
   I, you, he, she, it, we, they, who, which, etc.

2 **Determiners:**
   a, the, any, every, each, some
   this, that, these, those
   my, our, your, his, her, its, their, etc.

3 **Auxiliaries:**
   will, may, have, can, must, do, should, might, be, etc.

4 **Qualifiers:**
   very, rather, quite, too, somewhat, etc.

5 **Quantifiers:**
   many, a few, four, etc.

6 **Prepositions:**
   with, under, at, above, over, beside, in, etc.

7 **Conjunctions:**
   and, or, but, etc.

Content words
There are four forms called content words: **nouns** *(house)*, **verbs** *(eat)*, **adjectives** *(happy)* and **adverbs** *(happily)*. These words have meaning even when they stand alone.

NOUNS

In traditional grammar the **noun** was 'defined' by reference to its meaning. Thus a noun was said to be the name of a person, place or thing. But modern grammar points out that meaning may be too vague a criterion for defining English words. For example, is *wash* a noun or a verb? Is *end* a verb or a noun? In *Wash the end* and in *End the wash* it can be seen that the part of speech only emerges when the word is seen to occur in a sentence.

Nouns can be the **subject** or **object** of a sentence. In the basic sentence frame below, the nouns occupy key positions:

SUBJECT	PREDICATOR	OBJECT
noun phrase	verb phrase	noun phrase
The boy (noun)	kicked	the ball. (noun)
People (noun)	enjoy eating	chocolate. (noun)

In a **noun phrase** (NP) the noun is the *headword* (h) and the other words are modifiers (m):

NP	VP
John	laughed.

NP				VP
m	m	m	h	
The	poor	little	girl	wept.

NP							
m	m	m	h	m	m .	m	h
the (determiner)	stout (adjective)	old (adjective)	lady (noun)	(in (preposition)	the (determiner)	green (adjective)	hat) (noun)

Nouns can be sub-classified as:

1   **common nouns**   **or**   **proper nouns**
     girl   *John*
     table   *Edinburgh*
                                  the *Thames*

2   **count nouns**   **or**   **mass nouns**
     (can occur with
     numerals)
     a *girl*   *milk* (not 'a milk')
     three *tables*   *butter* (not 'three butters')
     some *meetings*   loud *applause*

3   **unit nouns**   **or**   **measure nouns**   **or**   **species nouns**
     a *piece* (of butter)   a *foot* (of rope)   a *type* (of cloth)
     a *lump* (of sugar)   a *yard* (of cloth)   a *species* (of mammal)
                                                                   a *make* (of car)

4   **abstract nouns**   **or**   **concrete nouns**
     happiness   *nails*

PRONOUNS

Pronouns have a noun-like function and are used to replace nouns in a sentence.

1   **Personal pronouns:** *I, me, you, he, him, she, her, it, we, us, they, them*
     Personal pronouns are sub-divided according to person, which classifies the
     relationship of the speaker:
     I ate *it*.   *We* like *them*.

2   **Demonstrative pronouns:** *this, that, these, those*
     Demonstrative pronouns are used to point out something:
     This train goes to London.   *Those* people are lucky.

3   **Indefinite pronouns:** *either, neither, each, both, all, some, many, few,*
                         something, somebody, someone, anything, anybody,
                         anyone, nothing, nobody, no-one, one, none
     Indefinite pronouns are used to refer to nouns whose number or quantity is
     not exactly defined:
     Many are called but *few* are chosen.
     Anybody can do *anything*.

4   **Reflexive pronouns:** *myself, ourselves, yourself, yourselves, himself, herself,*
                      itself, themselves

Reflexive pronouns refer back to the subject of the clause or sentence. They also act as pronoun intensifiers:

REFLEXIVE	INTENSIFIER
I satisfied *myself*.	I *myself* was satisfied.
She injured *herself*.	She *herself* was injured.
He gave *himself* to the cause.	He gave this to you *himself*.

5 Relative pronouns: *who, that, which, whom, whose*
Relative pronouns refer to the preceding noun and link it to the rest of the sentence:

This is the man *who* spoke to me.
We saw the house *which* had collapsed.
He joined the group *that* had been formed.

6 Possessive pronouns: *mine, yours, his, hers, its, ours, theirs*
Possessive pronouns are used to show ownership:

This book is *mine*.   *Theirs* is the fourth house on the right.

Note: 1 Do not confuse these with possessive adjectives: *my* book, *their* house.
2 An apostrophe is never used with the possessive pronoun (it's = it is).

7 Interrogative pronouns: *who, what, whose, which*
Interrogative pronouns are used for asking questions:

Who said that?   *Whose* are these shoes?

8 Impersonal pronouns: *you, one, they*
Impersonal pronouns act as subject in sentences referring to people in general:

You never know what will happen.
One must assume that . . .
They say that the British are very reserved.

Pronouns as subject or object
Like the noun, the pronoun can be the subject or object of a sentence:

SUBJECT	PREDICATOR	OBJECT
I (pronoun)	survived.	
We (pronoun)	rewarded	*her.* (pronoun)
Each (pronoun)	selected	*something.* (pronoun)

Pronouns as determiners

All demonstrative pronouns and some of the possessive pronouns (*his, hers, its*) can behave as determiners. Of the indefinite pronouns, *either, neither, each, both, all, some, many* and *few* also behave as determiners. These words are pronouns when they replace nouns and determiners when they modify nouns:

PRONOUN	DETERMINER
This is my friend.	*This* man is my friend.
Neither was satisfactory.	*Neither* book was satisfactory.

Reciprocal pronouns

Each other and *one another* are reciprocals, occurring as complements:

They hurt *each other.*   We must serve *one another.*

VERBS

Verbs are words or groups of words to denote actions performed by nouns or pronouns, or the state of being of a noun or pronoun:

She *sat* down.   They *are* disappointed.

Main verbs

A main verb is a word which forms the main part of the **predicator** in a sentence.

SUBJECT	PREDICATOR	OBJECT
NP	VP	NP
Cats (noun)	*purr.* (main verb)	
The cat (noun)	*scratched* (main verb)	my hand. (determiner) (noun)
Everyone (pronoun)	was *going* mad. (auxiliary (verb) (adjective) verb)	

There are four classes of main verb:

1   The verb be and its various forms link words in a sentence:

We   *were*   happy.
(pronoun) (main (adjective)
                 verb)

2 **Intransitive verbs** cannot be followed by a noun:

NP	VP
I (pronoun)	*stumbled.* (main verb)
The car (determiner) (noun)	*stopped.* (main verb)

3 **Transitive verbs** are normally followed by nouns:

NP	VP	NP
Everyone (pronoun)	*carried* (main verb)	a stick. (determiner) (noun)
The poor little girl (noun)	*saw* (main verb)	her long-lost mother. (noun)

4 **Copulative verbs** link the subject with the rest of the sentence and are followed by adjectives or nouns:

NP	VP
William (proper noun)	*seemed* excited. (main verb) (adjective)
They (pronoun)	*felt* sad. (main verb) (adjective)
The leader (noun)	*became* our friend. (main verb) (noun)

An English verb has five possible forms:

1 **Infinitive (or simple):** *walk, sing, run, try, fall,* etc.
2 **3rd person singular:** *walks, sings, runs, tries, falls,* etc.
3 **Present participle:** *walking, singing, running, trying, falling,* etc.
4 **Past tense:** *walked, sang, ran, tried, fell,* etc.
5 **Past participle:** *walked, sung, run, tried, fallen,* etc.

Regular and irregular verbs
English verbs can be regular or irregular.

Regular verbs have the following inflections:
    present participle: root plus *ing*   *walk(ing)*
    past participle: root plus *ed*   *walk(ed)*
    3rd person singular: root plus *s*   *walk(s)*

There are four regular exceptions as follows:

1 When the verb ends with a consonant, it is doubled before *ing* and *ed* if the preceding vowel is stressed and spelled with a single letter:
   fit — *fitting, fitted*
   prefer — *preferring, preferred*
   sob — *sobbing, sobbed*

2 Verbs ending with a consonant plus *y* change the *y* to *ie* before *s* (try — *tries*) and the *y* to *i* before *ed* (try — *tried*).

3 Verbs ending in a consonant plus *e* drop the *e* before *ing* and *ed*:
   debate — *debating, debated*
   love — *loving, loved*

4 Verbs ending in *ss*, *sh*, *z*, add an *e* before the *s* inflection:
   dress — *dresses*
   push — *pushes*
   buzz — *buzzes*

Irregular verbs form the past tense and past participle in different ways, for example:

INFINITIVE	3RD PERSON	PAST TENSE	PAST PARTICIPLE
fall	falls	fell	fallen
sing	sings	sang	sung
put	puts	put	put
drive	drives	drove	driven

There are some two hundred irregular verbs falling into three main types.

1 Infinitive, past tense and past participle are identical:

INFINITIVE	PAST TENSE	PAST PARTICIPLE	FURTHER EXAMPLES
bet	bet	bet	burst, cast, cost,
bid	bid	bid	hit, let, put, quit,
cut	cut	cut	set, shut, slit, split,
hurt	hurt	hurt	spread, thrust

2 Past tense and past participle are identical:

INFINITIVE	PAST TENSE	PAST PARTICIPLE	FURTHER EXAMPLES
burn	burned/burnt	burned/burnt	learn, smell, spell, spill, spoil
bend	bent	bent	build, lend, send, spend
bleed	bled	bled	breed, feed, flee, hold, lead
sleep	slept	slept	creep, deal, dream, feel, keep, lean, leap, leave, mean, meet, sweep, weep
cling	clung	clung	dig, fling, hang, sling, spin, stick, sting, strike, string, swing, wring
bring	brought	brought	buy, catch, fight, seek, teach, think
bind	bound	bound	find, grind, wind
get	got	got	
lose	lost	lost	
shine	shone	shone	
shoot	shot	shot	
sell	sold	sold	
tell	told	told	
become	became	became	
come	came	came	Other examples
run	ran	ran	of this type
hear	heard	heard	
light	lit	lit	
make	made	made	
say	said	said	
spit	spat	spat	
stand	stood	stood	
lay	laid	laid	
pay	paid	paid	

3 Infinitive, past tense and past participle are all different:

INFINITIVE	PAST TENSE	PAST PARTICIPLE	FURTHER EXAMPLES
hew	hewed	hewn/hewed	mow, saw, sew, show, sow, swell
break	broke	broken	awake, choose, freeze, speak, steal, wake, weave
bear	bore	born/borne	tear, wear
swear	swore	sworn	
blow	blow	blown	grow, know, throw
bite	bit	bitten	ride, rise, thrive
hide	hid	hidden	write
shake	shook	shaken	
take	took	taken	
drive	drove	driven	
begin	began	begun	drink, ring, shrink, sing, sink, spring, stink, swim
eat	ate	eaten	
fall	fell	fallen	
dive	dived/dove	dived	
do	did	done	
draw	drew	drawn	Other examples
fly	flew	flown	of this type
forget	forgot	forgotten	
give	gave	given	
go	went	gone	
lie	lay	lain	
see	saw	seen	

Auxiliary verbs
Auxiliary verbs contribute to the function of the main verb: as the name suggests, they 'help' the main verb. Auxiliaries do not normally form a verb phrase on their own.

The **primary auxiliary verbs** are *do, have, be*. They take the following forms:
do: do, does, did, doesn't, don't, didn't
have: have, has, had, having, 've, 's, 'd, haven't, hasn't, hadn't
be: be, am, 'm, is, 's, are, 're, was, were, being, been, aren't, ain't, isn't, wasn't, weren't

The **modal auxiliary verbs** are *can, may, might, shall, will, would, must, ought to, used to, need, dare.*

The **negative** is formed by adding **not** or **n't**: *can't, cannot, may not, mightn't, shan't, shouldn't, won't, wouldn't, mustn't, oughtn't to, needn't, daren't.*

Verb combinations
Verb combinations occur in four ways:

1   **Modal combinations** (modal auxiliary + infinitive): *can walk; used to visit*

2   **Perfective combinations** (*have* + past participle): *had walked; has gone*

3   **Progressive combinations** (*be* + present participle): *was walking; is going*

4   **Passive combinations** (*be* + past participle): *were being done; is being seen*

When a verb phrase consists of strings of auxiliaries and a main verb, the items always occur in the 1 to 4 order listed above:

1 + 2:   He *could have gone.*
2 + 3:   He *has been going.*
1 + 2 + 4:   He *must have been struck.*

ADJECTIVES

Adjectives are used to describe or give information about nouns or pronouns.

Functions of adjectives
Adjectives have two distinct functions:

1   **Attributive** (modify or 'qualify' nouns):
      This was an   *old*   house.
                   (adjective) (noun)

2   **Predicative** (act as complements of verbs):
      The house was   *old.*
              (verb)   (adjective
                        complement)

Some adjectives can only be used as attributives:
      his *former* leader   an *occasional* journey   the *late* president

But most adjectives can be either attributive or predicative:
      an *intelligent* man   — he was *intelligent*
      he's a *kind* person   — he's *kind*

Many noun forms can be used also as attributive adjectives:
      a *master* spy   a *giant* spider

Some adjectives are normally confined to the predicative function:
I felt *faint*.   I am *fond* of John.   Tom looked *ill*.
John looked *well*.   Are you *ready*?

Adjectives as postmodifiers
Some adjectives are used as postmodifiers, i.e. they are placed after the noun:
The people *concerned* . . .   a court *martial*
Something *special* to say . . .   the sum *easiest* to do
the president *elect*

Forms of adjectives
Many adjectives have the same form as **present participles** or **past participles**:

PREDICATIVE   ATTRIBUTIVE
The result was *surprising*.   a *surprising* result
I am *satisfied*.   a *satisfied* customer

Many adjectives are formed from the root of the verb or noun by adding **suffixes**:
able, al, en, esque, ful, ic, ish, ive, lar, less, like, ly, ous, some, worthy, y.
For example: *acceptable, seasonal, wheaten, picturesque, colourful, scenic, selfish, attractive, circular, expressionless, childlike, manly, adventurous, tiresome, seaworthy, greedy*.

Colour adjectives
Colour adjectives act like nouns in some contexts:
He doesn't like *blue*. *Blue* is a pleasant colour.   That shade of *purple* . . .

Comparative and superlative
Most adjectives can take comparative and superlative forms:

METHOD	POSITIVE	COMPARATIVE	SUPERLATIVE
1 by adding -er and -est	old fine friendly	older finer friendlier	oldest finest friendliest
2 by preposing *more* and *most*	extensive	more extensive	most extensive
3 by either method 1 or 2	wealthy	wealthier or more wealthy	wealthiest or most wealthy
4 by changing form altogether	good bad	better worse	best worst

Some adjectives have 'absolute' meanings: *real, right, perfect, equal, unique, white, black.* In normal Standard English these do not take comparative or superlative forms, though in colloquial or poetic English (for example in advertisements) these forms can occur:
This soap makes your clothes *whiter than white.*
A *blacker* night you never saw.
He's the *realest* guy I know.

Sequence of adjectives
Adjectives forming the modifiers of a noun phrase tend to occur in certain permissible sequences:

POSITION 2 (adjectives showing general characteristics)	POSITION 1 (adjectives of age, etc.)	HEADWORD (noun)
fierce	*old*	goat
nice	*new*	dress

ADVERBS

Adverbs are words or groups of words used to describe or give information about verbs, adjectives, or other adverbs.

Forms of adverbs
Many have the same form as adjectives:

ADVERB	ADJECTIVE
He was *late.*	He had a *late* breakfast.
He worked *hard.*	a *hard* sum
He stayed too *long.*	It was a *long* story.

Most adverbs are formed from adjectives with the suffix *-ly*:

ADJECTIVE	ADVERB
nice	*nicely*
beautiful	*beautifully*
happy	*happily*

But adverbs are not the only words which end in *-ly*; some adjectives also have this form:
an *elderly* man   a *friendly* face
a *manly* figure   a *lordly* gesture

Functions of adverbs
Adverbs have two distinct functions:

1 They modify **adjectives and other adverbs:**
  He is an *excessively*   slow   speaker.
    (adverb)   (adjective)

  He speaks *terribly* slowly.
    (adverb) (adverb)

  The house is *right* inside the city.
    (adverb) (adverb)

2 They act as adjuncts in the **verb phrase:**

NP	VP
The man	walked *slowly*. (adverb)
My aunt	came *yesterday*. (adverb)

Types of adverbs
In the verb phrase we can distinguish four types of adverbs:

1 **Adverbs of place or direction:**
  away, in, out, upstairs, down, etc.

2 **Adverbs of time:**
  often, usually, sometimes, never, occasionally, frequently, etc.

3 **Adverbs of manner:**
  bravely, quickly, reluctantly, fast, angrily, etc.

4 **Adverbs of degree:**
  really, thoroughly, entirely, wholly, fully, partially, etc.

ADVERBIALS

The function of the adverb can be implemented by other structures. There are four forms, called **adverbials**.

1 **Prepositional phrases:**
  The boy played *skilfully* / *with skill*.
      (adverb)   (prepositional
                    phrase)
  She came *early* / *before dawn*.
      (adverb) (prepositional
                  phrase)

2 Infinitives:

He played *eagerly* / *to win.*
           (adverb) (verb phrase)

They drove *fast* / *to be there* on time.
           (adverb) (verb phrase)

3 -ing participles:

Seeing red, he rushed forward.
(participle
phrase)

Angrily, he rushed forward.
(adverb)

4 -ed participles:

Urged on by determination, he ran forward.
(participle
phrase)

Courageously, she ran forward.
(adverb)

PREPOSITIONS

Prepositions relate nouns or noun phrases to other words in the sentence. They are phrase-makers, having no meaning by themselves.

Functions
Prepositions have four main functions:

1 They precede a noun, pronoun, etc. to indicate a **connection:**

John was   *in*   the *field.*
          (preposition)

2 They form a **prepositional phrase** which can modify a headword:

the man *in the office*   You can have it *for nothing.*
(prepositional phrase,   (prepositional phrase,
modifying *man*)   modifying *it*)

3 They modify **preceding verbs:**

He ran *round the field.*   He travelled *in Spain.*
(prepositional phrase,   (prepositional phrase,
modifying *ran*)   modifying *travelled*)

4 They combine with verbs to form **idiomatic expressions:**

The clock is *wound up.*   At last he *gave in.*

Many words can function as either adverbs or prepositions; usually you can identify a word as a preposition by looking for its object:

We turned *around*.
(adverb,
modifying the
verb *turned*)

We turned *around* the bay.
(preposition,
governing the
object noun *bay*)

Classification
Prepositions can be classified in accordance with how the **'place'** is perceived:

1   as a point in space:
   I walked *to my home*.
   John lived *at the crossroads*.

2   as a line:
   London is *on the Thames*.
   He ran *across the line*.
   They strolled *along the road*.

3   as a surface:
   The table stood *on the floor*.
   We strolled *across the field*.

4   as an area:
   They walked *through the park*.
   The mob ran *into the square*.
   He has a house *in the village*.

5   as a volume:
   He walked *into the house*.
   I put the paper *in the box*.
   They were *inside the building*.

Prepositions also show the relative **positions** of objects:
   Place your bag *below the seat*.
   He stood *behind the door*.
   The tree stood *between the house and the street*.
   His car was parked *opposite the shop*.

They also indicate **movement and direction**:
   The horse galloped *into the wood*.
   We ran *across the road*.
   He walked *down the hill*.

The inventory of English prepositions includes items of one, two or three words:

1   One-word prepositions:
   *about, above, across, after, against, along, amid(st), among(st), around, as,
   at, before, behind, below, beneath, beside, between, beyond, by,
   concerning, considering, despite, down, during, except, following, for,
   from, in, into, like, near, of, off, on, onto, opposite, out, outwith, over, per,
   regarding, round, save, since, then, through, throughout, till, to, toward,
   towards, under, underneath, unlike, until, up, upon, with, within, without*

2 Two-word prepositions:
   across from, along with, alongside of, apart from, away from, because of, down from, due to, except for, inside of, instead of, on to, out of, outside of, over to, together with, up to, up with, etc.

3 Three-word prepositions:
   in spite of, on account of, by means of, in addition to, in respect of, with regard to, in front of, on top of, on behalf of, etc.

CONJUNCTIONS

Conjunctions are joining words. **Co-ordinating conjunctions** connect words, phrases and sentences:

   boys *and* girls   going home *and* having fun
   horses *or* cattle   He came *and* he went.

The inventory of English conjunctions is a short one:
   and, but, or, nor, for, not, so, yet, rather than, sooner than, as well as

Subordinating conjunctions connect subordinate clauses to main clauses. The inventory of subordinators comprises *because, therefore, although, for, nevertheless, if, whether,* and includes some words which can also function as adverbs and/or prepositions: *after, before, since, so, when, whenever.*
   I drank it *because* I was thirsty.
   He attended classes *whenever* he felt like it.

INTERJECTIONS

Interjections are words which never fit into the grammatical structure of the sentence. Some are words which do have grammatical functions in other forms, but we indicate the fact that they are used as interjections by using an exclamation point:
   Good gracious! What! Oh, my!
Some forms exist only as interjections:
   Ugh! Whew! Psst! Nyuk!

5   SENTENCES

The English **sentence** consists of words combined into phrases or clauses.

BASIC SENTENCES

A **basic sentence** consists of a **subject** and a **predicator**. The subject position is usually occupied by a noun phrase or pronoun, and the predicator position is always occupied by a verb phrase.

SUBJECT	PREDICATOR
NP	VP
The boy	was happy.
Little girls	love dolls.
The President	arrived.
Everyone	sang.
I	went home.

The basic sentence can contain a noun phrase called the **object**, which follows the predicator:

SUBJECT	PREDICATOR	OBJECT
NP	VP	NP
The boy	ate	the sweets.
Little girls	love	dolls.
Everyone	sang	songs.
I	saw	my father.

The basic sentence can also contain an **adjunct** which consists of adverbs or adverbials.

SUBJECT	PREDICATOR	OBJECT	ADJUNCT
NP	VP	NP	**adv.**
The boy	ate	the sweets	greedily.
Little girls	love	dolls	passionately.
Everyone	sang	songs	with enthusiasm.
I	saw	my father	in the morning.

The adjunct can occur in different positions in the basic sentence:

ADJUNCT	SUBJECT	PREDICATOR	OBJECT	ADJUNCT
adv.	NP	VP	NP	**adv.**
Merrily	we	sang.		with much pleasure.
In 1985	the President	opened	the new building	

CLAUSES

When basic sentences are combined to form longer sentences, the parts can be joined by a **co-ordinating conjunction:**

BASIC SENTENCE	CONJUNCTION	BASIC SENTENCE
The boy ate the sweets	*and*	his mother was angry.
I saw my father	*but*	he did not see me.

MAIN CLAUSE

In a longer sentence the basic sentence is called a **main** (or **principal**) **clause.** Main clauses can stand alone as sentences. They can also be combined to form compound sentences.

COMPOUND SENTENCES

Compound sentences consist of two or more main clauses. They can be formed by:

1 **conjunction:** I agreed *and* I joined.

2 **semi-colon:** I agreed; I joined; my friend was pleased.

3 **transition words:** I agreed; *however,* my friend did not.
   (*also, accordingly, besides, consequently, furthermore, moreover, hence, however, still, subsequently, then, therefore, thus*)

PHRASES

Basic sentences can be combined by making one a main clause and the other a
phrase:

I saw my father. I felt happy.   My father was tired. He fell asleep.
Seeing my father, I felt happy.   My father, being tired, fell asleep.
       (phrase)   (phrase)

SUBORDINATE CLAUSES

The most common way of combining sentences is to make one a main clause and
the other a **subordinate clause**. A subordinate clause does not normally stand
alone as a sentence. There are several common types:

TYPE OF SUBORDINATE CLAUSE	MAIN CLAUSE	SUBORDINATE CLAUSE
adverb clause of reason	I went home	because I was tired.
,, ,, ,, time	My father arrived	before the letter came.
,, ,, ,, place	We sat down	where the rivers met.
,, ,, ,, condition	The President would be pleased	if the general joined him.
,, ,, ,, degree	He came to see us	as promptly as he could.
,, ,, ,, purpose	He walked quickly	so that he could catch the train.
,, ,, ,, manner	He danced	as if he were mad.
,, ,, ,, concession	He would not come	although he had been invited.
,, ,, ,, result	He walked so slowly	that he was late.
adjective clause	He saw the book	which she had written.
adjective clause	Here is the boy	who gave you the book.
noun clause	I asked him	what he wanted.
noun clause	We promised	that we would write home.

COMPLEX SENTENCES

Sentences consisting of one main clause and one or more subordinate clauses are called **complex sentences**.

MAIN CLAUSE	SUBORDINATE CLAUSE	SUBORDINATE CLAUSE
He was pleased	when he heard	that I had arrived.
Everyone was happy	because the girl found the dog	that had been lost.

SUBORDINATE CLAUSE	MAIN CLAUSE	SUBORDINATE CLAUSE
As soon as I arrived	I asked	what he had done.
When the train arrived	I saw the man	who had been invited.

COMPOUND-COMPLEX SENTENCES

These are sentences which consist of two or more main clauses and one or more subordinate clauses.

SUBORDINATE CLAUSE	MAIN CLAUSE	MAIN CLAUSE	SUBORDINATE CLAUSE
As soon as I arrived	I met my friend	and he told me	where he was going.
Because the work was finished	they went to the office	and asked for the money	they had earned.

THE PARAGRAPH

A **paragraph** is a section of a piece of extended writing which is marked off on the page by beginning a new line, often indented (that is, beginning a few spaces to the right of the margin). Many writers on English composition regard the paragraph as an 'expanded sentence', consisting of a group of sentences on the same topic. When you are ready to begin discussing a new topic, you begin a new paragraph.

Although few experienced writers would follow all these practices, the following features of paragraphing may be useful:

1   A paragraph ending signals a pause to the reader.

2   In fiction, a paragraph ending is necessary when dialogue is going to begin.

3   A new paragraph draws attention to a new character, scene, action, etc.

4   In discursive writing, a new paragraph signals a change of topic or a new argument.

5   Many older writers were careful to build each paragraph round a 'key' or 'topic' sentence. Each of the other sentences contributes to the central idea of the key sentence.

6   The sentences that comprise a paragraph should be coherent: that is, their content should be linked. This quality of coherence is gained by linking devices:

Cross-reference: i.e. a sentence contains words which echo those of the preceding sentence:
There was very little food in the stores. Nor was there food in the people's homes . . .

Sentence connectors: words such as *Thus, However, Moreover, Furthermore, Besides, Again, Next, First, Secondly,* etc.

Pronouns which refer to a noun, pronoun or noun phrase in the preceding sentence:
The President decided to resign. He took this step . . .
The storm raged for a week. It covered ten counties.

Conjunctions such as *But, And, Yet.*

Connecting phrases such as *In this way, To this end, For this reason, With this in mind, In this respect, In other words, For example.*

Most of these linking devices are also used to connect a new paragraph to a preceding paragraph.

6 SPELLING

PHONEMES

To understand English spelling it is necessary to know about **phonemes** and **morphemes**. A phoneme is the smallest meaningful sound in a language: the unit which makes the difference between *bat* and *hat*, *ban* and *bad*, *bin* and *bun*. Each of these words consists of three phonemes. In English the 26 letters in the alphabet can make between 43 and 48 phonemes: each of the 26 letters plus combinations making the sounds of *ng*, *th*, *ch*, *ow*, *aw*, and so on.

MORPHEMES

The spelling system of English (its **orthography**) is partly a sound-to-spelling system. But written English is not a wholly **phonetic** language. If it were, spellings and sounds would correspond exactly: for example the sentence *Phonetic spelling would improve education* would read something like *Fonetik speling wood improov ejukaishun*.

English spelling is also a partly morpheme-to-spelling system. A **morpheme** is the smallest unit of speech having a meaning or grammatical function. The morphemes which have semantic and grammatical functions, the prefixes, suffixes and inflections, are preserved in the spelling. If this were not the case, words such as *parked*, *goes*, *hidden* would look like *parkt*, *goz*, *hidn* and would lose the aids to meaning provided by the affixes *-ed*, *-es*, and *-en*.

STEMS

English orthography also preserves the **stems** of certain words: for example, in *electric*, *electrician* and *electricity*, the stem *electric* is the same in each, making it much easier to see the meaning and giving the spelling paradigm a greater consistency than it would have if a wholly phonetic system prevailed.

SPELLING ERRORS

At the same time, it is true that the correspondence between the spellings and the pronunciations of many English words is confusing. Such words as *tough*, *through*, *cough*, *bough*, *dough*, *heard*, *beard*, *great*, *threat* look alike but sound different. Students of the language must learn these sound/spelling facts by experience.

Much more difficult for the student are the words which have preserved original spelling patterns for purely historical reasons. For example, the *b* remains in *doubt*, *debt* and *subtle* because their Latin origins were *dubitare*, *debitum* and *subtilis*; the *p* remains in *receipt* because the Latin origin was *recepta*; the origin of *victuals* was the Latin *victualis*. Other words commonly misspelled by omitting 'historical' letters are:

acquire	except	psychology
adolescent	fascinate	reminisce
amateur	government	scenery
beautiful	marriage	schedule
cemetery	melancholy	sergeant
conscience	miniature	susceptible
conscious	paraffin	technique
disciple	parallel	
excellent	parliament	

Knowledge of English suffixes and their meanings helps to prevent the misspellings of many words, such as:

abundant	continuance	incidentally
academical	current	independent
acceptance	diligent	ingredient
accidentally	dominant	intelligent
actually	efficient	magnificent
admittance	entrance	performance
annually	existent	personal
apparent	financially	practical
attendant	fundamentally	principal
brilliance	hindrance	prominent
brilliant	ignorance	unusually
consistent	ignorant	

Knowledge of English prefixes helps to prevent the misspelling of words in which the prefix is a simple addition to a stem:

$$dis\text{-} + appoint = disappoint$$
$$grand\text{-} + daughter = granddaughter$$
$$un\text{-} + necessary = unnecessary$$

Other words in which the prefix and stem are clearly preserved are:
advantage, decide, definite, describe, discussion, encourage, enjoy, increase, inevitable, persuade

SPELLING RULES

The e rules
When a suffix begins with a vowel, drop the e.
When a suffix begins with a consonant, retain the e.

DROPPED e	RETAINED e
bride + al = bridal fame + ous = famous plume + age = plumage	grace + ful = graceful care + ful = careful rude + ness = rudeness

Exceptions to this rule occur when the e is retained to soften the pronunciation of c or g:
  notice – noticeable, courage – courageous, etc.

The gemination rules
If a suffix begins with a vowel, double the final single consonant for:

1 monosyllables:
  drop – dropping, pat – patting, sit – sitting

2 stressed last syllables:
  admit – admittance, repel – repelled, regret – regrettable

3 a consonant following a single vowel:
  grit – gritting, refer – referring, infer – inferring

But refer – reference, infer – inference, etc., because here the second syllable is not stressed.

The e-i rule

1 When the sound is ee write ie, except after c:
  chief, field, priest, relieve

2 After c, write ei:
  ceiling, conceive, deceive, receipt

3 When the sound is not ee write ei:
  eight, foreign, vein, weigh

Exceptions: either, neither, financier, seize, species, weird.

The y rule
Change final *y* to *i* except when the suffix is -*ing*:

defy: *defiance*   – *defying*
happy: *happiness*
petrify: *petrified* – *petrifying*

Vowel + gh rules

1 The **gh** is pronounced *f* when *au* is pronounced as in:
   draught, laugh

2 The **gh** is silent when *au* is pronounced as in:
   caught, daughter, fraught, naught, naughty, taught, slaughter

3 The **gh** is pronounced *f* when *ou* is pronounced as in:
   clough, enough, rough, slough, sough, tough, trough

4 The **gh** is silent when *ou* is pronounced as in:
   bought, brought, sought
   or as in:
   borough, thorough
   or as in:
   dough, furlough, though
   or as in:
   through
   or as in:
   bough, drought, slough, sough

Note: *slough* and *sough* can be pronounced as in 3 or 4 above.

MISPRONUNCIATION

Spelling errors can result from the mispronunciation of words:

1 by omitting a phoneme:
   accidentally, arctic, boundary, generally, geography, liable, library, literature, occasionally, strictly, temperament, valuable, veteran

2 by inserting a phoneme:
   disastrous, helm, entrance, handled, hindrance, lightning, remembrance, suffrage, umbrella

3 by transposing letters:
   children, hundred, hospital, irrelevant, preservation, prescribe, revelry

HOMONYMS

Homonyms can sometimes be confused with one another. Examples of words and phrases misspelled by this error:

ascent, assent	dual, duel
affect, effect	dying, dyeing
all ready, already	forth, fourth
allusive, elusive, illusive	fillip, Philip
berth, birth	hear, here
born, borne	holy, wholly
cache, cash	passed, past
canon, cannon	precede, proceed
canvas, canvass	principal, principle
capital, Capitol	right, rite, write, wright
carat, carrot	stationary, stationery
carbine, carbon	threw, through
cite, sight, site	their, there
coarse, course	to, too, two
complement, compliment	whose, who's
counsel, council	your, you're
descent, dissent	

COMMONLY MISSPELLED WORDS

Letters where mistakes are often made are printed in bold type:

a bit (2 words)	ach**ie**vement
a lot (2 words)	acknow**ledge**
abundance, abund**a**nt	ac**q**uaintance
ac**a**demic, academi**cally**, academy	acquie**sce**
ac**c**elerate	ac**q**uire
ac**c**eptable, acceptance, accepting	ac**q**uit**(**ted**)**
ac**c**essible	actu**a**lity, actual**ly**
accident**a**l, accidentally	ad**d**ress
accom**m**odation	adequately
accomp**a**nied, accomp**a**nies,	admi**ss**ion, admi**tt**ance
accomp**a**niment	adol**esce**nce, adol**esc**ent
accomp**a**nying	advant**age**ous
accompl**i**sh	advert**ise**ment, advert**ise**r,
accuracy, **acc**urate, accurately	advert**ising**
ac**c**user, ac**c**uses, accusing	ad**vice** (noun)
accus**t**om	ad**vise** (verb)

aerial
affect
afraid
against
aggravate
aggregate
aggressive, aggressor
agreeable
alcohol
allege
alleviate
allotment
allot(ted)
all right (2 words)
already
altar
altogether
amateur
amount
analysis, analyse (analyze)
ancillary
annihilate
annually
anticipated
apologetically, apologised (ized)
apology (apologies)
appal, appalling
apparatus
apparently
appearance
applying
appreciate, appreciation
approaches
appropriate
approximate
Arctic
arguing, argument
arouse
arrangement
article
assassinate
associate

atheist
attach
attachment
attempts
attendance, attendant, attended
attitude
audience
author
authoritative, authority
available
awkward

bachelor
balloon
bargain
barrenness
basically
battalion
beauteous, beautified
beautiful, beauty
becoming
beginner, beginning
belief, believe
beneficial
benefit, benefited, benefitting
bicycle
biggest
boisterous
boundary
breath, breathe
brilliance, brilliant
Britain
burglar
burial, buried, bury
business

calendar
campaign
career
careful, careless
caricature
carriage
catarrh

category
caterpillar
cemetery
century
challenge
changeable
changing
chaos
character, characteristic,
    characterised (characterized)
Christian, Christianity
choose, chose
cigarette
circuit
cite
collaborate
colleague
college
colonel
commemorate
commercial
commission
committee
comparative(ly)
comparison
compatible
competent
competition, competitive,
    competitor
computer
concede
conceivable, conceive
concentrate
concern
condemn
conjure
connotation, connote
conscience, conscientious
conscious
consensus
consequently
considerably

consistency
consistent
conspiracy
contemporary
continuous(ly)
controlled, controlling
controversial, controversy
convenience, convenient
correlate
correspondence
corroborate
council
counsellor
counterfeit
courteous
criticism, criticise (criticize)
cruelly, cruelty
curiosity, curious
curriculum
cynicism

dealt
deceit, deceive
decision
defence, defensive
definite(ly), definition
degradation
democracy
dependent
descendant
descent
describe, description
desiccated
despair, desperately
detached
deteriorate
deterrent
detriment
devastating
develop(ed), development
device
diarrhoea

die, died, dying
difference, different
difficult
dilapidated
dilemma
diligence
dining
disappear
disappoint
disastrous
disciple
discipline
discrimination
discussion
disease
disgusted
disillusioned
disobeyed
dissatisfied
dissolve
distributor
doesn't
dominant
dropped
duly

ecstasy
eerie
effect
efficiency, efficient
eighth
elegant
eliminate
embarrass
emperor
emphasise (emphasize)
encourage
endeavour
enormous
entrance
environment
equatorial

equipped
escapade
especially
estuary
evidently
exaggerate
exceed
excellence, excellent
except, exceptionally
excitable, excitement
exercise
exhibition
exhilarating
existence, existent
expense
experience
experiment
explanation
extremely

Fahrenheit
fallacy
familiar
families, family
fantasies, fantasy
fascinate
fashion
favourite
feasible
February
fictitious
field
fiery
finally
financially, financier
fluorescent
foreigner
forfeit
fortunately
forty
fourteen
fourth

friend, friendliness
fulfil, fulfilled
fundamentally
furniture

gaiety
galloped
gauge
generally
genius
goddess
government, governor
grammar, grammatically
grandeur
grievous
guaranteed
guard
guidance, guiding

handkerchief
handled
happened
happiness
harass
heaven
height
heir
hero, heroes
heroic, heroine
hindrance
hopeless, hoping
hospitalisation (hospitalization)
humorist, humorous
hundred
hungrily, hungry
hygiene
hypocrisy, hypocrite

ideally
identical
ignorance, ignorant
illegible, illegibly
imaginary, imagination, imagine

immediately
immense
imminent
importance
in between (2 words)
incidentally
indefinite
independence, independent
indispensable
individually
in fact (2 words)
infinite
in front (2 words)
ingenious
ingredient
initiative
innocence
innuendo
inoculate
in spite of (3 words)
install, instalment
insurrection
intellect, intellectual
intelligence, intelligent
intention
interest, interested
interference
interpretation
interrupt
involve
irrelevant
irreparable
irresistible
irreverent
irritable
isosceles
its (it's)

jealousy
jeopardy
jewellery (jewelry)

keenness

knowledge, knowledgeable
laboratory
labourer, laboriously
led
leisurely
lengthening
liaison
licence (noun)
license (verb)
lieutenant
lightening
lightning (flash)
likelihood, likely, likeness
listener
literary, literature
liveliest, livelihood, liveliness
loathsome
loneliness, lonely
loose
luxury

magazine
magnificence, magnificent
maintain, maintenance
manageable, management
manoeuvre, manoeuvring
manufacturers
marriage
marvellous
material
mathematics, mathematician
mechanics
medicine
medieval (mediaeval)
Mediterranean
melancholy
messenger
metaphor(s)
mimic, mimicked
miniature
minute
miscellaneous

mischief, mischievous
monastery
morale
morally
murmured, murmuring
mysterious
mystifying

naive
narrative
naturally
navigate
Negroes
neighbour
ninety
ninth
no one (2 words)
noticeable, noticing
nuisance
numerous

obstacle
occasionally
occur, occurred, occurrence
offered
old-fashioned
omit, omission
operate
opinion
opponent
oppose
opposite
optimism
ordinarily
organisation (organization)
original(ly)
overrule

paid (never payed)
pamphlet
panic-stricken
paraffin
parallel(ed)

paralysed (paralyzed)
parliament(ary)
particularly
passed
past
pavilion
peculiar(ly)
perceive
permanent
permissible
persistent
personal
personnel
persuade
phenomenon
philosophy
physical
piece
pigeon
planned
plausible
playwright
pleasant
poisonous
political, politician
possible
possession
practice (noun)
practise (verb)
practical
precede
predecessor
predominant
preferred
prejudice
preparation
presence
prestige
pretence
pretension
prevalent
primitive

principal
principle
prisoner
probably
procedure, proceed
professor
programme
prominent
pronunciation
proof
propaganda
propagate
propeller
protrude
prove
psychiatrist
psychoanalysis
psychology
psychopathic
publicly
punctuation
pursue

quantity
quarrel, quarrelling
quarter
queue
quietly

realise (realize)
really
rebel
receipt
receive, receiving
recommend
reconnoitre
refer, referred
refrigerator (fridge)
relative
relieve
religion, religious
reminisce, reminiscence
represent

reservoir
resistance
resources
responsibility
restaurant
revealed
rhyme
rhythm
ridicule, ridiculous
rogue
roommate
rouge

sacrifice
sacrilegious
safety
sandal
satire
satisfied, satisfy
scenery
schedule
scissors
secretary
seize
sentence
separate, separation
sergeant (serjeant)
several
shepherd
sheriff
shining
significance
silhouette
similarly
simile
sincerely
skilful
sociology
soldier
solicitor
soliloquy (-quies)
souvenir

sovereignty
speech
sponsor
stabilisation (stabilization)
statistics
stepped
straight
strength
stretch
stubborn
studying
substantial
subtle, subtlety, subtly
succeed, successfully, succession
sufficient
summarise (summarize), summary
summed
supersede
suppose
suppress
surfeit
surprise
surrounding
susceptible
suspense
swimming
symbol
symmetry
synonymous
systematic

technical
technique
temperament
temperature
temporary
tendency
terrifying
their
themselves
theories, theory
there

therefore
they're
thorough
thought
tie, tied, tying
to (too, two)
tobacco
toboggan
tomorrow
tongue
tragedy
tragic
tranquillity
transferred
tremendous
truly
twelfth
tyranny

undoubtedly
unnecessary
until (but till)
unusually
useful, useless

vacuum
valley(s)

valuable
vegetable
vehicle
vengeance
veterinary
vicious
vigorous
villain
virtually

warrant
weather
weird
where
whether
whole, wholly
whose
wield
wilful
wiry
withhold
witticism
woollen
worship

yacht
yield
you're

WORDS OFTEN CONFUSED

accent, ascent, assent
accept, except
adapt, adopt
advice, advise
affect, effect
all ready, already
all together, altogether
allusive, elusive, illusive, delusive
allowed, aloud
alter, altar
alternate, alternative

always, all ways
amiable, amicable
astrology, astronomy

bail, bale
bare, bear
berth, birth
board, bored
boarder, border
borne, born
break, brake

breath, breathe
Britain, Briton, Breton
brooch, broach, broch

canon, cannon
canvas, canvass
capital, Capitol
ceremonious, ceremonial
choose, chose
check, cheque
cite, sight, site
civil, civic
coarse, course
compliment, complement
conscience, conscious
contemptible, contemptuous
continual, continuous
council, counsel, consul
credible, credulous, creditable
currant, current

decease, disease
decent, descent, dissent
defective, deficient
dependant, dependent
deprecate, depreciate
derisive, derisory
desert, dessert
distract, district, detract
disperse, disburse
draft, draught
duel, dual
dyeing, dying

effective, effectual
elicit, illicit
eligible, illegible
emigrant, immigrant
eminent, imminent, immanent
ensure, insure
exceptional, exceptionable

faint, feint
fair, fare

formerly, formally
foregoing, forgoing
forth, fourth
fortunate, fortuitous

gentle, gentile

hear, here
holy, wholly, holly
hoard, horde
human, humane

idle, idol
imaginary, imaginative
imperial, imperious
industrial, industrious
ingenious, ingenuous
instance, instants
intelligent, intelligible
it's, its

judicial, judicious

knew, new
know, no

lead, led
leant, lent
lessen, lesson
lightening, lightning
loose, lose
luxuriant, luxurious

marshal, martial
meter, metre
moral, morale

negligent, negligible

observant, observance
of, off
official, officious

past, passed
peace, piece
persecute, prosecute
personal, personnel

plain, plane
pray, prey
precede, proceed
precipitate, precipitous
presence, presents
prescribe, proscribe
principal, principle
prophecy, prophesy

quiet, quite

rain, reign, rein
raise, raze
respectfully, respectably,
    respectively
review, revue
right, rite, wright, write

sense, since
sensible, sensitive
sensual, sensuous

sew, sow, so
sociable, social
shone, shown
stationary, stationery
statue, stature, statute
stimulant, stimulus
superficial, superfluous

taught, taut
temporal, temporary
there, their, they're
threw, through
to, too, two

waist, waste
waive, wave
weak, week
were, we're
who's, whose

your, you're

7 PUNCTUATION

Punctuation helps you to convey meaning in writing. It is often the only way there is in modern English to indicate emphasis, or to show that you are asking a question.

THE COMMA

The **comma** has the following seven functions:

1 It is used to signal the separation of main clauses from non-restrictive clauses: that is, clauses which do not restrict the meaning of the main clause but merely comment on it, or give more information about it:

We looked eagerly for the men, who were to be our guides.
This is our new home, in which we hope to live for many years.
The leader silently raised his hand, which looked thin and cold.

Note: The following example illustrates the difference between restrictive and non-restrictive clauses:

Restrictive:
He was reading the book which had a red cover. 'which had a red cover' is a restrictive clause and is part of the definition of book, perhaps to distinguish it from another book of a different colour.

Non-restrictive:
He was reading the book, which had a red cover. 'which had a red cover' here, by the use of the comma, is a non-restrictive clause giving additional information about the book.

2 It sets off non-restrictive phrases:

The girl, her hair tossing in the wind, ran quickly into the field.
His eyes shining, Joe told us he had won the game.

3 It sets off appositive phrases, that is, phrases which give a further description of a noun or pronoun:

Joe, our new captain, explained his plan.
We hurried to meet Mr Tang, our new cook.

4 It separates clauses joined by *and, but, or, nor, for*:

He asked for an explanation, and I told him what had happened.
He asked for an explanation, but we could not give him one.
He asked for an explanation, or at least some hint of what had happened.
He would tell us nothing, nor would he let his friend speak.
He would not tell us his plan, for that might spoil the fun.

5 It sets off introductory clauses and phrases:
While the food boiled gently in the pot, the children sat by the fire and told stories.
Their hides being hard and tough, elephants can roam among thorny bushes without being hurt.

6 It separates the items in a list of words, phrases or clauses:
Boars, baboons, giraffes and birds all live peacefully together on the plains.
They were tall, powerful, fierce-looking, and they were approaching fast.
These plants can be found among trees, on river-banks, on the sides of hills, and indeed wherever there is ample shelter.
The messenger said that the enemy had retreated, that they were moving fast, and that they were leaving their stores behind.

7 It is used to signal the separation of direct speech:
"Come over here," said Harry, "and bring the map with you."
William's boss said, "If you were less careless, you would find the work easier."

THE FULL STOP

The **full stop**, which is also called the **period**, signals the end of a sentence. In formal, correct English, a sentence is usually what the writer intends to be a unified, complete thought. In grammatical terms a sentence consists of one or more main clauses with or without one or more subordinate clauses:

right: The giraffe stood still, looking at us.
wrong: Looking at us.

right: The giraffe stood still and looked at us.
wrong: Looked at us.

The full stop can also mark the end of abbreviations:
Jones and Co., Ltd., etc.
We placed an ad. in the paper.

Note: When the last letter of a word forms the last letter of the abbreviation, the full stop is not needed in modern English: *Mr, Dr, Ltd*
The full stop is normally omitted from initials: *BBC, TV, OAU*

Another use of the full stop is to show that something has been omitted from a sentence. This is called an **ellipsis**:

1 Three stops in combination show an omission in the middle of a sentence:
'What did he . . . I cannot go on!'

2 Four stops at the end of a sentence show that the sentence is intended to tail off:
'As the day came to an end, the children lay down, hoping to sleep . . . .'

3 Three stops show that part of a quotation has been omitted:
'Banquo said, "My noble partner . . . seems rapt withal." '

4 A row of stops indicate the omission of a line of verse, a whole passage, etc.

THE QUESTION MARK

The **question mark** indicates a question. It should not be used unless there is a direct question asked by the writer or by someone quoted.

right: Who led the army?
right: He asked, "Who led the army?"
wrong: He asked who led the army?

THE EXCLAMATION POINT

The **exclamation point** is used to mark interjections or to strengthen the force of an exclamation:
Yes! That's right! Help! Tell me the truth!

THE SEMI-COLON

The **semi-colon** marks off parts of a sentence that have equal grammatical patterns. It has three main functions:

1 It separates main clauses in a sentence:
The ambassador will come tomorrow; he hopes to arrive by train.
Everything was quiet; it was as if the village was deserted.

2 It separates a main clause from a following main clause which begins with a connector:
The ambassador is late; in fact, he should have been here hours ago.
Everything has been carefully planned; however, we cannot be too confident.

3 It marks a series of main clauses with a common subject:
The device gives much pleasure to children; provides hours of amusement improves the learning of mathematical skills.

THE COLON

The **colon** is an introduction signal, whereas the semi-colon is a separator. These marks cannot be used in place of one another. The colon has five main functions:

1   It introduces a list:
    We have several kinds of book in our library: works of fiction, reference books, dictionaries and volumes of poetry.

2   It introduces a quotation:
    'Macbeth said: "Speak, if you can. What are you?" '

3   It introduces an explanation:
    I knew why he was late: he had been sleeping.
    His need was clear: he was thirsty.

4   It marks a logical connection not openly stated:
    The general ordered the retreat: he had lost confidence.

5   It balances two comparisons or contrasts:
    Dogs bark: cats miaow.
    Cats love themselves: dogs love their masters.

THE DASH

The **dash** has five main uses:

1   It marks a sudden change of direction in the writer's flow of thought:
    The sun shone as we set out — it was a late summer that year.
    The president spoke for many hours — but this was not unusual.

2   It can indicate that a thought has broken off:
    Oh, what a disaster — .
    There could be no other way — !

3   It introduces a summary:
    We had books, food, tools, clothes — everything we needed.

4   Two dashes mark off an inserted thought:
    The whole family came — I remember it all so well — and we were so happy.
    It was obvious — no other explanation was possible — that he had camped there.

5   It separates a list from a main clause:
    Hammer, spade, nails, saw — these were all packed.
    All were present — father, mother, brothers, sisters.

THE HYPHEN

The **hyphen** is used to form certain kinds of compound words. Some words which were originally hyphenated are now usually written as solid words in modern English: *postman, football, headline, oilrig,* etc.

With many words it is still optional to hyphenate or not: *catch-phrase, flow-chart, play-group,* etc.

Hyphens are usually still necessary when verbs are combined with nouns or prepositions: *never-to-be-forgotten, couldn't-care-less, running-in,* etc.

With the prefix *re-* a hyphen is used to distinguish words which could otherwise be confused: *re-sign* (resign), *re-form* (reform), etc.

THE APOSTROPHE

The **apostrophe** has two functions.

1 It denotes possession:

the boy's ball	the lady's coat	men's lives
the boys' toys	the ladies' coats	women's rights

2 It indicates contractions:

The boy's in the house.   He doesn't want to come.
It's Monday today.   We can't go.
They didn't see the ball.

Note: The apostrophe is seldom used nowadays to form the plurals of numbers and letters: the modern forms are *the 90s, the 3 Rs, Ps and Qs.*

CAPITAL LETTERS

These are also called **upper case initials**. They are used:

1 to mark the beginning of a sentence

2 to begin proper nouns

3 in titles

4 to begin lines of verse

5 to indicate an abstraction:
    'O what a foolish thing is Man!'   'We must avoid Pride.'

INVERTED COMMAS

These are also called **quotation marks**. They are used:

1 to begin a quotation:
   Macbeth cried: 'Is this a dagger which I see before me . . .'

2 to show that a word is used as if it were being quoted:
   It is no 'crime' to pick these flowers.

3 to indicate a title:
   He was known as 'Captain'.
   The essay is called 'On Study'.
   We went to see 'David Copperfield'.

Note: In modern English writing it is more usual to underline titles, and in print to set them in italics.

4 to mark off direct speech:
   He said, 'I am tired.'
   'It is my wish,' he said calmly, 'that my daughter should marry her cousin.'

Note: It is more common nowadays to use single inverted commas wherever possible. Double inverted commas may be used for quotations within quotations:
   He said, 'We distinctly heard him say "Go home" before he entered the house.'

8 PRONUNCIATION

STANDARD AND NON-STANDARD ENGLISH

The term **Standard English** (SE) is used to denote the 'correct' English used by educated speakers of English all over the world. **Non-standard English** takes various forms: it is used by people who live in a particular district, or by people who share a particular way of life, or by people when they are relaxed or at home. Most native English speakers can use SE well enough for their own purposes. SE is the form of the language used in schools, in text-books, in business and so on; and it is SE that students must learn if they wish to be considered educated users of English.

Standard English has nothing to do with *accent*, or the way you form the basic sounds. Speakers of SE in various parts of the world speak the language with different habits of pronunciation, but the grammar and vocabulary are common to all. When learning to speak English, however, students should learn the sounds of Received Pronunciation (RP), which is the sound system common to most educated people in the south of England; or General American (GA) which is used by educated speakers of English in North America. It is not necessary however, to speak *exactly* like RP or GA speakers: regional English, Scots, Welsh, Irish, Australian and many other varieties of spoken SE will serve any student very well.

LETTERS AND SOUNDS

Written English has 26 letters: of these 5 are vowels and 21 are consonants. The vowels are *a, e, i, o, u* and the consonants are *b, c, d, f, g, h, j, k, l, m, n, p, q, r, s, t, v w, x, y, z.*

These letters appear in words with many more than 26 sound forms. In English there are between 43 and 48 **phonemes**, which are the smallest meaningful sounds. There is no exact number of phonemes in English, because different speakers use different numbers of sounds (see page 139).

The phonetic alphabet

In order to describe the sounds of language, scholars in this subject (phoneticians) have invented symbols to stand for all the different phonemes. The system used almost everywhere now is the **International Phonetic Alphabet (IPA)**, which was developed between the end of the 19th century and 1951. This may be found in any major English dictionary.

HOW THE SOUNDS ARE MADE

The **labial consonants** (p b f v w m) are produced by closing the lips. For f and v the upper teeth contact the lower lip.

The **dental consonants** (t d n th) are produced by the action of the tongue against the teeth-ridge (that is, the ridge of bone at the back of the upper teeth). The teeth-ridge is also called the dental ridge or the alveolar ridge.

The **lateral consonant** (l) is produced by lowering the sides of the tongue from the teeth-ridge and letting air flow past the sides of the tongue.

The **post-alveolar** (or **post-dental**) **consonants** (s z) are produced by the front (or blade) of the tongue approaching the front of the palate just behind the teeth-ridge.

The **alveolar** r is also produced in this way by RP speakers. Some speakers, for instance Scottish people, pronounce r by a 'dental trill': that is, they vibrate the tip of the tongue against the teeth-ridge.

The **palatal consonants** (ch dge) are produced by raising the tongue higher against the hard palate.

The **velar consonants** (k g ng) are produced with the back of the tongue against the soft palate (also called the velum).

The **aspirate** h is produced by hissing air through a small opening made by bringing together the vocal chords. (This opening is called the glottis.)

N = nasal cavity
H = hard palate
B = blade of tongue
T = tip of tongue
A = teeth-ridge
S = velum or soft palate
VC = vocal chords
L = larynx
G = glottis

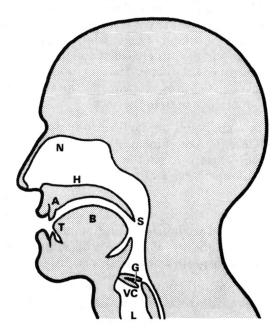

The **stops** (or **plosives**) (p b t d k g) are caused by letting the air escape with a 'pop'. This is called a *closure*. p b are produced by labial closures and t d are produced by dental closures.

The **affricates** (ch dge) are also stops but the closure is released gradually.

The **fricatives** (f v th) are produced by hissing air through a narrow channel.

The **nasal consonants** (m n ng) are produced by letting air into the nasal cavities.

The **semi-vowels** (w r j) are produced as follows:

w is formed by rounding the lips and raising the back of the tongue towards the soft palate.

r is produced by the tip of the tongue turned up to the teeth-ridge.

j is produced by pushing the tongue up to the hard palate.

The **lateral** l is produced by the blade of the tongue against the teeth-ridge and the lowering of the sides of the tongue to let the air pass.

Voiced and voiceless sounds

Voiced sound is produced by vibration of the vocal chords, and a voiceless sound is produced with the vocal chords apart.

The *voiced stops* are b d g. The *voiceless stops* are p t k.

The *voiced fricatives* are v th z s. The *voiceless fricatives* are f th s sh.

Vowels

All the vowels are voiced in the larynx and there is no restriction of the air as it passes through the vocal chords. From the larynx to the lips, the mouth and throat form a kind of tube, which is called the **vocal tract**. The actions of the tongue and the lips give the vocal tract the different shapes which produce the different vowel sounds. The tongue forms itself into a hump in the mouth, and it moves on two axes, one from the floor of the mouth to the roof and one from the front of the mouth to the back.

The main points on the floor-to-roof axis are:

close (to roof of mouth): ee in *see*, oo in *too*

half-close: o in *rotating*

half-open: e in *met*

open: a in *far*

The main points on the front-to-back axis are:

front (beneath hard palate): ee in *see*, ai in *bait*

central (below where hard and soft palates meet): i in *bird*

back (beneath soft palate): a in *far*, oo in *too*

Two categories of lip-shape are significant:

rounded: corners of lips are forward: oo in *too*

unrounded: corners of lips are pulled back: ee in *see*

Diphthongs

Diphthongs are two vowels blended in one syllable, and they are produced by changing the positions of tongue and lips. Vowels that do not change in this way are called **monophthongs**. Most native English speakers have many diphthongs in their speech, while others, such as the Scots, Welsh, Indian speakers of English, produce monophthongs, for example for such words as *day, close, no.*

VOWEL SOUNDS IN MODERN ENGLISH

VOWEL	NAME	EXAMPLES
a	long a (diphthong)	ale, bay, break, gauge, make, pain
a	short a	back, bat, hat, landed
a	broad a	alms, arm, barred, father, hearth
a	long o	all, swarm, talk
a	short o	austere, authority, quality, swan, wash
a	half-long a	chaotic, duplicate, vacation
au	long o	caught, haul, maul
aw	long o	awful, dawn, hawk, law
e	long e	be, eke, eve
e	short e	met, send, well; friend, heifer, leopard
e	unaccented short e	college, enlarge, excuse, kindness
e	accented e	fern, herd, verge
ee	long e	keeper, meet, see
ei	long e	deceit, receive
ey	long a (diphthong)	obey, they
i	long i (diphthong)	child, ice, sight, time
i	short i	bit, ill, pity, remit
i	unaccented short i	charity, possible, respiration
o	long o (diphthong)	go, note, old, over, owe
o	short o	botany, not, probable, proper, rob, sorry
oi	diphthong oi	coil, oil, point
oo	long o (diphthong)	food, pool, school, shoo, sure, tour
ou	diphthong ou	out, pout, shout
ow	diphthong ow	cow, how, now, scowl
u	long u	cue, dispute, use, yule
u	short u	bunch, fun, sun, under

INTONATION

Intonation is the 'tunes' or 'melody' of English speech. Its main features are **stress** and **tone**.

Stress

Stress is shown by placing ' in front of the stressed syllable. One-syllable words in English have stress patterns as follows:

Stressed are one-syllable **content** words, i.e. nouns, verbs, adjectives, adverbs.

Unstressed are one-syllable **function** words, i.e. prepositions, pronouns, determiners, conjunctions, etc.

Note: When a preposition is used in an idiomatic expression or is used as an adverb it will normally carry stress, because this makes it a content word:
He was 'brought to the 'room. (*to* = preposition)
He 'fainted but was 'soon brought 'to. (*to* = idiom)
The 'table was 'carried through the 'hall. (*through* = preposition)
The 'table was carried 'through. (*through* = adverb)

In English the stress pattern of a word of more than one syllable (**polysyllabic**) is a signal of its meaning to the experienced speaker, but unfortunately there are no easily-described rules showing how the stress is selected for different words. The stressing of syllables must be learned along with learning each word's meaning.

In English sentences the content words, which carry the main information, carry stress, and the function words do not. In the following sentences, for example, the main stresses are carried by the content words:
The 'elephants 'escaped from the 'compound 'early 'yesterday 'morning.
'Everyone in the 'garden 'decided to 'join the 'group who were 'singing.

Tone

Tones are changes of intonation, shown by rising or falling in the pitch of the voice, which help to convey the meaning of an utterance, the speaker's intention, mood and so on.

Falling tones generally indicate finality, certainty, assertion, contrast, etc. (Falling tones are shown by ˋ over the syllables affected.)

finality:	That's all there is.
	Now we go home.
certainty:	I told you so.
	You may go but I can't.
assertion:	The boy's a fool.
	It's hard to say.

contrast: Her bag is whìte. (Not red or blue, etc.)
                       His name is Jòe. (Not anything else!)

Rising tones generally indicate uncertainty, questioning, incompleteness, etc.
(Rising tones are shown by ´ over the syllables affected.)

uncertainty: Are you súre?
                       Aren't you comíng?
questioning: What are you doíng?
                       What would you líke to eat?
incompleteness: If you líke, I'll còme.
                       I wónder, would you líke to còme?

Falling and rising tones can be combined to produce different effects. (The
fall-rise tone is shown by ˇ or ` ´ over the syllables affected.)

hesitation: Are you comíng? I think̆ s̆o.
                       Here's your tennis ràcket. That's not mỳ rácket.
implication: You thìnk you're ríght. (But you may not be!)
                       I knòw he cáme. (But he may leave again.)
unexpectedness: He refúsed? (I expected him to accept.)

9 COMMON ERRORS

<u>AGREEMENT</u>

1 A verb must agree in number with its subject:

wrong: (singular subject) (plural verb)
The   *ship*   *sail.*
right: The ship *sails.*

wrong: (plural subject)   (singular verb)
The *elephants*   *was*   running.
right: The elephants *were* running.

wrong: (singular subject)   (plural verb)
One   of the boys   *were*   eating sweets.
right: One of the boys *was* eating sweets.

wrong: (singular subject)   (plural verb)
The   *sound*   of the bells   *were*   heard in the distance.
right: The sound of the bells *was* heard in the distance.

wrong: (singular subject)   (plural verb)
The   *leader,*   as well as his followers,   *were*   tired.
right: The leader, as well as his followers, *was* tired.

wrong: (singular verb)   (plural subject)
In the van there   *was*   a dozen   *boxes.*
right: In the van there *were* a dozen boxes.

2 A pronoun must agree in number with the noun or pronoun that antecedes it:

wrong: (singular)   (plural)
Each   of the girls ate *their* cakes.
right: Each of the girls ate *her* cakes.

wrong: (singular)   (plural)   (plural)
Anyone can play if *they* pay *their* share.
right: Anyone can play if *he* pays *his* share.

wrong: (singular)   (plural)
One   must always pay *their* share.
right: One must always pay *one's* share.

3 A collective noun is followed by a singular verb:

wrong: (collective noun) (plural verb)
          The whole *company*   *were*   leaving the building.
right: The whole company *was* leaving the building.

wrong: (collective noun)   (plural verb)
          A *thousand*   dollars   *were*   a good price.
right: A thousand dollars *was* a good price.

4 A verb in an adjective clause must agree in number with the noun or pronoun in the main clause to which it refers:

wrong: (plural)   (singular)
          She was one of the tallest *women* who   *has*   lived here.
right: She was one of the tallest women who *have* lived here.

wrong: (plural)   (singular)
          We shall climb every one of the *trees* which   *has*   fruit.
right: We shall climb every one of the trees which *have* fruit.

5 A title is treated as singular and takes a singular verb:

wrong: 'The Good Companions' *were* showing at the Tivoli.
right: 'The Good Companions' *was* showing at the Tivoli.

wrong: 'Happy Days' *are* my favourite show.
right: 'Happy Days' *is* my favourite show.

6 A word quoted as a word takes a singular verb:

wrong: 'We' *are* the first person plural.
right: 'We' *is* the first person plural.

wrong: 'Thousands' *are* often misspelled.
right: 'Thousands' *is* often misspelled.

ADJECTIVES

1 Do not confuse the *positive, comparative* and *superlative* forms of adjectives. The *comparative* compares or contrasts between two. The *superlative* relates to more than two.

wrong: (superlative)
     He was the   *best*   soldier of the two.
right: (comparative)
     He was the   *better*   soldier of the two.

wrong: (comparative)
     He was the   *better*   player of the three.
right: (superlative)
     He was the   *best*   player of the three.

2   Use adverbs, not adjectives, to modify verbs:

wrong: (adjective)
     He performed the trick *perfect*.
right: (adverb)
     He performed the trick *perfectly*.

wrong: (adjective)
     She said it could be done as *easy* as anything.
right: (adverb)
     She said it could be done as *easily* as anything.

3   Use the correct adjective with count and mass nouns:

wrong: There were not *much* soldiers in the village.
right: There were not *many* soldiers in the village.

wrong: How *many* flour do you need?
right: How *much* flour do you need?

4   Do not confuse *few* and *a few*, *little* and *a little*, etc:

wrong: There was *a little* need to return the letter.
right: There was *little* need to return the letter.

wrong: The hill was so high that *a few* succeeded in climbing to the top.
right: The hill was so high that *few* succeeded in climbing to the top.

5   Do not confuse *each* and *every*. *Each* relates to separate items and *every* to items in a group. *Each* is also used for one of two.

wrong: *Each* leaf in the tree turned yellow.
right: *Every* leaf in the tree turned yellow.

wrong: *Every* one of my two friends came to see me.
right: *Each* one of my two friends came to see me.

6 Do not confuse *less* and *fewer*:

wrong: I had *less* apples than he had.
right: I had *fewer* apples than he had.

wrong: I had *fewer* bread than he had.
right: I had *less* bread than he had.

7 Place two or more adjectives in the most logical order:

wrong: These are the *four first* numbers.
right: These are the *first four* numbers.

wrong: Seated on the bench were *old little two* men.
right: Seated on the bench were *two little old* men.

ADVERBS

1 Place an adverb near the verb it modifies:

wrong: We travel on this bus *never*.
right: We *never* travel on this bus.

wrong: He *cheerfully* stood up and smiled.
right: He stood up and smiled *cheerfully*.

2 Do not confuse *very* and *much*, *very* and *too*, *very much* and *too much*:

wrong: The hill was *much* high.
right: The hill was *too* high.

wrong: I was *too* hot but it was not uncomfortable.
right: I was *very* hot but it was not uncomfortable.

wrong: It was *very* hot to run quickly.
right: It was *too* hot to run quickly.

wrong: I loved reading that book *too* much.
right: I loved reading that book *very* much.

3 Do not confuse *very* and *so*:

wrong: She told me that the tree was *so* tall.
right: She told me that the tree was *very* tall.

wrong: The tree was *very* tall that we could not climb it.
right: The tree was *so* tall that we could not climb it.

4 Do not use the wrong adverb to indicate time:

wrong: She says she arrived an hour *before*.
right: She says she arrived an hour *ago*.

wrong: I told her I would join her *just now*.
right: I told her I would join her *soon*.
right: I told her I would join her *presently*.

wrong: I am *presently* a member of two clubs.
right: I am *at present* a member of two clubs.

DEMONSTRATIVES

Do not confuse *this, that, these, those*:

wrong: Let us use *this* boat on the other side of the river.
right: Let us use *that* boat on the other side of the river.

wrong: *Those* books in my bag are for you.
right: *These* books in my bag are for you.

wrong: *These* is my brother.
right: *This* is my brother.

NOUNS

1 Do not use the plural form for mass nouns:

wrong: She asked him for some *informations*.
right: She asked him for some *information*.

wrong: The *evidences* were clear.
right: The *evidence* was clear.

wrong: He found he had lost all his *baggages*.
right: He found he had lost all his *baggage*.

Note: Other mass nouns: *advertising, advice, butter, character, damage, fruit, furniture, gravel, luggage, milk, resentment, work*, etc.

2 Some nouns appear to be plural but are singular:

wrong: Mathematics *are* my favourite subject.
right: Mathematics *is* my favourite subject.

wrong: Measles *are* a common ailment.
right: Measles *is* a common ailment.

Note: Other singular nouns ending in -s: *Athens, billiards, Brussels, classics, darts, measles, mumps, news,* etc.

PREPOSITIONS

1 Do not use the wrong preposition in a verb phrase, learn the whole phrase:

PREPOSITION	VERB PHRASES	
	right	**wrong**
about	be happy about	to be happy at/be happy for
	to brag about	to brag for
	to dream about	to dream at
at	to aim at	to aim on
	to hint at	to hint on
	to arrive at	to arrive to
	be good at	be good in
by	to benefit by	to benefit from
	to travel by (air, etc.)	to travel with (air, etc.)
for	to allow for	to allow to
	to care for	to care with
	be exchanged for	be exchanged by
	to play for (a team, etc.)	to play with (a team, etc.)
	to hope for	to hope to
	to shout for	to shout at
	to wait for	to wait on
from	be different from	be different than
in	be interested in	interested at
	to believe in	believe to
	have confidence in	have confidence to
	be disappointed in	be disappointed from
	to fail in (exam)	to fail from/at

PREPOSITION	VERB PHRASES	
	right	**wrong**
of	be accused of (a crime)	be accused for (a crime)
	to approve of	to approve in
	be afraid of	be afraid from
	be ashamed of	be ashamed with
	be proud of	be proud with
	to brag of (a skill)	brag for (a skill)
	be careful of	be careful for
	to complain of	to complain from
	to consist of	to consist in/from
	be composed of	be composed from
	be made of	be made from
	be cured of	be cured from
	be full of	be full with
	be glad of	be glad with/from
on	to call on (someone)	to call at (someone)
	to congratulate on (an achievement)	to congratulate for
	to enlarge on (a subject)	to enlarge in
	to depend on	to depend from
	to live on (a salary)	to live by
	to insist on	to insist to
to	to add to	to add in
	be accustomed to	be accustomed with
	to attend to (someone or something)	to attend at
	to conform to	to conform with
	to refer to (a book)	to refer in/at
	be an exception to	be an exception of
	be indifferent to	be indifferent from/for
	be married to	be married with
	be opposite to	be opposite from
	be related to	be related with
	be similar to	be similar with
	be inferior to	be inferior from
	be superior to	be superior than
	to tie (something) to	to tie (something) on

2 Do not omit the preposition in a prepositional verb phrase:

right	**wrong**
to apply *for* a job	to apply a job
to ask *for* something	to ask something
to add *to* something	to add something
to amount *to* a sum	to amount a sum
to attend *to* something	to attend something
to dream *of* something	to dream something
to explain *to* someone	to explain someone
to explain *about* something	to explain something
to care *for* someone	to care someone
to listen *to* someone	to listen someone
to reply *to* someone	to reply someone
to wait *for* someone	to wait someone

PRONOUNS

1 Use *who* and *whom* correctly:

wrong: *Who* did you follow in the race?
right: *Whom* did you follow in the race?

wrong: The new president was a leader *whom* was bound to succeed.
right: The new president was a leader *who* was bound to succeed.

wrong: He promoted *whomever* was loyal.
right: He promoted *whoever* was loyal.

2 After the conjunctions *as* or *than*, the pronoun should not be in the objective form:

wrong: He was successful as well as *her*.
right: He was successful as well as *she*.

wrong: She was taller than *him*.
right: She was taller than *he*.

3 The objective form of the pronoun must be used in a phrase which is the object:

wrong: He told my wife and *I* to go.
right: He told my wife and *me* to go.

wrong: The choice lay between you and *I*.
right: The choice lay between you and *me*.

4 Indefinite pronouns should be followed by a singular verb and the appropriate possessive:

wrong: No one can say what *their* future will bring.
right: No one can say what *his* future will bring.

wrong: Nobody can do *their* best unless *they* are properly encouraged.
right: Nobody can do *his* best unless *he* is properly encouraged.

Note: *One* is followed by *one* in British Standard English, but may be followed by *he* in American Standard English:
right: One should do one's best. (British SE)
right: One should do his best. (American SE)
wrong: One should do your best.
wrong: You should do one's best.
right: You should do your best.

VERBS

1 Ensure that you have learned the correct form of irregular verbs:

wrong: The wind *blowed* . . .
right: The wind *blew* . . .

wrong: I have *drinked* the wine.
right: I have *drunk* the wine.

2 Do not confuse tense forms in a sentence:

wrong: I *stop* speaking when he came in.
right: I *stopped* speaking when he came in.

wrong: He *had* reported that he is ill.
right: He *has* reported that he is ill.

or: He *had* reported that he *was* ill.

3 Do not use an inappropriate verb part with the infinitive:

wrong: He was pleased *to have seen* you last night.
right: He was pleased *to see* you last night.

wrong: She said that she would have liked *to have seen* him.
right: She said that she would have liked *to see* him.

wrong: He said that he hoped *to have gone* to the village.
right: He said that he hoped *to go* to the village.

4 Do not confuse the following verbs:

be and be found
wrong: The president *was found* in his office.
right: The president *was* in his office.
or: The president *could be found* in his office.

be and *have*
wrong: The gun *was* with the leader.
right: The leader *had* the gun.
or: The gun *was* in the leader's possession.

borrow and *lend*
wrong: He decided to *lend* some money from his brother.
right: He decided to *borrow* some money from his brother.
wrong: He agreed to *borrow* money to his brother.
right: He agreed to *lend* money to his brother.

bring and *take*
wrong: He *took* the ball back to me.
right: He *brought* the ball back to me.
wrong: He *brought* the ball from here to there.
right: He *took* the ball from here to there.

can and *may*
wrong: She asked, "*Can* I have some bread?"
right: She asked, "*May* I have some bread?"
wrong: We decided that we should go if we *might*.
right: We decided that we should go if we *could*.

care and *take care*
wrong: He told us that he did not *take care* for that fruit.
right: He told us that he did not *care* for that fruit.
wrong: We decided to *care more* for the horses.
right: We decided to *take more care* of the horses.
wrong: She said that if her brother *cared* for his dog it would survive.
right: She said that if her brother *took care* of his dog it would survive.

could and *be able*
wrong: As she had already eaten the apples, she *could not* eat the meal.
right: As she had already eaten the apples, she *was not able* to eat the meal.
wrong: He ran so fast that he *could* reach home long before dark.
right: He ran so fast that he *was able* to reach home long before dark.

eat and ate
wrong: As soon as we sat down we *eat* the fruit.
right: As soon as we sat down we *ate* the fruit.

know and learn
wrong: He worked hard to *know* his lesson.
right: He worked hard to *learn* his lesson.
wrong: As soon as we *knew* what he had to tell us we went home.
right: As soon as we *learned* what he had to tell us we went home.

learn and teach
wrong: The old man *learned* us to hunt.
right: The old man *taught* us to hunt.

learn and study
wrong: He sat down to *learn* the subject.
right: He sat down to *study* the subject.

lie and lay
wrong: The old man *laid* down to sleep.
right: The old man *lay* down to sleep.
wrong: He *lay* the book down.
right: He *laid* the book down.

leave and let
wrong: *Leave* me tell the rest of the story.
right: *Let* me tell the rest of the story.
wrong: He would not *let* me to continue the journey.
right: He would not *leave* me to continue the journey.

like and want
wrong: She asked if we *liked* to see her picture.
right: She asked if we *wanted* to see her picture.
wrong: Would you *want* to be the leader in this game?
right: Would you *like* to be the leader in this game?

make and do
wrong: Remember not to *do* a mistake.
right: Remember not to *make* a mistake.
wrong: He *made* his best to succeed.
right: He *did* his best to succeed.

must and ought
wrong: Everyone *must* remember the date of his own birthday.
right: Everyone *ought* to remember the date of his own birthday.

remember and *remind*
  wrong: *Remind* me to all my friends.
  right: *Remember* me to all my friends.
  wrong: The music *remembered* me of my childhood.
  right: The music *reminded* me of my childhood.

rise and *raise*
  wrong: As soon as dawn came he *raised* and washed.
  right: As soon as dawn came he *rose* and washed.
  wrong: When the sun came out the temperature *raised*.
  right: When the sun came out the temperature *rose*.

see and *look*
  wrong: The old man bent down to *see* into the hole.
  right: The old man bent down to *look* into the hole.

hear and *listen to*
  wrong: We had to *hear* every word to understand the message.
  right: We had to *listen to* every word to understand the message.
  wrong: At 4.00 a.m. I was annoyed that I could still *listen to* the noise of the party next door.
  right: At 4.00 a.m. I was annoyed that I could still *hear* the noise of the party next door.

sleep and *go to bed*
  wrong: I *sleep* at ten o'clock every night.
  right: I *go to bed* at ten o'clock every night.

stay and *live*
  wrong: How long have you *stayed* in this town?
  right: How long have you *lived* in this town?
  wrong: We *lived* in the hotel for a month.
  right: We *stayed* in the hotel for a month.

take and *get*
  wrong: We arranged for him to *take* the biggest share.
  right: We arranged for him to *get* the biggest share.

want and *wish*
  wrong: The little girl was given the doll she *wished*.
  right: The little girl was given the doll she *wanted*.
  wrong: He said he *wanted* we would help him.
  right: He said he *wished* we would help him.

SENTENCES

1 In formal written English, do not write a fragment for a complete sentence.

wrong: Hoping you are well.
right: I hope you are well.

wrong: She was very tall. And stout.
right: She was very tall. She was also stout.
right: She was very tall and stout.

2 Do not join sentences with only a comma.

wrong: The mountain was high, we could not climb it in one day.
right: The mountain was high, and we could not climb it in one day.
right: The mountain was high, so we could not climb it in one day.

wrong: He was our leader, we did not obey him.
right: He was our leader, but we did not obey him.

3 Do not place a phrase in the wrong position.

wrong: In America he told us that everyone plays baseball.
right: He told us that in America everyone plays baseball.

4 Do not place an adjective clause in the wrong position.

wrong: A book about Africa caught my eye which I decided to give my friend.
right: I decided to give my friend a book about Africa which caught my eye.

10   LITERARY TERMS

abridged	shortened, condensed: as in *abridged edition*
abstract (adj.)	expressing a meaning which is general or non-specific; the opposite of *concrete*, e.g. *milk* is concrete while *milkiness* is abstract
abstract (noun)	summary of a written work
accent	stress on a syllable, e.g. in *invent* the accent is on the second syllable
accidence	inflections in words
acrostic	poem in which the first letters in each line form a word
act	section of a play
action	storyline of a play
adaptation	changed form, e.g. a screen play may be an adaptation of a stage play
addendum	addition
address	speech
aesthetic	concerning art and artistic quality
affective	concerning feeling
afflatus	inspiration (usually in the expression 'the divine afflatus')
Age of Reason	period roughly from 1680 to 1780, when poets and other artists favoured classical forms, logical arguments and rational thought
air	song or melody
alexandrine	line of twelve syllables
alienation effect	deliberate reminders to the audience that they are watching a play (as in Bertholt Brecht's plays)
allegory	story, poem or play in which there is meaning below the surface, such as Bunyan's *The Pilgrim's Progress*
alliteration	figure of speech in which the sounds of certain letters are repeated to create an effect, e.g. 'the murmuring of innumerable bees'
allusion	reference to some person or thing
ambiguity	writing with more than one meaning
anachronism	referring to something which is not appropriate to the time in which a story is set
anacoluthon	breaking off a sentence and ending it in another way, e.g. 'He walked over — but that's another story.'
anagram	rearrangement of letters to form a different word, e.g. *draw, ward*

analysis	detailed description of a work
anatomy	old term for *analysis*
anecdote	short, interesting or amusing story
annals	accounts of events year by year over a period
anonymous	having no known author
anthology	collection of poems, stories, etc.
anti-climax	effect of something dignified being followed by something ridiculous, in a play or line of verse, e.g. 'Scotland is a land of mountains, rivers and porridge.'
anti-hero	central character who is *not* admirable
antithesis	use of opposites for effect
antonomasia	figure of speech in which a label or title is used to refer to a person, e.g. 'He was a Napoleon of business.'
antonym	word of opposite or contrasting meaning
aphorism	brief expression containing some truth or wise idea
apocryphal	of doubtful authenticity
apology (or *apologia*)	defence of someone's ideas or works
apophthegm	terse saying (similar to *aphorism*)
apostrophe	figure of speech in which the speaker or writer addresses someone (or something) not present
Arcadia	legendary land where all is peace and beauty (adj. *Arcadian*)
archaic; archaism	obsolete; the use of an old expression for effect
archetype	model to be copied or followed
argument	intended message conveyed by a poem or essay, etc.
aside	remarks directed by a character in a play to the audience
assonance	repetition of vowel sounds for effect
atmosphere	mood created by a writer in a work
aubade	love-song supposed to record lovers' sadness at parting in the morning
Augustan	pertaining to the period roughly from 1680 to 1780, when writers aspired to the classical styles of Roman poets, such as Virgil and Horace, in the reign of the Emperor Augustus
autobiography	story of a person written by himself or herself
avant-garde	writing, art, etc. which is recent and seems to be the beginning of a new style
ballad	song or poem, usually anonymous, handed down by oral tradition
bard	in Celtic history, a king's poet

bathos	writing in which the intention is to achieve elegance or nobility but which falls into absurdity
best-seller	book that has achieved great success among the reading public
biography	art of writing about the lives of the famous; account of someone's life
blank verse	poetry written in iambic pentameters without rhyming
blue-stocking	woman of scholarly tastes
blurb	publisher's brief indication of what a book is about
bombastic	over-elaborate or extravagant in style
bowdlerise	to rewrite poetry, drama, etc. and remove anything thought distasteful, as was done by T. Bowdler in his *Family Shakespeare*, 1818
broadside; broadsheet	song, ballad, etc. printed on one sheet of paper, usually sold by street vendors
brochure	pamphlet, usually listing items for sale, often with illustrations
burden	refrain of a song or poem; meaning of a poem
burlesque	strongly-styled parody, making fun of some established form of art
Byronic	pertaining to the poet Lord Byron; in the style of Byron's poetry
cadence	rhythm; the pattern of stresses in the language of poetry or prose
caesura	break in a line of verse
calypso	West Indian song
canon	established body of works by a writer
canticle	kind of hymn
canto	section of a narrative poem
canzone	kind of lyric from Italy or Provence
caricature	crude portrait in writing or drawing which ridicules someone
carol	Christmas song
Caroline	pertaining to the reign of Charles I
catastrophe	tragic outcome of a play
catch	song sung by three or more singers
catharsis	release from tension after experiencing a great emotional scene in a play
Cavalier	label for writers in the reign of Charles I, e.g. Lovelace, Herrick, Suckling
chanson	love song in the style of the troubadours of Provence in the Middle Ages

chapbooks	pamphlets peddled in the streets during the 17th and 18th centuries, containing ballads, songs, etc.
Chaucerian	pertaining to the work or style of the poet Geoffrey Chaucer, *c* 1340-1400
chorus	character (or group of characters) who are used to comment on the action of a play, e.g. in Greek drama, Shakespeare, Brecht
chronicle	a history, often in verse, e.g. the *Anglo-Saxon Chronicles*; the term is also sometimes used by novelists, e.g. the *Pasquier Chronicles*
circumlocution	writing or speech which skirts round the main theme; the use of too many words to say something
classic	work of established importance
classicism	forms and styles of writing which are modelled on the classical writings of the Greeks and Romans, or the use of themes, settings, etc. from classical times
clerihew	comic verse consisting of four lines, e.g.

> If you think Uccello
> Was a clever fellow
> Take a dekko
> At El Greco

cliché	idiomatic expression which has lost its force by being over-used
climax	part of a play, novel, etc. in which a crisis emerges and is resolved
colloquy	discussion
colloquium	meeting for discussion; the recorded speeches of such a meeting
colophon	information about date of printing, etc. on the title page of a book; a publisher's emblem
comedy	any written work designed to inspire laughter
comedy of humours	17th century plays which hinged around the quirks and fancies of the main characters, e.g. Molière's comedies about a miser, a hypochondriac, etc.
comedy of manners	17th, 18th and 19th century plays which hinged around social fashions, e.g. the plays of Sheridan and Wilde
comic relief	parts of a tragic play designed to relieve the tension
complaint	poem expressing a lover's regret or disappointment
conceit	witticism or figure of speech in a poem
confidant; confidante	character in a play whose main function is to listen to the confidences of a central character
conflict	tension created between characters with opposing natures, ideas or purposes in a play or novel

content	ideas and feelings conveyed in a poem, novel, etc.
convention	device used in a play which the audience can accept as indicating some necessary feature of time, place or action, e.g. the use of asides, chorus, etc.; any feature of composition that links the author's meaning to a traditional style or mode of thought
couplet	pair of lines of verse
crisis	part of a play, poem or story at which tension is highest
dénouement	part of a play or story at which the crisis is resolved, or the mystery unravelled
detective fiction	stories about crime and the solution of mysteries by a professional or amateur sleuth
deus ex machina	character who enters a story to bring relief or help, but who has not had an integral part to play in the plot
dialect	manner of speech characteristic of a particular region or social group
dialectic	method of arguing; the sequence of ideas in a work
dialogue	speech exchanged between characters in a play or story
diarist	writer of a published diary
diction	speech; the use of vocabulary
didactic	conveying a message; teaching
digest	abridgement of a written work
digression	part of a written work which strays from the main theme, plot or thread of argument
dirge	lament
discourse	scholarly discussion of a topic
discursive writing	writing to discuss a topic
dissertation	written discussion of a topic
dissonance	intentionally discordant sounds in poetry
ditty	short song
divertissement	short composition (usually a play or operetta) designed for entertainment
documentary novel	novel which uses real facts, documents or excerpts, etc.
documentary play	dramatic representation of factual events or persons
doggerel	bad verse
dramatic irony	action or dialogue which has meaning for the audience but not for the characters in a play
dramatis personae	list of the characters in a play
dramatisation	rendering of a story in play form
dumb show	part of a play in mime
duologue	dialogue between two characters

eclogue	poem in the form of a dialogue
edition	the number of copies of a book produced at one time
Edwardian	pertaining to the reign of Edward VII
elegy	poem lamenting the death of someone or group of persons (adj. *elegiac*)
Elizabethan	pertaining to the reign of Queen Elizabeth Tudor, 1558-1603
ellipsis	figure of speech in which a word or expression is omitted, e.g. 'Youth's a stuff will not endure.'
emend	to alter a text
emotive	designed to arouse the reader's or audience's feelings
encomium	piece of writing in praise of someone
enjambement	extension of the meaning beyond the second line of a couplet
entr'acte	entertainment given between acts of a play
envoi	stanza additional to the main poem
epic	long poem, usually telling the story of a hero and his followers
epic simile	(also called *Homeric simile*) a long elaborate simile which provides a comparison between two actions
epigram	witty saying, e.g. 'Happiness is the absence of sorrow.'
epilogue	speech to the audience given at the end of a play, usually by one of the characters or by the chorus
episode	separate event in a story; separate part of a serial
epistle	letter; a poem in the form of a letter
epitaph	verse written for a tomb
epithalamion	poem celebrating a wedding
epithet	descriptive adjective
eponymous	term signifying that the central character's name is also the name of the book, e.g. 'David Copperfield is the eponymous hero of that book.'
essay	prose work written to amuse or instruct the reader
euphemism	expression in which a pleasant word or idea is given in place of an unpleasant version, e.g. 'passed away' for 'died'
euphony	use of pleasant-sounding syllables
euphuism	highly elaborate, flowery language
exegesis	analysis or explanation of a poem, essay, etc.
explication	analysis of a text, discussing the imagery, grammar, meaning, etc.
eye-rhyme	term meaning that the words do not rhyme although they look as though they should, e.g. *crown, flown*

fable	moral story in which animals represent humans
farce	comedy in which situations, actions, etc. are exaggerated
feminine rhyme	term meaning that both syllables of the words rhyme, e.g. *faster, master*
fiction	general term for novels, short stories, etc.
figure of speech	expression designed to produce a certain effect, such as *metaphor, simile, personification,* etc.
flyting	sequence of poems in which the poets attack one another
folio	set of four pages; the term is also used for an early edition of Shakespeare's plays
folk song	song or ballad handed down orally from one generation to another until finally recorded by a 'collector'
foot	unit of rhythm in verse. The number of feet per line is labelled thus:

one foot	monometer
two feet	dimeter
three feet	trimeter
four feet	tetrameter
five feet	pentameter
etc.	

Within the foot there is a pattern of stress labelled thus:

anapaestic	∪ ∪ —	e.g. intercede
trochaic	— ∪	e.g. marry
dactylic	— ∪ ∪	e.g. marrying
iambic	∪ —	e.g. betray
spondaic	— —	e.g. long road
etc.		

∪ = weak stress

— = strong stress

foreword	introduction to a book, often written by someone other than the author
form	combination of words, word order, rhyme and rhythm chosen by a writer for conveying what he has to say (the ideas and feelings conveyed are the *content*)
format	make-up of a page or book
free verse	verse which does not have a regular metrical pattern
gazette	old name for a newspaper; now a list of appointments, etc.
gazetteer	dictionary of place names

genre	type or kind of literature, e.g. *the novel, poetry, biography,* etc.
Georgian	pertaining to the early reign of George V
georgic	poem about country life and work, e.g. Virgil's *Georgics*
geste	medieval story of the adventures of a heroic group of warriors
ghost writer	author who writes a book which appears under the authorship of someone else, usually someone famous
glossary	list of terms and their meanings
gothic	term originally used for ghost stories set in the early Middle Ages and later for any story of exaggerated mystery and drama
haiku	verse of seventeen syllables, originating in Japan but now found in English writing
half-rhyme	imperfect rhyming, e.g. *hail, whole,* or *frost, past*
handbook	book providing information, guidance, etc.
heroic verse	meter generally used in epic poems, usually consisting of pentameter, rhyming in couplets or unrhymed
holograph	text written in a person's own hand
homily	written work of religious instruction
Homeric	pertaining to Homer; having some of the features of an epic
hymn	religious song
hyperbole	figure of speech in which exaggeration is used for effect, e.g. 'I could eat a horse.'; 'The actress got millions of bouquets.'
iamb	metrical foot consisting of two syllables, the second carrying the stress, e.g. re$\overset{\cup}{\text{f}}$r$\overline{\text{ain}}$
ibid.	short for *ibidem,* Latin for 'in the same place' — used in footnotes and references
idiom	expression with a particular meaning not evident by its constituent parts, e.g. 'a long shot' meaning 'a risk'
imagery	use of language to convey effects; the representativeness of language
index	alphabetical list of the items in a book
indirect speech	rendering of direct speech into reported speech
inflection	word-parts used to add to the meaning of the word's root
interlude	short entertainment given between the acts of a play; part of an activity in a story

inversion	changing round the parts of a sentence or phrase, e.g. 'Never was I so relieved.'
invoke	to appeal for help of a spirit, etc.
irony	conveying a meaning by saying or doing something contrary, e.g. 'You are a fine one, aren't you!'
Italian sonnet	sonnet (poem of fourteen lines) consisting of an octave (eight lines) and a sestet (six lines) with conventional rhyme schemes
Jacobean	pertaining to the reign of James I and VI, 1603-1625
jingle	verse with short lines and many rhymes
Johnsonian	in the manner of Dr Samuel Johnson, 1709-1784
journalese	having features of the style of newspaper writers, such as short sentences, clichés, etc.
juvenilia	work written when the author was very young
kitchen sink	term used for the realist drama of the 1950s, such as the plays of Osborne and Wesker
Lake poets	Wordsworth, Coleridge and Southey, who wrote c. 1790-1820
lament	work mourning someone's death
lampoon	rough satire
lay	short narrative poem
legend	story about some long-ago event or person, usually not historical
limerick	form of verse with a regular pattern of rhyme and meter, e.g.

> There was a young man from Japan
> Whose limericks never would scan
> When they said it was so
> He replied, 'Yes, I know,
> But I always try to get as many words into the last line
> as ever I possibly can.'

litotes	figure of speech in which under-statement is used for effect, e.g. 'London's a busy little town.'
loose sentence	sentence consisting of a main clause followed by subordinate clauses or phrases
lyric	song; also a poem expressing the poet's feeling; any poetry other than epic or narrative
madrigal	lyric set to music for several voices
magnum opus	author's most important work

malapropism	use of the wrong word in a context; after the character Mrs Malaprop in Sheridan's *The Rivals*, who said her daughter should learn 'geometry, that she might know something of the contagious countries', etc.
manifesto	declaration of policies, usually issued by a political party
masculine rhyme	one-syllable rhymes, e.g. *back, tack*
masque	entertainment in song and dance, as performed at the court of Elizabeth or James in the 16th and 17th centuries
maxim	wise saying
measure	old term for meter
medieval	pertaining to the Middle Ages
meiosis	figure of speech in which understatement is the main feature, e.g. 'This food is not bad', meaning that it is good
melodrama	play in which emotions and actions are exaggerated, usually not intentionally
metaphor	figure of speech in which something is compared with something else without the use of such words as *like* or *as*, used to give the reader a striking mental picture of an object or person, or to convey a meaning vividly, e.g. *The Moon's A Balloon*
metaphysical	term used for the poetry of Herbert, Vaughan, Marvell and other 17th century poets: they were mostly religious and their poetry abounded in striking imagery
meter	pattern of stresses in verse
metonymy	figure of speech in which one thing represents another, e.g. 'The pen is mightier than the sword'; 'You can reach your goal by putting your shoulder to the wheel'
miracle plays	medieval plays recounting the stories of saints
mixed metaphor	expression in which two contrasting or unrelated images are used together, e.g. 'Put your shoulder to the wheel and stand up for yourself'
mock-heroic	poetry written in the epic manner but with trivial or absurd content
monograph	essay on a scholarly subject
monologue	speech by one person without interruption by another
morality play	allegorical play originating in medieval times, in which good triumphs over evil
mummers	old term for actors

mystery play	medieval play recounting Biblical events, performed on wagons during holidays by members of craft guilds
myth	story with deep meaning, generally explaining the origin of the world or of some important part of life
narrative	writing in which telling a story is the main purpose
narrator	story-teller
naturalism	showing a love of nature; the effort of a writer to show things as they really are
near-rhyme	same as *half-rhyme*
neoclassical	pertaining to the period 1670-1780
neologism	new word, e.g. *sputnik, teleprinter*
nom de plume	pen-name; a name adopted by an author
novel	work of fiction of some length
novella	very short novel; or a long short story
numbers	old word for verses or lines of poetry
nursery rhyme	poem or song for very young children
obiter dicta	observations in speech or writing which are thought to be incidental
occasional verse	verse written for a special occasion
octameter	line of eight feet
ode	long lyric poem
officialese	language characteristic of civil servants or administrators
onomatopoeia	use of words to represent sounds, e.g. *cockadoodle-doo, putt-putt-putt*
opera	play in music and song
operetta	opera with a light theme and treatment
ottava rima	Italian term used for a stanza of eight lines in iambic feet: the rhyme scheme is always a b a b a b c c
oxymoron	figure of speech in which words of opposite meaning are used together, e.g. 'a beloved enemy'
pageant	series of dramatic sketches, mimes, tableaux, etc. depicting historic events
palindrome	word or phrase which reads the same backwards as forwards, e.g. *rotor, Madam, I'm Adam.*
panegyric	speech, poem or essay in praise of someone
pantomime	entertainment for children, consisting of drama, singing, dancing, jokes, etc., usually based on nursery rhymes or fairy tales
parable	story which conveys a moral message

paradox	statement which seems absurd but conveys a truth, e.g. 'The child is father of the man.'
paragraph	section of an essay consisting of one or more connected sentences
paraphrase	rendering of a text into other words, usually simpler to read
para-rhyme	same as *half-rhyme*
parenthesis	word or phrase or clause inserted in a sentence, e.g. 'He walked over (at least, so he says) and gave her the jewel.'
parody	writing which imitates the style, content, etc. of a well-known model and which ridicules the original
passion play	medieval play presenting the crucifixion of Jesus Christ
pastiche	mock-up of different pieces from texts, put together to amuse the reader
pastoral	pertaining to rural life
pathos	tender feeling in a work of writing or speech
pentameter	verse line of five feet (units of rhythm)
periphrasis	roundabout manner of speaking or writing; same as *circumlocution*
peroration	concluding passage of a speech
persona	identity adopted by a writer in a poem or story
personification	figure of speech in which inanimate things are given human attributes, e.g. 'The mountain's mighty heart faltered.'; 'Rebellion reared its head.'
Petrarchan sonnet	same as *Italian sonnet*: so called after the Italian poet Petrarch (1304-1374)
philippic	spoken or written attack on someone
picaresque	telling the story of a lovable rogue, usually in episodes
plagiarism	theft of some other author's work; unlawful deliberate borrowing of some other writer's words, plot, etc.
platitude	trite expression
plot	pattern of action in a story
poetaster	inferior versifier
poetic diction	kind of language used in poetry, i.e. use of figures of speech, rhyming, rhythm, etc.
poetic justice	due punishment of evil and reward of virtue
poetic licence	liberty that seems proper for a writer to take, e.g. with language, or treatment of life, character, etc.
poetic prose	prose writing that has features of poetic language, e.g. rhythm, figures of speech, etc.
polemic	dispute or quarrel conducted in published writing

polysyllabic	having more than two syllables
précis	summary
preface	introductory section of a book
prologue	introductory section of a play or novel
proverb	wise saying handed down by tradition
pun	play on the meaning of a word, e.g. 'When is a sailor not a sailor? When he's aboard.'
psalm	sacred song
pseudonym	pen-name; a false name adopted by a writer
quartet	four lines of verse
quatrain	four-line stanza
quintain	(also quintet) five-line stanza
realism	style, treatment or outlook on life which is close to reality; a deliberate effort to represent things as they are
refrain	line or part of a line that is repeated at intervals in a poem, usually at the end of each stanza
Renaissance	pertaining to the period from the 14th to the 16th centuries and the art of that period
Restoration	pertaining to the reign of Charles II
review	report on a work, written to give prospective audience or readers some idea of its content, quality, etc.
revue	modern stage entertainment, including singing, dancing, sketches, etc.
rhapsody	emotional poem
rhetoric	art of affecting people by means of language; the devices of language used for this purpose
rhetorical question	question which evidently does not require to be answered
rhyme royal	form of stanza which has seven ten-syllabled lines
rhyming slang	use of rhymed expressions to convey special meanings, e.g. plates of meat (for 'feet')
riddle	puzzle in words, e.g. 'What gets wet when drying?' — answer, a towel
romance	story of adventure or love, or both
romantic	having features of poems, novels, etc. in which the writers are preoccupied by love, adventure, natural beauty, etc.
romance languages	languages of France, Spain, Portugal, Rumania
rondeau	type of poem fashionable in 16th century France, consisting of three stanzas of thirteen or fifteen lines and a refrain

roundelay	medieval song which provided the rhythms for dancing
saga	medieval narratives from Norway, Denmark and Iceland, relating the adventures of heroes
satire	writing which holds up to ridicule persons, customs, etc. which the writer considers to be worthy of attack
scansion	analysis of the patterns of meter in verse, usually employing the following symbols:

∪ unstressed or weakly stressed syllable

— stressed syllable

| division of the feet

e.g. So all | day long | the noise | of bat | tle rolled.

scenario	outline of the action, scenes, etc. of a film or play
school	group of writers who share similar tastes, themes, styles, etc.
science fiction	genre of writing set in or dealing with the future or some fantastic era, place, etc., so called because most science fiction employs scientific knowledge and devices
sensibility	quality of being sensitive to suffering, or to beauty; tenderness of feelings
sentimental	excessively prone to sensibility; full of feeling
sermon	discussion, usually of a religious or moral topic
sestet	group of six lines of verse
Shakespearian sonnet	sonnet consisting of three quatrains and a couplet
simile	figure of speech in which two or more things are compared by using *like* or *as*, e.g. 'My love is like a red, red rose'; 'Mary had a little lamb, Its fleece was white as snow.'
sketch	description in writing; short play
skit	short parody or satire
slice of life	writing which sets out to represent exactly some aspect of real life
Socratic dialogue	form of discussion which proceeds by question and answer
solecism	glaring error in grammar, usage, etc.
soliloquy	speech in a play in which a character talks alone or to himself
sonnet	form of poem, consisting of fourteen lines, usually in iambic pentameter, with a conventional rhyme schem
source book	work from which an author has drawn plots, characters, etc.
spondee	metrical foot of two equally stressed syllables

Spoonerism	expression in which letters are transposed, with comic effect, e.g. kinquering congs (for 'conquering kings')
stanza	set of lines of verse
stock character	kind of character in plays or novels, appearing in many versions, e.g. the Clown, the Village Idiot, etc.
stock situation	situation which occurs in many different plays or novels, e.g. a girl masquerading as a boy, or someone mistaken for someone else
stream of consciousness	writing which represents the thoughts flowing through the writer's mind
style	characteristic features of a writer's work
sublime	term used to describe the elevated language of certain great writers
sub-plot	plot subordinate to the main plot of a play or novel
syllabic verse	verse in which an important requirement of style is that the number of syllables in the lines should be regular
symbolism	writing or plot construction which has the power of conveying a second, deeper meaning
symposium	collection of essays by different authors, usually sharing a common theme
synecdoche	figure of speech in which a part of something represents the whole, e.g. 'All hands on deck!'
tableau	group of actors representing a still picture
tetralogy	four plays connected by a theme
textual criticism	study of literary texts
theme	central ideas or messages of a work
thesis	argument; essay
thriller	story which sets out to involve the reader's imagination in a story of adventure, mystery, or conflict
tone	quality in a work which reveals the author's attitudes, outlook, etc.; mood created by the work
tract	pamphlet, usually religious
tragedy	form of drama or fiction in which the central character, mostly of admirable nature, suffers some terrible fate
tragi-comedy	tragic play which contains some comic features or a tragedy which ends happily, at least for some of the central characters
transferred epithet	figure of speech in which a descriptive adjective is used unexpectedly to qualify a different noun, e.g. 'I lay on a sleepless pillow'; 'They spent an anxious day.'
treatise	scholarly discussion of a subject

trilogy	sequence of three connected plays or novels
triplet	three-line verse
trochee	metrical foot consisting of two syllables, the first carrying the stress, e.g. happy
unities	dramatic convention requiring that the action, setting and time of a play should all coincide
utopian	pertaining to an ideal world, as in Sir Thomas More's *Utopia*
vade mecum	handbook carried around for ready reference
verisimilitude	appearing to be true or natural; an impression of reality conveyed by the writer
vernacular	common language of a country or district
vers libre	*free verse* which is not tied to ordinary conventions of meter, rhyme, etc.
viewpoint	writer's outlook, philosophical position; or the stance taken up by a narrator, i.e. his relationship to his characters or to the action
vignette	brief picture created by a writer
whodunit	(*who done it*) a story of mystery and detection

11 GENERAL KNOWLEDGE

NAMES FROM ENGLISH LITERATURE

Abou ben Adhem — character in a poem by Leigh Hunt

Abrahams, Peter H. (b. 1919) — South African coloured writer, author of *Dark Testament* (1942), *Mine Boy* (1946), *A Wreath for Udomo* (1956), etc.

Achebe, Chinua (b. 1930) — Nigerian novelist; author of *Things Fall Apart* (1958), *No Longer at Ease* (1960), *Arrow of God* (1964), *Don't Let Him Die* (1978), etc.

Addison, Joseph (1672-1719) — author of essays on 'Sir Roger de Coverley' and other works which appeared in *The Spectator* and the *Tatler*

Ahab, Captain — character in Herman Melville's novel, *Moby Dick*

Alcott, Louisa M. (1832-88) — American novelist; author of *Little Women* (1868), etc.

Alice's Adventures in Wonderland (1865) — children's story by Lewis Carroll

All's Well That Ends Well (c. 1595) — play by Shakespeare

Amis, Kingsley (b. 1922) — novelist and poet; author of *Lucky Jim* (1954), etc.

Ancient Mariner, The Rime of the (1798) — poem by Coleridge

Antiquary, The (1816) — novel by Sir Walter Scott

Antony and Cleopatra (1606-7) — play by Shakespeare

Areopagitica (1644) — essay by John Milton in defence of artistic freedom

Armstrong, William (c. 1590) — known as 'Kinmont Willie'; hero of Border ballads

Arnold, Matthew (1822-88) — poet and literary critic; author of *Sohrab and Rustum, The Scholar-Gipsy, The Forsaken Merman, Thyrsis*, etc.

Artful Dodger — character in Dicken's novel *Oliver Twist*

As You Like It (c. 1599) — comedy by Shakespeare

Aubrey, John (1626-97) — author of *Lives* of famous contemporaries

Auden, Wystan Hugh (1907-73) — poet and writer; author of *Look, Stranger* (1936), etc.

Austen, Jane (1775-1817)

author of famous novels: *Sense and Sensibility* (1811), *Pride and Prejudice* (1813), *Mansfield Park* (1814), *Emma* (1815), *Northanger Abbey* (1818), *Persuasion* (1818)

Bacon, Francis (1561-1626)

influential statesman and essayist

Banquo

character in Shakespeare's play *Macbeth*

Barbour, John (c. 1316-96)

Scottish poet, author of *The Bruce*

Barchester Towers (1857)

novel by Anthony Trollope; one of the *Barsetshire Novels*

Barnaby Rudge (1841)

novel by Charles Dickens

Barrie, Sir James M. (1860-1937)

Scottish playwright and writer; author of *Quality Street* (1901), *The Admirable Crichton* (1902), *Peter Pan* (1904), *What Every Woman Knows* (1908), etc.

Beckett, Samuel (b. 1906)

playwright; author of *Waiting for Godot* (1954), *Endgame* (1958), *Happy Days* (1962), etc.

Beerbohm, Sir Max (1872-1956)

essayist and critic

Beggar's Opera, The (1728)

musical play by John Gay

Behan, Brendan (1923-64)

Irish playwright, author of *The Quare Fellow*, etc.

Belloc, J. Hilaire (1870-1953)

poet, essayist and novelist; author of *Cautionary Tales*, *The Path to Rome* (1902), *Hills and the Sea* (1906), etc.

Bellow, Saul (b. 1915)

Canadian-American novelist; author of *Dangling Man* (1944), *The Adventures of Augie March* (1953), *Humboldt's Gift* (1975), etc.

Bennett, Arnold (1867-1931)

novelist; author of *The Old Wives' Tale* (1908), the *Clayhanger* series, *Riceyman Steps* (1923), etc.

Beowulf

Old English poem dating from the 10th century

Betjeman, Sir John (1906-84)

poet laureate 1972-84; famous for his direct style

Bierce, Ambrose (c. 1842-1914)

American author of short stories

Bilbo Baggins

character in Tolkien's epic fantasy, *The Fellowship of the Ring*

Binyon, Laurence (1869-1943) — poet; his most famous work is For the Fallen (1914), in memory of the dead of the First World War

Blackmore, R. D. (1825-1900) — novelist; his most famous work is Lorna Doone (1869)

Blake, William (1757-1827) — poet and artist; author of Songs of Innocence (1789), Songs of Experience (1794), etc.

Bleak House (1852-3) — novel by Charles Dickens

Blunden, Edmund (1896-1974) — poet and literary scholar

Borrow, George (1803-81) — author of The Bible in Spain (1843), Lavengro (1851) and The Romany Rye (1857)

Boswell, James (1740-95) — biographer of Dr Samuel Johnson

Bottom, Nick — comic character in Shakespeare's play A Midsummer Night's Dream

Bride of Lammermoor, The (1819) — novel by Sir Walter Scott

Bridges, Robert (1844-1930) — poet, playwright and literary essayist

Brontë, Anne (1820-49) — sister of Charlotte and Emily Brontë; author of Agnes Grey (1847) and The Tenant of Wildfell Hall (1848)

Brontë, Charlotte (1816-55) — novelist; author of Jane Eyre (1847), Shirley (1849), Villette (1853) and The Professor (1857)

Brontë, Emily (1818-48) — author of the novel Wuthering Heights (1847) and notable poems

Brooke, Rupert (1887-1915) — First World War poet; his best-known poems are Grantchester and the sonnet If I should die, think only this of me

Browning, Elizabeth Barrett — poetess wife of Robert Browning

Browning, Robert (1812-89) — poet; his most famous works are Pippa Passes (1841), Dramatis Personae (1864), Dramatic Idyls (1879-80), etc.

Brutus — tragic hero of Shakespeare's play Julius Caesar

Buchan, John (1875-1940) — novelist and biographer; author of The Thirty-Nine Steps (1915), Greenmantle (1916), Mr Standfast (1919), etc.

Bunyan, John (1628-88) — author of The Pilgrim's Progress, a religious allegory

Burgess, Antony (b. 1917)   novelist and essayist; author of *A Clockwork Orange* (1962), *Earthly Powers* (1980), etc.

Burns, Robert (1759-96)   Scottish poet; author of *The Cottar's Saturday Night*, *Tam O'Shanter*, and many well-known lyrics and satires

Butler, Samuel (1835-1902)   author of *Erewhon* (1872), *Erewhon Revisited* (1901) and *The Way of All Flesh* (1903)

Byron, George Gordon, Lord (1788-1824)   poet; his most famous works are *Childe Harold's Pilgrimage*, *The Corsair*, and *Don Juan*; he also wrote many lyrics and satires

Caliban   monster in Shakespeare's play *The Tempest*

Campbell, Thomas (1777-1844)   poet; author of *Hohenlinden*, *The Battle of the Baltic*, *Ye Mariners of England*, etc.

Canterbury Tales, The (c. 1387) Geoffrey Chaucer's great series of poetic tales preceded by *The Prologue*

Carlyle, Thomas (1795-1881)   essayist, scholar and historian; author of *Sartor Resartus* (1833-4), *The French Revolution* (1837), etc.

Carroll, Lewis (1832-98)   (real name Charles L. Dodgson) writer and nonsense poet; author of *Alice's Adventures in Wonderland* (1865), etc.

Charley's Aunt (1892)   farce by Brandon Thomas

Chaucer, Geoffrey (c. 1340-1400) author of *The Book of the Duchess*, *The Romaunt of the Rose*, *Troilus and Criseyde*, *The Canterbury Tales*, etc.

Cheshire Cat, The   figure in Carroll's children's story *Alice's Adventures in Wonderland*

Chesterton, G. K. (1874-1936)   novelist; author of *The Father Brown Stories* (1929), etc.

Childe Harold's Pilgrimage (1812-18)   epic poem by Byron in four cantos

Christie, Agatha (1891-1975)   popular and prolific detective novelist

Christmas Carol, A (1843)   long 'short' story by Dickens

Clare, John (1793-1864)   author of *Poems Descriptive of Rural Life* (1820), *The Shepherd's Calendar* (1827), etc.

Clark, John Pepper (b. 1935)	Nigerian poet and playwright; author of Poems (1962), Song of a Goat (1964), The Raft (1964), etc.
Claudius	character in Shakespeare's play Hamlet
Clayhanger series	novels about life in the English Potteries, by Arnold Bennett
Cobbett, William (1763-1835)	journalist, satirist, writer of political tracts
Coleridge, Samuel Taylor (1772-1834)	poet and critic; author of The Rime of the Ancient Mariner (1798), Christabel (1816), Kubla Khan (1816), etc.
Collins, W. Wilkie (1823-89)	novelist; author of The Woman in White (1860), The Moonstone (1868), etc.
Comedy of Errors, The (1594)	play by Shakespeare
Compleat Angler, The (1653)	book on fishing by Izaak Walton
Compton-Burnett, Ivy (1892-1969)	novelist; author of Brothers and Sisters (1929), Elders and Betters (1944), etc.
Congreve, William (1670-1729)	Restoration playwright; his most famous work is The Way of the World (1700)
Conrad, Joseph (1857-1924)	novelist; his most famous works are Almayer's Folly (1895), The Nigger of the Narcissus (1898), Lord Jim (1900), Nostromo (1904), and The Secret Agent (1907)
Cooper, James Fenimore (1789-1851)	American novelist; author of The Pioneers (1823), The Last of the Mohicans (1826), The Deerslayer (1841), etc.
Cordelia	character in Shakespeare's play King Lear
Coriolanus (1608)	play by Shakespeare
Coward, Noël (1899-1973)	playwright; author of Private Lives (1930), Blithe Spirit (1941), etc.
Cowper, William (1731-1800)	poet, author of John Gilpin (1782), The Task (1785), etc.
Crabbe, George (1754-1832)	poet; author of The Village (1783), The Borough (1810), etc.
Crane, Stephen (1871-1900)	novelist, author of The Red Badge of Courage (1895), etc.
Cymbeline (1611)	play by Shakespeare

David Copperfield (1850)	novel by Charles Dickens
Day-Lewis, Cecil (1904-72)	Irish poet, novelist and critic, poet laureate 1968-72; author of Overtures to Death (1938), The Abbey that Refused to Die (1967), etc.
De la Mare, Walter (1873-1956)	poet and writer; his work includes The Listener, The Veil, etc. and the novel Memoirs of a Midget (1921)
Decline and Fall of the Roman Empire, The (1776-88)	masterly historical narrative in six volumes by Edward Gibbon
Defoe, Daniel (1660-1731)	writer; author of Robinson Crusoe (1719), Moll Flanders (1722), etc. and many pamphlets and other prose works
Dekker, Thomas (c. 1570-1632)	playwright; author of The Shoemaker's Holiday (1600), etc.
Diary of a Nobody, The (1892)	humorous stories by George and Weedon Grossmith
Dickens, Charles (1812-70)	one of the greatest English writers; author of many famous novels and short stories including The Pickwick Papers (1836), Oliver Twist (1838), Nicholas Nickleby (1839); his last book was the unfinished Edwin Drood, begun in 1870
Dickinson, Emily (1830-86)	American poet; author of many fine lyrics
Disraeli, Benjamin (1804-81)	statesman and writer; his novels include Coningsby (1844), Sybil (1845), and Lothair (1870)
Dombey and Son (1846-7)	novel by Charles Dickens
Don Juan (1819-24)	epic poem by Byron
Donne, John (1572-1631)	poet and preacher; known for satires, elegies and lyrics written in the 'metaphysical' style
Doyle, Sir Arthur Conan (1859-1930)	novelist; author of the Sherlock Holmes stories and historical novels
Dreiser, Theodore (1871-1945)	American novelist; author of Sister Carrie (1900), An American Tragedy (1925), etc.
Dr Faustus, The Tragedy of (c. 1590)	play by Christopher Marlowe, in which the hero sells his soul to the devil

Dryden, John (1631-1700)	poet and dramatist; author of *Annus Mirabilis* (1667), *All for Love* (1678); *Absalom and Achitophel* (1681), etc.
Du Maurier, George (1834-96)	novelist; author of *Trilby* (1894) and other works
Dunbar, William (c. 1460-1513)	Scottish poet; his works include *The Dance of the Sevin Deidlie Synnis* (1503-8), *Tretis of the Twa Mariit Wemen and the Wedo* (1508), etc.
Dunciad, The (1728 & 1742)	satirical poem in four volumes by Alexander Pope
Durrell, Lawrence (b. 1912)	novelist and poet; author of *The Alexandria Quartet* (1957-60), etc.
Edwin Drood (1870)	unfinished novel by Charles Dickens, which he was working on at the time of his death
Ekwensi, Cyprian (b. 1921)	Nigerian novelist; author of *People of the City* (1954), *Burning Grass* (1962), *Beautiful Feathers* (1963), etc.
Elia	pen-name of the essayist Charles Lamb
Eliot, George (1819-80)	(real name Mary Ann Evans) novelist; works include *Scenes of Clerical Life* (1857), *Adam Bede* (1859), *The Mill on The Floss* (1860), *Silas Marner* (1861), *Daniel Deronda* (1876) and her greatest novel, *Middlemarch* (1872)
Eliot, Thomas Stearns (1888-1965)	great poet; author of *The Waste Land* (1922), *Ash Wednesday* (1930), a verse play *Murder in the Cathedral* (1935), etc.
Emerson, Ralph Waldo (1803-82)	American essayist
Emma (1815)	novel by Jane Austen
Evelyn, John (1620-1706)	Elizabethan diarist, contemporary of Samuel Pepys
Faerie Queene, The (1589-96)	great poetic work by Edmund Spenser
Fagin	character in Dickens's novel *Oliver Twist*
Fair Maid of Perth, The (1828)	novel by Sir Walter Scott
Falstaff, Sir John	character in Shakespeare's plays *Henry IV* and *The Merry Wives of Windsor*
Far from the Madding Crowd (1874)	novel by Thomas Hardy

Faulkner, William (1897-1962)

American novelist; author of *The Sound and the Fury* (1931), *Sanctuary* (1931), *Light in August* (1932), etc.

Fergusson, Robert (1750-74)

Scottish poet; Burns acknowledged a debt to his vernacular verse

Fielding, Henry (1707-54)

novelist; his works include *Joseph Andrews* (1742), *Tom Jones* (1749)

Fitzgerald, Edward (1809-83)

poet; author of a poetic (and free) translation of *The Rubaiyat of Omar Khayyam*

Fitzgerald, F. Scott (1896-1940)

American novelist; author of *The Great Gatsby* (1925), *Tender is the Night* (1934), etc.

Forster, Edward Morgan (1879-1970)

novelist and critic; author of *A Room with a View* (1908), *Howard's End* (1910), *The Celestial Omnibus* (1911), *A Passage to India* (1924), etc.

Fortunes of Nigel, The (1822)

novel by Sir Walter Scott

Frankenstein (1818)

story by Mary Shelley

Galsworthy, John (1867-1933)

novelist; author of *The Forsyte Saga* (1906-28), a sequence of connected novels

Galt, John (1779-1839)

Scottish novelist; author of *Annals of the Parish* (1821), *The Entail* (1823), etc.

Gaskell, Elizabeth C. (1810-65)

novelist; author of *Mary Barton* (1848), *Cranford* (1853), *North and South* (1855), etc. and a number of short stories

Gawayne and the Green Knight, Sir

chivalrous romance in verse by unknown 14th century writer

Gay, John (1685-1732)

minor poet and playwright whose most famous work is *The Beggar's Opera* (1728)

Gibbon, Edward (1737-94)

historian and writer; author of *The Decline and Fall of the Roman Empire*

Gibbons, Stella (b. 1902)

novelist; author of *Cold Comfort Farm* (1932), etc.

Golding, William (b. 1911)

novelist; author of *Lord of the Flies* (1954), *The Inheritors* (1955), *Pincher Martin* (1956), *Free Fall* (1959), etc.

Goldsmith, Oliver (1730-74)

Irish poet, playwright and novelist; author of *The Vicar of Wakefield* (1766), *The Deserted Village* (1770), *She Stoops to Conquer* (1773), etc.

Gordimer, Nadine (b. 1923)

South African novelist and short story writer; author of *Face to Face* (1949), *A Guest of Honour* (1971), *A Soldier's Embrace* (1980), *July's People* (1981), etc.

Gormenghast

epic trilogy by Mervyn Peake, comprising *Titus Groan* (1946), *Gormenghast* (1950) and *Titus Alone* (1959)

Grahame, Kenneth (1859-1932)

author of *The Wind in the Willows*, a famous story for children

Graves, Robert (b. 1895)

poet and novelist; author of *Goodbye to All That* (1929), *I, Claudius* (1934), etc.

Great Expectations (1861)

novel by Charles Dickens

Greene, H. Graham (b. 1904)

novelist; author of *Stamboul Train* (1934), *Brighton Rock* (1938), *The Power and the Glory* (1940), *The Heart of the Matter* (1948), *Our Man in Havana* (1958), etc.

Grossmith, George and Weedon

authors of *The Diary of a Nobody* (1892)

Gulliver's Travels (1726)

famous satire by Jonathan Swift

Guy Mannering (1815)

novel by Sir Walter Scott

Haggard, Rider (1856-1925)

Victorian romance writer; author of *King Solomon's Mines* (1885), *She* (1887), etc.

Hamlet (1604)

tragedy by William Shakespeare

Hard Times (1854)

novel by Charles Dickens

Hardy, Thomas (1840-1928)

poet and novelist; author of *Under the Greenwood Tree* (1872), *Far from the Madding Crowd* (1874), *The Mayor of Casterbridge* (1886) and many other great novels

Hawthorne, Nathaniel (1804-64)

American novelist; author of *The Scarlet Letter* (1850), *The House of the Seven Gables* (1851), etc.

Hazlitt, William (1778-1830)

English essayist and critic

Heart of Midlothian, The (1818)

novel by Sir Walter Scott

Heller, Joseph (b. 1923)   American novelist; author of *Catch 22* (1961), *Something Happened* (1974), *Good as Gold* (1979), etc.

Hemingway, Ernest (1898-1961)   American novelist; author of *A Farewell to Arms* (1929), *The Sun Also Rises* (1926), *The Old Man and the Sea* (1952), etc.

Hobbes, Thomas (1588-1679)   influential philosophical writer

Hobbit, The (1937)   story by J. R. R. Tolkien; the forerunner to his *Lord of the Rings*

Hogg, James (1770-1835)   (the 'Ettrick Shepherd') Scottish writer; author of *Private Memoirs and Confessions of a Justified Sinner* (1824), etc.

Holmes, Sherlock   fictional detective created by Sir Arthur Conan Doyle

Hopkins, Gerard Manley (1844-89)   poet; famous for religious lyrics with highly original rhythms and rhymes

Hughes, Ted (b. 1930)   poet and writer; appointed poet laureate 1985, author of *The Hawk in the Rain* (1957), *Lupercal* (1960), *Crow* (1970), etc.

Hunt, Leigh (1784-1859)   journalist, essayist and poet; editor of *Leigh Hunt's London Journal*, etc.

Huxley, Aldous (1894-1963)   novelist; author of *Crome Yellow* (1921), *Brave New World* (1932), etc.

Idylls of the King, The (1859-85)   series of connected poems by Alfred Lord Tennyson

Il Penseroso (c. 1630)   poem by John Milton

Importance of Being Earnest, The (1895)   play by Oscar Wilde

Irving, Washington (1783-1859)   American writer; his works include *The Sketch Book* (1820) which contains the famous stories *Rip Van Winkle* and *The Legend of Sleepy Hollow*

Ivanhoe (1819)   novel by Sir Walter Scott

James, Henry (1843-1916)   novelist; author of *Daisy Miller* (1878), *Portrait of a Lady* (1881), *The Spoils of Poynton* (1897), *The Ambassadors* (1903), etc.

Jane Eyre (1847)   novel by Charlotte Brontë

Jerome, Jerome K. (1859-1927) author of the humorous story *Three Men in a Boat*, etc.

Johnson, Dr Samuel (1709-84) poet, critic, biographer and lexicographer; author of *Johnson's Dictionary* (1755), *Rasselas* (1759), *The Lives of the Poets* (1781), etc.

Johnson, The Life of Samuel (1791) famous biography by James Boswell

Jonson, Ben (1572-1637) playwright; author of *Every Man in his Humour* (1598), *Volpone* (1606), *The Alchemist* (1610), *Bartholomew Fayre* (1614), etc.

Joseph Andrews (1742) novel by Henry Fielding

Joyce, James (1882-1941) novelist; author of *Dubliners* (1914), *Portrait of the Artist as a Young Man* (1916), *Ulysses* (1922), *Finnegans Wake* (1939), etc.

Julius Caesar (1599) play by Shakespeare

Jungle Books (1894-5) children's stories by Rudyard Kipling

Keats, John (1795-1821) poet; author of *The Eve of St Agnes, La Belle Dame Sans Merci*, the great odes *On a Grecian Urn, To a Nightingale, To Autumn*, etc.

Kenilworth (1821) novel by Sir Walter Scott

Kidnapped (1886) novel by Robert Louis Stevenson; the sequel, *Catriona*, appeared in 1893

King Lear (1606) tragedy by Shakespeare

Kingsley, Charles (1819-75) novelist; author of *Westward Ho!* (1855), *The Water Babies* (1863), etc.

Kipling, Rudyard (1865-1936) poet and novelist; author of novels set in India, children's stories such as the *Jungle Books* (1894-5), *Just So Stories* (1902), and many works of poetry, travel, history, etc.

Kubla Khan (1816) famous poem by Coleridge

Kyd, Thomas (1558-94) Elizabethan dramatist; author of *The Spanish Tragedy*, etc.

Lady of Shalott, The (1833) poem by Alfred Lord Tennyson

Lady of the Lake, The (1810) narrative poem by Sir Walter Scott

Lamb, Charles (1775-1834) essayist; author of *Essays of Elia*

Lawrence, David Herbert (1885-1930) — poet and novelist; author of Sons and Lovers (1913), Lady Chatterley's Lover (1928), The Rainbow (1929), etc.

Lawrence, Thomas Edward (1888-1935) — author of The Seven Pillars of Wisdom (1926), an account of the Arab revolt against the Turks

Leacock, Stephen (1869-1944) — author of Nonsense Novels (1911) and other humorous works

Lear, Edward (1812-88) — author of The Book of Nonsense and other works; famous for his limericks

Lee, Laurie (b. 1914) — novelist; author of the autobiographical novel Cider with Rosie (1959), etc.

Lewis, C. S. (1898-1963) — novelist and literary critic

Lewis, Sinclair (1885-1951) — American novelist; author of Main Street (1920), Babbitt (1922), Elmer Gantry (1927), Dodsworth (1929), etc.

Lewis, Wyndham (1884-1957) — artist and novelist; author of Time and Western Man (1927), etc.

Life and Opinions of Tristram Shandy, The — series of volumes by Laurence Sterne, published between 1759 and 1767

Lilliput — land of tiny people in Swift's novel Gulliver's Travels

Linklater, Eric (1899-1974) — Scottish novelist; author of Poet's Pub, Juan in America, etc.

Little Dorrit (1857-8) — novel by Charles Dickens

Locke, John (1632-1704) — philosopher and essayist

London, Jack (1876-1916) — American novelist; author of The Call of the Wild (1903), White Fang (1906), etc.

Longfellow, Henry Wadsworth (1807-82) — American poet; author of Hiawatha and other narrative and lyric poems

Lord of the Rings, The (1954) — part of the mythical epic by J. R. R. Tolkien, The Fellowship of the Ring

Love's Labour's Lost (1598) — play by Shakespeare

Lyndsay, Sir David (1490-1555) — Scottish poet; author of Ane Pleasant Satyre of the Thre Estaitis (1540), a satire on the church and state

Macaulay, Thomas Babington (1800-59) — essayist and historian; author of a History of England and Essays, he also wrote verse, the most famous being Lays of Ancient Rome (1862)

Macbeth, The Tragedy of (c. 1606) — tragedy by Shakespeare

McDiarmid, Hugh (1892-1978)

MacDonald, George (1824-1905)

McGonagall, William (1830-1902)

Mackenzie, Compton (1883-1972)

MacNeice, Louis (1907-63)

Malory, Sir Thomas (c. 1408-71)
Mansfield, Katherine (1888-1923)

Mansfield Park (1814)
Marlowe, Christopher (1564-93)

Marryat, Frederick (1792-1848)

Martin Chuzzlewit (1844)
Marvell, Andrew (1621-78)

Masefield, John (1878-1967)

Maugham, W. Somerset (1874-1965)

Mayor of Casterbridge, The (1886)
Measure for Measure (c. 1604)
Melville, Herman (1819-91)

Merchant of Venice, The (c. 1596)
Meredith, George (1828-1909)

(real name Christopher M. Grieve)
Scottish poet; author of A Drunk Man
Looks at the Thistle, etc.
novelist, preacher and poet; author of
Phantastes and other mystical works
Scottish versifier, famous for his bad
verse
Scottish novelist; author of Carnival
(1912), Sinister Street (1914), Whisky
Galore, etc.
poet; author of Autumn Journal (1939),
The Collected Poems of Louis MacNeice
(pub. 1966), etc.
author of Le Morte Darthur, etc.
essayist and short story writer; author
of The Garden-Party (1922),
Something Childish (1924), etc.
novel by Jane Austen
playwright; author of Tamburlaine,
The Tragedy of Dr Faustus, The Jew of
Malta, etc.
novelist; author of Mr Midshipman Easy
(1836), Masterman Ready (1841), etc.
novel by Charles Dickens
poet; his best known works are The
Garden and Last Instructions to a
Painter
poet laureate 1930-67; two of his best
known works are Salt Water Ballads
(1902) and the narrative poem Reynard
the Fox (1919)
novelist and playwright; author of Of
Human Bondage (1915), Cakes and Ale
(1930), etc.
novel by Thomas Hardy
play by Shakespeare
American novelist; author of Moby Dick
(1851), Billy Budd (pub. 1924), etc.
play by Shakespeare
novelist; author of The Ordeal of
Richard Feverel (1859), The Egoist
(1879), etc.

Merry Wives of Windsor, The (1600)	play by Shakespeare
Middlemarch (1872)	novel by George Eliot
Midsummer Night's Dream, A (1600)	play by Shakespeare
Milne, A. A. (1882-1956)	children's writer; creator of Winnie the Pooh, etc.
Milton, John (1608-74)	poet; his greatest works are Paradise Lost, L'Allegro, Il Penseroso, and his sonnets
Mitford, Nancy (1904-73)	author of The Pursuit of Love (1945), Love in a Cold Climate (1949), also historical biographies
Moby Dick (1851)	novel by Herman Melville
More, Sir Thomas (1478-1535)	author of Utopia, a political fantasy
Much Ado About Nothing (c. 1598)	comedy by Shakespeare
Muir, Edwin (1887-1959)	Scottish poet and novelist; author of The Horses, The Labyrinth, etc.
Munro, H. H. (1870-1916)	(pen-name 'Saki') short story writer
Murdoch, Iris (b. 1919)	novelist; author of The Bell (1958), A Severed Head (1961), etc.
Naipaul, V. S. (b. 1932)	Caribbean novelist; author of A House for Mr Biswas (1961), In a Free State (1971), Among the Believers: An Islamic Journey (1981), etc.
Nairn, Lady (1776-1845)	Scottish poet; author of The Laird o'Cockpen and other Scots ballads
Nash, Ogden (1902-71)	humorous poet; author of The Face is Familiar, etc.
Newbolt, Sir Henry (1862-1938)	poet; author of Drake's Drum and other songs
Ngugi, Wa Thiongo (b. 1938)	Kenyan writer; author of Weep Not Child (1964), The River Between (1965), Petals of Blood (1974), etc.
Nicholas Nickleby (1839)	novel by Charles Dickens
Nineteen Eighty-Four (1949)	futuristic novel by George Orwell
Northanger Abbey (1818)	novel by Jane Austen
O'Casey, Sean (1880-1964)	Irish playwright; his works include Juno and the Paycock (1924), The Plough and the Stars (1926), etc.
O. Henry (1862-1910)	(real name William Sydney Porter) American short story writer
Old Curiosity Shop, The (1841)	novel by Charles Dickens

Old Mortality (1816)	novel by Sir Walter Scott
Oliver Twist (1838)	novel by Charles Dickens
O'Neill, Eugene (1888-1953)	American playwright; author of The Emperor Jones (1920), Mourning Becomes Electra (1931), etc.
Orwell, George (1903-50)	(real name Eric Blair) novelist and essayist; author of Animal Farm (1945), Nineteen Eighty-Four (1949), etc.
Osborne, John (b. 1929)	playwright; author of Look Back in Anger (1956), etc.
Ossian	Celtic hero; in 1762 James Macpherson published what he claimed were verse translations of Ossian's works
Othello, the Moor of Venice (c. 1604)	tragedy by Shakespeare
Owen, Wilfred (1893-1918)	poet; famous for his writings on the First World War
Pamela: or Virtue Rewarded (1740)	novel by Samuel Richardson
Paradise Lost (1667)	great epic poem by John Milton, followed by Paradise Regained (1671)
Paton, Alan S. (b. 1903)	South African writer; author of Cry the Beloved Country (1948), Too Late the Phalarope (1953), Ah, But Your Land is Beautiful (1981), etc.
P'Bitek, Okot (b. 1931)	Ugandan poet; author of Song of Lawino, Song of Ocol, etc.
Peake, Mervyn (1911-68)	artist and novelist; author of epic Gormenghast trilogy
Peggoty	family in Charles Dicken's novel David Copperfield
Pepys, Samuel (1633-1703)	the great Elizabethan diarist
Pericles (c. 1608)	play by Shakespeare
Persuasion (1818)	novel by Jane Austen
Peter Pan (1904)	children's story by J. M. Barrie
Pickwick Papers, The (1837)	novel by Charles Dickens
Piers the Plowman (c. 1400)	allegorical poem attributed to William Langland, a contemporary of Chaucer
Pilgrim's Progress, The (1678)	allegorical story by John Bunyan
Pinero, Sir Arthur Wing (1855-1934)	playwright; author of The Second Mrs Tanqueray (1893), Trelawny of the Wells (1898), etc.

Pinter, Harold (b. 1930)   playwright; author of The Caretaker
                                    (1959), The Hothouse (1980), etc.
Plath, Sylvia (1932-63)   American poet and writer; author of
                                    The Colossus (1960) and the novel The
                                    Bell Jar (1963), etc.
Poe, Edgar Allan (1809-49)   American writer of verse and short
                                    stories; author of The Murders in the
                                    Rue Morgue, The Gold Bug, The Bells,
                                    Annabel Lee, etc.
Pope, Alexander (1688-1744)   poet; author of The Rape of the Lock
                                    (1712), The Dunciad (1728 & 1742),
                                    Essay on Man (1733-34), etc.
Potter, Beatrix (1866-1943)   writer of children's books, creator of
                                    Peter Rabbit, etc.
Potter, Stephen (1900-69)   humorist; creator of 'Gamesmanship'
Pound, Ezra (1885-1972)   American poet; his major work is
                                    Cantos (1925)
Powell, Anthony (b. 1905)   novelist; author of a sequence of novels
                                    with the general title of The Music of
                                    Time, etc.
Pride and Prejudice (1813)   novel by Jane Austen
Priestley, J. B. (1894-1984)   novelist and playwright; author of The
                                    Good Companions (1929), Angel
                                    Pavement (1930), An Inspector Calls
                                    (1947), etc.
Pygmalion (1913)   famous play by George Bernard Shaw
                                    on which is based the musical My Fair
                                    Lady

Quentin Durward (1823)   novel by Sir Walter Scott

Ramsay, Allan (1686-1758)   Scottish poet; author of The Tea-table
                                    Miscellany, The Gentle Shepherd, etc.
Ransome, Arthur (1884-1967)   children's writer; author of Swallows
                                    and Amazons (1931), etc.
Rasselas (1759)   romance by Dr Samuel Johnson
Rattigan, Terence (1911-77)   playwright; author of The Winslow Boy,
                                    The Browning Version, etc.
Reade, Charles (1814-84)   novelist; author of It is Never Too Late
                                    to Mend (1856), The Cloister and the
                                    Hearth (1861), etc.

Redgauntlet (1824) — novel by Sir Walter Scott

Reeves, James (1909-78) — writer of verse and prose for children

Richardson, Samuel (1689-1761) — novelist; author of *Pamela* (1740), *Clarissa Harlowe* (1747-8), etc.

Rivals, The (1775) — comic play by Sheridan

Rob Roy (1817) — novel by Sir Walter Scott

Robinson Crusoe (1719) — novel by Daniel Defoe

Romeo and Juliet (1599) — play by Shakespeare

Rosencrantz and Guildenstern — characters in Shakespeare's play *Hamlet*

Roy, Raja Rammohun (1774-1833) — Indian writer; father of Indo-Anglian literature, author of *Precepts of Jesus* (1820), etc.

Runyon, Damon (1884-1946) — American short story writer; author of *Guys and Dolls* (1932), *Runyon on Broadway* (pub. 1950), etc.

Samson Agonistes (1671) — poetic tragedy by John Milton

Sassoon, Siegfried (1886-1967) — poet and novelist; author of *Memoirs of a Foxhunting Man* (1928), etc.

Sayers, Dorothy L. (1893-1957) — novelist; author of detective stories *The Nine Tailors, Murder Must Advertise*, etc.

Scott, Sir Walter (1771-1832) — poet and novelist; author of many famous novels, including *Waverley* (1814), *Guy Mannering* (1815), *The Antiquary* (1816), *Old Mortality* (1816), etc.

Sense and Sensibility (1811) — novel by Jane Austen

Sewell, Anna (1820-78) — children's writer, author of *Black Beauty* (1877)

Shakespeare, William (1564-1616) — author of some of the world's greatest poetic dramas: *Hamlet, Macbeth, King Lear, Othello, Twelfth Night*, etc.

Shaw, George Bernard (1856-1950) — playwright; author of *Candida* (1895), *Pygmalion* (1913), *Saint Joan* (1923), etc.

Shelley, Mary W. (1797-1851) — author of *Frankenstein, or the Modern Prometheus* (1818), etc.

Shelley, Percy Bysshe (1792-1822) — poet; author of *Queen Mab, Alastor, The Revolt of Islam* and many fine lyrics

Sheridan, Richard Brinsley (1751-1816)

playwright; author of *The Rivals* (1775); *The School for Scandal* (1777), *The Critic* (1779), etc.

Shute, Nevil (1899-1960)

(real name Nevil Norway) Australian novelist; author of *No Highway*, *A Town Like Alice*, etc.

Shylock

character in Shakespeare's play *The Merchant of Venice*

Sillitoe, Alan (b. 1928)

author of *Saturday Night and Sunday Morning* (1958)

Sitwell, Edith (1887-1964)

poet; author of *Façade* (1922), *Selected Poems* (1936), etc.

Smollett, Tobias (1721-71)

novelist; author of *Roderick Random* (1748), *Peregrine Pickle* (1751), *Humphry Clinker* (1771), etc.

Snow, C. P. (b. 1905)

novelist; chronicler of men in power, as in *Strangers and Brothers* (1940)

Songs of Innocence (1789)

volume of lyric poetry by William Blake

Songs of Experience (1794)

counterbalancing volume to *Songs of Innocence*

Sons and Lovers (1913)

autobiographical novel by D. H. Lawrence

Southey, Robert (1774-1843)

writer and poet; his popular short poems include *After Blenheim*, *The Inchcape Rock*, etc. and his miscellany *The Doctor* (1834-7) gave children 'The Story of the Three Bears'

Soyinka, Wole (b. 1934)

Nigerian writer; author of *The Lion and the Jewel* (1959), *The Trials of Brother Jero* (1960), *Kongi's Harvest* (1964), *The Road* (1965), etc.

Spark, Muriel (b. 1918)

novelist; author of *The Ballad of Peckham Rye* (1960), *The Prime of Miss Jean Brodie* (1962), *Loitering with Intent* (1981), etc.

Spenser, Edmund (1552-99)

poet; author of *The Faerie Queene*, etc.

Spring, Howard (1889-1965)

novelist; author of *Fame is the Spur*, *My Son*, *My Son*, etc.

Steinbeck, John (1902-68)

American novelist; author of *The Grapes of Wrath* (1939), *Cannery Row* (1944), *East of Eden* (1952), *The Winter of Our Discontent* (1961), etc.

Sterne, Laurence (1713-68)   novelist; author of *The Life and Opinions of Tristram Shandy* in nine volumes, and *A Sentimental Journey through France and Italy* (1768), etc.

Stevenson, Robert Louis (1850-94)   novelist and essayist; author of *Treasure Island* (1883), *Kidnapped* (1886), *Catriona* (1893), etc. and many short stories and essays

Stoker, Bram (1847-1912)   novelist; author of *Dracula*, etc.

Stoppard, Tom (b. 1937)   playwright; author of *Rosencrantz and Guildenstern are Dead* (1966), *Every Good Boy Deserves Favour* (1978), *Squaring the Circle* (1983), etc.

Stowe, Mrs Harriet Beecher (1811-96)   American novelist; author of *Uncle Tom's Cabin* (1852), etc.

Swift, Jonathan (1667-1745)   essayist and satirist; author of *The Drapier's Letters* (1724), *Gulliver's Travels* (1726), etc.

Synge, John M. (1871-1909)   playwright; author of *Riders to the Sea* (1904), *The Playboy of the Western World* (1907), etc.

Tagore, Rabindranath (1861-1941)   Indian writer and poet; translated some of his own work into English, e.g. *Collected Poems and Plays* (1936)

Tale of Two Cities, A (1859)   novel by Charles Dickens

Talisman, The (1825)   novel by Sir Walter Scott

Taming of the Shrew, The (c. 1594)   play by Shakespeare

Tempest, The (c. 1611)   comedy by Shakespeare

Tennyson, Alfred Lord (1809-92)   poet; author of *The Idylls of the King*, *In Memoriam* and many other famous poetic works

Thackeray, William Makepeace (1811-63)   novelist; author of *Vanity Fair* (1848), *Pendennis* (1848), *Henry Esmond* (1852), etc.

The Fellowship of the Ring (1954-5)   mythical epic in three parts by J. R. R. Tolkien; *The Lord of the Rings*, *The Two Towers*, and *The Return of the King*

Thomas, Dylan (1914-53)   Welsh poet and playwright; author of *Deaths and Entrances* (1946), the play *Under Milk Wood* (1954), etc.

Thompson, Francis (1859-1907)	poet; author of The Hound of Heaven, a long religious poem (1893), etc.
Thomson, James (1700-48)	poet; author of The Seasons (1730), etc.
Thoreau, Henry David (1817-62)	American writer; author of Walden (1854), Journals and Writings (pub. 1906), etc.
Tolkien, John R. R. (1892-1973)	novelist; author of The Hobbit (1937), The Fellowship of the Ring (1954-5), etc.
Tom Jones (1749)	novel by Henry Fielding
Treasure Island (1883)	adventure story by R. L. Stevenson
Troilus and Cressida (c. 1602)	tragedy by Shakespeare
Trollope, Anthony (1815-82)	novelist; author of the Barsetshire Novels, Phineas Finn (1869), The Eustace Diamonds (1873), etc.
Tutuola, Amos (b. 1920)	Nigerian novelist; author of The Palm-Wine Drinkard (1952), My Life in the Bush of Ghosts (1954), Feather Woman of the Jungle (1962), etc.
Twain, Mark (1835-1910)	(real name Samuel L. Clemens) American novelist; author of Tom Sawyer (1876), Huckleberry Finn (1884), A Connecticut Yankee in King Arthur's Court (1889), etc.
Twelfth Night (1623)	comedy by Shakespeare
Ulysses (1922)	epic novel by James Joyce
Under the Greenwood Tree (1872)	novel by Thomas Hardy
Updike, John H. (b. 1932)	American novelist; author of Rabbit, Run (1960), The Centaur (1963), Problems and Other Stories (1979), etc.
Utopia (1516)	political fantasy by Sir Thomas More
Vanity Fair (1848)	Thackeray's greatest novel
Vidal, Gore (b. 1925)	American novelist; author of The City and the Pillar (1948), Myra Breckinridge (1968), etc.
Waiting for Godot (1954)	play by Samuel Beckett
Wallace, Edgar (1875-1932)	writer of mystery stories, including The Terror, The Squeaker, etc.
Walpole, Horace (1717-97)	author of The Castle of Otranto (1764), an early example of the 'gothic' novel
Walton, Izaak (1593-1683)	author of The Compleat Angler (1653)

War of the Worlds, The (1898) — early 'science fiction' story by H. G. Wells

Waste Land, The (1922) — famous poem by T. S. Eliot

Waugh, Evelyn (1903-66) — novelist; author of Brideshead Revisited (1945), Men at Arms (1952), etc.

Waverley (1814) — novel by Sir Walter Scott

Webster, John (c. 1580-1625) — playwright; author of The White Devil, The Duchess of Malfi, etc.

Wells, Herbert George (1866-1946) — novelist; author of early 'science fiction', The Time Machine (1895), The War of the Worlds (1898), etc.; and novels of character, Kipps (1905), The History of Mr Polly (1910), etc.

West, Nathanael (1903-40) — American novelist; author of Miss Lonelyhearts (1933), The Day of the Locust (1939), etc.

Weyman, Stanley (1855-1928) — historical novelist; author of A Gentleman of France (1893), Under the Red Robe (1894), etc.

White, Patrick (b. 1912) — Australian novelist; author of The Aunt's Story (1946), The Tree of Man (1954), etc.

White, T. H. (1906-64) — novelist; author of the Arthurian tetralogy, The Once and Future King (1958), etc.

Whitman, Walt (1819-92) — American poet; author of Leaves of Grass, Drum-Taps, etc.

Wilde, Oscar (1854-1900) — playwright; author of Lady Windermere's Fan (1892), The Importance of Being Earnest (1895), etc.

Williams, Tennessee (b. 1911) — American playwright; author of A Streetcar Named Desire (1947), Cat on a Hot Tin Roof (1955), etc.

Winter's Tale, The (1609) — play by Shakespeare

Wodehouse, P. G. (1881-1975) — novelist; author of The Inimitable Jeeves and many other humorous stories

Woolf, Virginia (1882-1941) — novelist; author of Mrs Dalloway (1925), To the Lighthouse (1927), etc.

Wordsworth, William (1770-1850) — poet; among his works are The Prelude, Intimations of Immortality, The Excursion and a large body of narrative and lyric poems

Wuthering Heights (1847)	novel by Emily Brontë
Wyatt, Sir Thomas (c. 1503-42)	poet; author of sonnets, lyrics and satires
Xanadu	the city in Coleridge's poem Kubla Khan
Yahoos	humanoid creatures in Swift's satire Gulliver's Travels
Yeats, William Butler (1865-1939)	poet; author of poetical dramas and many books of poems, including The Wild Swans at Coole (1919), Sailing to Byzantium (The Tower) (1928)
Zangwill, Israel (1864-1926)	Jewish novelist; author of Children of the Ghetto, Dreamers of the Ghetto, etc.

NAMES FROM HISTORY

Adam, Robert (1728-92)	Scottish designer of houses, furniture
Aga Khan (1877-1957)	head of a Moslem sect; a fabulously wealthy Indian prince
Alfred, King (849-99)	king of the West Saxons
Appleton, Sir Edward (1892-1965)	British physicist; discovered the radio waves called the 'Appleton layers'
Asoka (c. 300-232 BC)	Indian emperor; made Buddhism the state religion
Astaire, Fred (b. 1899)	American film star; a great modern dancer
Baden-Powell, Robert (Lord) (1857-1941)	British soldier; founded the Boy Scouts
Baedeker, Karl (1801-59)	German publisher of early travel books
Baird, John Logie (1888-1946)	Scottish inventor of television
Barnardo, Thomas (1845-1905)	British philanthropist; founded children's homes
Beatles, The	English popular musicians in the 1960s
Beethoven, Ludwig van (1770-1827)	German composer
Beeton, Isabella Mary (1836-65)	writer of cookery and household management books
Bell, Alexander Graham (1847-1922)	Scottish-American inventor of the telephone
Bligh, William (1754-1817)	British naval officer; his crew mutinied on HMS Bounty

Bogart, Humphrey (1899-1957) — American film actor
Bonaparte, Napoleon (1769-1821) — French general and emperor of France
Boudicca (or Boadicea) (d. AD 62) — queen of the Iceni; warrior-leader in Roman Britain
Brummel, George (Beau) (1778-1840) — leader of fashion during the Regency period
Brunel, Isambard K. (1806-59) — English civil engineer
Buddha, Gautama (c. 560-480 BC) — Indian religious leader; founder of the Buddhist faith

Calvin, John (1509-64) — French theologian; influenced the Scottish Reformation
Carnegie, Andrew (1835-1919) — Scottish-American philanthropist
Carson, 'Kit' (1809-68) — American Indian fighter
Caruso, Enrico (1873-1921) — Italian opera singer
Catherine the Great (1729-96) — empress of Russia (Catherine II), 1762-96
Caxton, William (c. 1422-91) — brought printing from the Continent to England
Chaplin, Charles (1889-1977) — British-American film producer, actor, comedian
Charlemagne (c. 742-814) — king of the Franks and, as Charles I, Holy Roman Emperor
Chippendale, Thomas (1718-79) — English furniture designer
Churchill, Sir Winston (1874-1965) — British statesman
Columbus, Christopher (1451-1506) — Italian navigator and explorer; discovered the New World for Spain
Confucius (K'ung Fu-tse) (c. 550-479 BC) — Chinese teacher and philosopher
Constable, John (1776-1837) — English painter
Cook, Captain James (1728-79) — English navigator and explorer
Cook, Thomas (1808-92) — English travel agent
Cortés, Hernando (1485-1547) — Spanish conquistador; conquered Mexico 1523
Crockett, Davy (1786-1836) — American frontiersman
Cromwell, Oliver (1599-1658) — English soldier and statesman
Curie, Marie (1867-1934) and Pierre (1859-1906) — French scientists; Madame Curie discovered radium and polonium

Darwin, Charles (1809-82) — English naturalist; author of *The Origin of Species*
Da Vinci, Leonardo (1452-1519) — artist and inventor; genius of the Italian Renaissance

Davy, Sir Humphrey (1778-1829)	English chemist; inventor of the Davy safety lamp for miners
De Gaulle, Charles (1890-1970)	French general and statesman
De Mille, Cecil B. (1881-1959)	American film producer
Disney, Walt (1901-66)	American film producer; pioneered animated cartoons
Drake, Sir Francis (c. 1540-96)	English navigator and explorer
Edison, Thomas A. (1847-1931)	American scientist and inventor
Eisenhower, Dwight D. (1890-1969)	American general and US president
Elizabeth I (1533-1603)	queen of England, 1558-1603
Engels, Friedrich (1820-95)	German socialist leader and collaborator with Karl Marx
Epstein, Sir Jacob (1880-1959)	British sculptor
Faraday, Michael (1791-1867)	English physicist and chemist; discovered electromagnetic induction
Fawkes, Guy (1570-1606)	English conspirator; the plot to blow up the Houses of Parliament is still remembered on 5 November
Fleming, Sir Alexander (1881-1955)	Scottish bacteriologist; discovered penicillin
Franklin, Benjamin (1706-90)	American statesman
Fry, Elizabeth (1780-1845)	English Quaker; prison reformer
Gainsborough, Thomas (1727-88)	English painter
Galilei, Galileo (1564-1642)	Italian scientist and astronomer
Gandhi, Mahatma (1869-1948)	Indian political and spiritual leader, social reformer
Gandhi, Mrs Indira (1917-84)	Indian political leader and prime minister, daughter of Pandit Nehru
Garibaldi, Guiseppe (1807-82)	Italian patriot; led his countrymen against the Austrians and French
Grace, Dr W. G. (1848-1915)	English cricketer
Halley, Edmund (1656-1742)	English astronomer
Harvey, William (1578-1657)	English scientist; discovered circulation of the blood
Henry VIII (1491-1547)	king of England, 1509-47
Hereward the Wake (fl. 1070)	English warrior-leader; fought William the Conqueror
Hillary, Sir Edmund (b. 1919)	New Zealand mountaineer; first successful climber of Everest, 1953
Hirohito (b. 1901)	emperor of Japan since 1926

Hitchcock, Alfred (1899-1982)	British-American film director
Hitler, Adolf (1889-1945)	German dictator; leader of Nazi party
Houdini, Harry (1874-1926)	American escape artist
Irving, Sir Henry (1838-1905)	English actor and theatre manager
James I and VI (1566-1625)	king of England and Ireland (1603-25) and, as James VI, king of Scotland (1567-1625)
James, Jesse (1847-82)	American outlaw
Jeanne d'Arc (Joan of Arc) (1412-31)	French patriot and martyr
Jeans, Sir James (1877-1946)	English astronomer and author
Jeffreys, Judge (1645-89)	English judge known for arbitrary and harsh sentences
Jenner, Edward (1749-1823)	English medical scientist; discovered vaccination
Jesus Christ (0-33 AD)	Jesus of Nazareth; regarded by Christians as the son of God
Jex-Blake, Sophia (1840-1912)	pioneer woman physician
Johnson, Amy (1903-41)	English aviator
Jones, Inigo (1573-1652)	English architect
Joule, James P. (1818-89)	English physicist; studied heat and electricity
Kaunda, Kenneth (b. 1924)	first president of Zambia
Keaton, Buster (1895-1966)	American film producer and comedian
Kelly, Ned (1855-80)	Australian outlaw
Kennedy, John F. (1917-63)	American statesman and US president
Kennedy, Robert F. (1925-68)	American statesman
Kenyatta, Jomo (1891-1978)	first president of Kenya
Kitchener, Lord (1850-1916)	British general
Knox, John (1505-72)	Scottish church leader
Lauder, Sir Harry (1870-1950)	Scottish singer and comedian
Lawrence, T. E. (1888-1935)	British soldier in Arabia
Lenin, Vladimir Ilyich (1870-1924)	Russian Communist leader
Lincoln, Abraham (1809-65)	American president
Lister, Joseph (Baron) (1827-1912)	English surgeon and research scientist; introduced the use of antiseptics
Livingstone, David (1813-73)	Scottish explorer of Africa
Luther, Martin (1483-1546)	German leader of the Protestant Reformation
McAdam, John (1757-1836)	Scottish engineer; invented 'macadamised' road surfaces

Macbeth (d. 1057)	Scottish king, 1040-57
Mackintosh, Charles Rennie (1868-1928)	Scottish architect and designer of furniture, etc.
Mao Tse-Tung (1893-1976)	Chinese Marxist theoretician and leader of the Chinese Communist Party
Marconi, Guglielmo (Marchese) (1874-1937)	Italian physicist; developed radio telegraphy
Marx, Karl (1818-83)	German-British philosopher, author of Das Kapital
Mary, Queen of Scots (1542-87)	Scottish queen, 1542-67
Menuhin, Yehudi (b. 1916)	American-British musician
Mesmer, Friedrich (c. 1733-1815)	German physician; pioneered hypnotism
Michelangelo (Buonarroti) (1475-1564)	Florentine sculptor, painter and architect
Mohammed (c. 570-632)	The Prophet and founder of Islam
Monroe, Marilyn (1926-62)	American film actress
Montgomery, Bernard (Lord) (1887-1976)	British general
More, Sir Thomas (1478-1535)	English statesman
Mussolini, Benito (1883-1945)	Italian Fascist dictator
Nehru, Pandit Jawaharlal (1889-1964)	first prime minister of independent India
Nelson, Horatio (Lord) (1758-1805)	British naval commander
Newton, Sir Isaac (1643-1727)	English mathematician, physicist, etc. formulated law of gravitation
Nightingale, Florence (1820-1910)	English pioneer of hospital nursing
Nkrumah, Kwame (1909-72)	first president of Ghana
Nyerere, Julius (b. 1922)	first president of Tanzania
Pankhurst, Emmeline (1857-1928)	English pioneer of women's political rights
Pasteur, Louis (1822-95)	French research chemist; his work on microorganisms resulted in process of 'pasteurisation'
Pepys, Samuel (1633-1703)	English diarist
Peter the Great (1672-1725)	tsar of Russia (Peter I), 1682-1725
Polo, Marco (1254-1324)	Venetian explorer of Asia
Quisling, V. (1887-1945)	Norwegian traitor; collaborated with Hitler in the Second World War

Raleigh, Sir Walter (1552-1618)   English navigator and explorer
Reagan, Ronald (b. 1911)   president of USA; elected for second
                                    term in 1984
Reynolds, Sir Joshua (1723-92)   English painter
Rhodes, Cecil (1853-1902)   British colonialist in South Africa
Richard the Lionheart (1157-99)   English king (Richard I), 1189-99
Rob Roy MacGregor (1671-1734)   Scottish outlaw
Robert the Bruce (1274-1329)   Scottish king (Robert I), 1306-29
Robespierre, Maximilien de   French revolutionary leader
  (1758-94)
Roosevelt, Franklin D. (1882-1945) American president and statesman

Scott, Robert F. (1868-1912)   English naval officer and Antarctic
                                    explorer
Simpson, Sir James Young (1811-70) Scottish physician; introduced the use
                                    of chloroform
Sinatra, Frank (b. 1917)   American singer and film actor
Smith, Adam (1723-90)   Scottish economist
Stalin, Joseph (1879-1953)   successor to Lenin as Soviet leader
Stephenson, George (1781-1848)   English pioneer of railways
Stuart, Charles Edward (1720-88)   ('Bonnie Prince Charlie'); Scottish
                                    prince who led the 1745 Rebellion

Tchaikovsky, Pyotr Ilyich (1840-93) Russian composer
Telford, Thomas (1757-1834)   Scottish civil engineer
Tenzing, Norgay (b. 1914)   Nepalese Sherpa who reached the peak
                                    of Everest with Hillary, 1953
Thatcher, Margaret H. (b. 1925)   first woman prime minister of Britain
Thomas a Becket (1118-70)   English churchman; now canonised
Turner, Joseph (1775-1851)   English painter
Turpin, Dick (1706-39)   English highwayman
Tussaud, Madam (1760-1850)   founded the London Waxworks
Tyler, Wat (d. 1381)   English rebel, leader of Peasants'
                                    Revolt, 1381

Victoria (1819-1901)   British queen, 1837-1901

Wagner, Wilhelm R. (1813-83)   German composer
Walpole, Sir Robert (1676-1745)   English statesman and first British
                                    prime minister, 1721-42
Washington, George (1732-99)   American general and statesman, first
                                    president of USA, 1789-97

Watt, James (1736-1819)	Scottish engineer and inventor; introduced use of steam power in industry
Wellington, Arthur Wellesley, Duke of (1769-1852)	British general and statesman
Wesley, John (1703-91)	English founder of the Methodist church
Wilberforce, William (1759-1833)	English politician and philanthropist; fought slavery
William the Conqueror (c. 1027-87)	first Norman king of England (William I), 1066-87
William the Lion (1143-1214)	Scottish king
Wolfe, James (1727-59)	British general
Wolsey, Thomas (c. 1475-1530)	English statesman and churchman
Wren, Sir Christopher (1632-1723)	English architect
Wright, Orville (1871-1948) and Wilbur (1867-1912)	American aviation pioneers; flew the first aircraft
Wycliffe, John (c. 1328-84)	English religious heretic
Young, Brigham (1801-77)	American Mormon leader
Zeppelin, Ferdinand von (Count) (1838-1917)	German inventor of airships
Ziegfeld, Florenz (1869-1932)	American designer of theatre revues

CLASSICAL NAMES

Academia	home of the Academic Philosophers (followers of Plato near Athens
Achates	faithful friend of the Trojan hero Aeneas
Acheron	river in the lower world, mentioned in Homer's Odyssey
Achilles	in Homer's Iliad, the chief Greek hero in the Trojan war
Aeneas	hero of Virgil's Aeneid
Aeolus	god or king of the winds, in Homer's Odyssey
Aeschylus	great tragic poet
Aesop	traditional author of Greek fables
Aetna (or Etna)	volcanic mountain in Sicily
Agamemnon	leader of the Greek army which fought Troy
Agricola	Roman governor of Britain, AD 78-85
Ajax	Greek warrior in the Trojan War, character in Homer' Iliad

Alaric	king of the Visigoths, who invaded Italy in AD 402
Alcibiades	450-404 BC; leading Greek politician
Alexander the Great	356-323 BC; Macedonian soldier who gained power over most of the known world
Alexandria	capital of Egypt under the Ptolemies
Amazons	mythical race of female warriors
Anacreon	Greek poet; fl. 520 BC
Androcles	Roman slave thrown to the lions. A lion greeted him with affection because, years before in Africa, he had pulled a thorn from its paw. Androcles was pardoned.
Antigone	according to Sophocles, daughter of Oedipus by his own mother
Antony, Marcus	consul with Caesar, 44 BC (character in Shakespeare's plays *Julius Caesar* and *Antony and Cleopatra*)
Aphrodite	Greek goddess of beauty and love
Apollo	Greek god of prophecy, sender of plagues, and god of the sun
Arachne	mythical weaver, turned into a spider by Athene
Arcadia	Peloponnesian country, land of mountains and of shepherds famed for their music
Archimedes	287-212 BC; Greek mathematician, inventor of the screw for pumping water
Argonauts	Greek heroes who sailed with Jason to fetch the Golden Fleece
Ariadne	daughter of Minos: in Homer's *Odyssey*, she loved Theseus and helped him escape from the Labyrinth
Aristophanes	Greek comic poet; fl. 300 BC
Aristotle	384-322 BC; Greek philosopher
Artemis	maiden warrior goddess, huntress, spirit of nature
Asclepius	Greek god of medicine
Athene	Greek goddess of wisdom, war, industry, crafts; protector of Athens
Atlantis	legendary island, swallowed up by the sea
Atlas	Titan who rebelled against Zeus and was condemned to stand holding up heaven on his head and hands
Attica	area of Greece
Attila	king of the Huns, invader of Italy, c. 450 BC
Augustus	the first Roman emperor, c. 29 BC
Aurelius, Marcus	Roman emperor AD 161-180, philosopher, author of *Meditations*
Avernus	lake, supposed to be the entrance of the underworld

Bacchus	nature god; god of wine and fruitfulness, also known as *Dionysus*
Bellerophon	Homeric hero who rode the winged horse Pegasus and killed the monster Chimaera
Bellona	Roman goddess of war
Boreas	North wind
Brigantes	British tribe inhabiting Eboracum (York)
Britannia	Roman name for Britain
Brutus, Marcus	one of the leading conspirators and assassins of Caesar
Bucephalus	Alexander the Great's horse
Caesar, Julius	102-44 BC; Roman soldier, statesman, poet and historian, author of *Commentarii*
Caligula	Roman emperor AD 37-41, notorious for madness, debauchery and cruelty
Calypso	in Homer's *Odyssey*, a nymph who fell in love with Odysseus
Caractacus	king of the British tribe, the Silures
Carthage	city in North Africa
Casca	one of the assassins of Caesar in 44 BC
Cassandra	Trojan prophetess, daughter of Priam
Cassius	leading conspirator and assassin of Caesar
Castor	brother of Pollox; they were heroes in Homer's works
Cato	234-149 BC; Roman soldier, statesman, writer
Catullus	c. 87-54 BC; Roman poet
Centaurs	mythical race of half-horse, half-men creatures
Cerberus	dog that guarded the entrance to Hades
Charon	boatman who conveyed the shades of the dead across the river into the underworld
Chimaera	a fire-breathing monster, part lion, part dragon, part goat, killed by Bellerophon
Cicero	106-43 BC; great Roman orator and statesman
Cincinnatus	soldier who returned from retirement to save Rome from defeat, 458 BC
Circe	a sorceress in the *Odyssey*; she changed Odysseus' companions into swine, but her magic failed with him
Cleopatra	69-30 BC; queen of Egypt, lover of Caesar and of Antony
Clusium	Etruscan city
Clytaemnestra	Agamemnon's wife; she and her lover murdered her husband
Cnossus (or *Knossos*)	Cretan town, capital of King Minos
Concordia	Roman goddess symbolising harmony

Constantine	AD 306-337; Roman emperor who established Constantinople as new imperial headquarters in AD 330
Coriolanus	legendary Roman hero. Exiled, he returned with an army and threatened Rome, but spared the city on the entreaties of his mother and his wife
Corybantes	dancing priests
Croesus	king of Lydia 560-546 BC; noted for his wealth
Cyclops	giant shepherds in Homer; they had only one eye each and they devoured human beings
Cynosura	nymph, one of the nurses of Zeus
Cyrus	founder of the Persian empire
Daedalus	mythical Greek sculptor who made wings for himself and his son Icarus. Icarus flew too near the sun and perished when the heat melted the wax with which the wings were fastened.
Damocles	Syracusan who was placed under a naked sword hanging by a single thread
Daphne	goddess loved by Apollo, who changed into a laurel tree to escape him
Darius	king of Persia 521-485 BC
Delos	small island in the Aegean sea
Delphi	small Greek town containing the oracle of Apollo, in which the god communicated his revelations
Demeter	Greek goddess of agriculture (called *Ceres* by the Romans)
Democritus	Greek philosopher; fl. 450 BC
Demosthenes	Greek general in the Peloponnesian war, c. 426 BC
Diana	Roman goddess of the moon and fruitfulness
Dido	mythical founder of Carthage; in Virgil's *Aeneid* she falls in love with Aeneas
Diocletian	Roman emperor AD 284-305
Diogenes	cynic philosopher, fl. 400 BC; he took to living in a large tub
Dionysius	rich and powerful Syracusan tyrant of the 5th century BC
Dionysus	god of wine and fruitfulness; also known as *Bacchus*
Draco	author of an extremely strict code of laws for Athenians
Eboracum	Roman name for York
Echidna	mythical monster, half-woman, half-serpent; mother of the Chimaera and other monsters

Egeria	goddess of fountains and a prophetess
Electra	legendary mother of Dardanus; she tore out her hair with grief when Troy was destroyed; she became a comet
Elysium	(The Elysian Fields) in Homer, a happy land where the weather is always perfect and immortal heroes dwell
Empedocles	scientist and magician of Sicily; fl. 490 BC
Endymion	legendary youth famed for beauty; the moon goddess Selene sent him to sleep for ever so that she could kiss him without his knowledge
Enyo	goddess of war
Eos	goddess of morning (called Aurora by the Romans)
Epicurus	342-270 BC; Greek philosopher who taught that the greatest good was the absence of pain, attained by peace of mind
Erebus	spirit of darkness
Eros	god of love (called Amor or Cupido by the Romans)
Etruria	country in Italy, inhabited by the Etruscans
Euclid	3rd century BC Greek mathematician, inventor of geometry
Eumenides	Greek goddesses of vengeance, also known as Furies
Euripides	480-406 BC; Greek tragic poet
Europa	in Homer's Iliad, daughter of Phoenix. Also, Greek name for the mainland of Hellas (Greece).
Eurus	East wind
Eurydice	wife of Orpheus
Flora	Roman goddess of flowers and spring
Fortuna	Roman goddess of fate
Gaea	in Homer, a divine being, the Earth
Ganymede	in Homer, a beautiful human being who was carried of to be a cupbearer of Zeus
Gigantes	in Homer, a race of giants
Gordius	king whose wagon, dedicated to Zeus, was fastened to the yoke by a knot of bark; it was foretold that whoever untied the knot would rule Asia. Alexander the Great cut the Gordian knot with his sword.
Hades	god of the underworld (also called Pluto)
Hamilcar	name given to several Carthaginian generals
Hannibal	247-183 BC; Carthaginian general who invaded Italy in 218 BC
Hebe	goddess of youth

Hecate	goddess of night, magic and the underworld
Hector	eldest son of Priam, king of Troy; he was a heroic warrior but he fled from Achilles, who killed him
Hecuba	wife of Priam and mother of Hector, Paris, Cassandra and many others
Helen	in Homer, the beautiful wife of Menelaus who was carried off to Troy by Paris and thus became the cause of the Trojan war
Helios	Greek god of the sun (called Sol by the Romans)
Hellas	Greece
Hera	wife of Zeus (called Juno by the Romans)
Heracles	legendary warrior, performer of many heroic deeds (called Hercules by the Romans)
Hermaphrodite	son of Hermes and Aphrodite; his body was that of a youth and a nymph combined
Hermes	the gods' messenger; inventor of the lyre (called Mercury by the Romans)
Herodotus	Greek historian; fl. 440 BC
Hesiod	Greek poet; fl. 735 BC
Hesperides	guardians of the golden apples which Ge (Earth) gave to Hera when she married Zeus
Hippocrates	460-357 BC; great Greek physician
Homer	Greek epic poet, author of the Iliad and the Odyssey, fl. 800 BC
Horae	goddesses of the weather, the seasons, clouds, etc.
Horace	65-8 BC; Roman poet and satirist (in Latin, Quintus Horatius Flaccus)
Hygiea	Greek goddess of health
Hymen	Greek and Roman god of marriage
Hyppolyte	queen of the Amazons
Icarus	son of Daedalus
Ilium	Troy
Irene	goddess of peace (called Pax by the Romans)
Iris	in Homer's Iliad, the messenger of the gods
Isis	one of the greatest Egyptian deities
Isocrates	436-338 BC; Athenian orator
Ithaca	island in the Ionian Sea; said to be the birthplace of Odysseus
Janus	Roman god of beginnings; of man's birth, of the year's starting, etc.
Jason	leader of the Argonauts

Jocasta	mother of Oedipus; she married Oedipus, unaware that he was her son
Juno	the Roman version of *Hera*, the queen of the heavens
Jupiter	called *Zeus* by the Greeks; king of the heavens, ruler of the gods
Juvenal	Roman satirist, fl. AD 120
Laertes	king of Ithaca, father of Odysseus
Laocoon	Trojan who warned the people not to pull in the Trojan horse. He and his son were killed by serpents.
Lares	Roman household gods
Laverna	Roman goddess of thieves
Leander	youth who loved Hero, the priestess of Aphrodite. He swam every night across the Hellespont to visit her, and back again to Abydos in the morning, but one night he perished in stormy seas.
Leda	queen of Sparta; Zeus came to her as a swan and she bore two eggs, one yielding Helen and the other Castor and Pollux
Leonidas	king of Sparta 491-480 BC; with a small army he held the pass of Thermopylae against the might of Persia's invading army
Lesbos	large island in the Aegean sea
Lethe	river in the underworld; drinking its water caused the dead to forget all their mortal experiences
Londinium	Roman name for London
Longinus	Greek grammarian of the 3rd century BC
Lucretia	wife of Tarquin
Luna	goddess of the moon (called *Selene* by the Greeks)
Lupercus	god who protected sheep from wolves and caused them to multiply
Manes	spirits of the dead
Marathon	battleplace where the Athenians defeated the Persians in 290 BC
Mars	Roman god of war
Martial	c. AD 40-104; Roman poet
Menander	342-291 BC; Athenian poet
Menelaus	Helen's husband and a leading Greek warrior in the siege of Troy
Mentor	friend and adviser of Odysseus
Mercury	Roman god of commerce; the Roman version of *Hermes*

Midas	king of Phrygia; Dionysus granted him the 'touch of gold'
Milo	great Greek athlete
Minerva	Roman goddess of invention and thought
Minos	king of Crete, resident at Cnossus; when he died he was said to have become a judge in Hades
Minotaur	half-man/half-bull kept in the Labyrinth at Cnossus; slain by Theseus
Mithridates	great king of Pontus c. 130-63 BC
Moira	in Homer, the personification of fate
Morpheus	god of dreams
Mors	Roman god of death; the Greeks called him *Thanatos*
Muses	goddesses of song, poetry, the arts, sciences, etc.
Myrmidons	people who followed Achilles to war against Troy; they were said to have been ants turned into men
Naiads	nymphs of rivers and lakes
Narcissus	beautiful youth who spurned the love of Echo, who died of grief. As a punishment he was made to fall in love with his own reflection.
Necessitas	Roman goddess of inexorable fate
Nemesis	Greek goddess of punishment for wrongdoing
Neptune	Roman god of the sea; the Greeks called him *Poseidon*
Nereids	sea-nymphs
Nero	Roman emperor, AD 54-68
Nessus	centaur shot by Heracles for carrying off his wife Deianira
Nestor	very aged Greek who took part in the siege of Troy
Nike	Greek goddess of victory (called *Victoria* by the Romans)
Niobe	queen of Thebes; her six sons and six daughters were slain by Apollo and Artemis. Niobe was changed into stone, and her tears of grief caused streams to trickle down the rocks.
Notus	South wind
Nox	the Roman personification of night; the Greek version is *Nyx*
Nymphs	spirits inhabiting springs, rivers, trees, etc.
Oceanus	in Homer, the source of all things, even the gods

Odysseus	Homeric hero of the *Odyssey*, an epic poem recounting his adventures as he sailed for home after the destruction of Troy (called *Ulysses* by the Romans)
Oedipus	mythical tragic hero of Greek drama
Olympia	plain in Elis where the Olympic Games were held
Olympus	mountain on which the Greek gods dwelt
Orestes	in Homer and later writers, a hero who struggled against many adversities, including madness
Orion	in Homer, a giant hunter slain by Artemis
Orpheus	mythical composer and lyre player who could enchant wild beasts and even stones and trees with his music. He went to Hades to recover his dead wife Eurydice, but lost her by turning round to see her and thus disobeying the condition by which he had been granted her life.
Ovid	43 BC-AD 18; Roman poet
Paean	in Homer, the gods' physician
Pallas	giant, slain by Athene in a battle with the gods
Pan	god of shepherds and their flocks
Pandora	first woman on earth; she opened the lid of a jar which her husband Epimetheus had been forbidden to open, and all man's evils flew out
Paris	second son of Priam and Hecuba; he carried off Helen and thus caused the Trojan war
Parnassus	sacred mountain where the Muses dwelt
Parthenon	temple of Athena on the Acropolis in Athens
Patroclus	friend of Achilles
Pegasus	winged horse who carried thunder and lightning for Zeus. Bellerophon rode him to kill the Chimaera.
Pelops	grandson of Zeus, and subject of many legends
Penates	household gods in Italy
Penelope	wife of Odysseus. During his absence she held off a horde of suitors by saying she must first finish weaving a robe.
Pericles	great Athenian statesman; fl. 450 BC
Persephone	daughter of Zeus, and queen of the underworld (called *Proserpina* by the Romans)
Perseus	son of Zeus and the subject of many legendary adventures
Petronius Arbiter	friend of Nero, and the author of the *Satyricon*, a work of prose and verse

Phaedra	wife of Theseus
Phaedrus	Epicurean philosopher; fl. 80 BC
Phaeton	son of Helios (the sun) who was killed by Zeus because he recklessly drove the chariot of the sun too near the earth and almost destroyed it
Phidias	c. 490-432 BC; great Greek sculptor
Philip of Macedonia	father of Alexander the Great
Phoenix	in Homer, the father of Europa. Also a mythical bird with red and gold feathers; it was said that when it died a new phoenix rose from the ashes
Pindar	522-442 BC; great lyric poet of Greece
Plato	428-347 BC; great Greek philosopher
Pleiades	daughters of Atlas; after death they were said to become stars
Pliny the Elder	AD 23-79; Roman author of Natural History
Plutarch	biographer and philosopher; fl. AD 66
Polyphemus	one of the Cyclops; in Homer, Odysseus put out his single eye and thus he and his men escaped
Pompeii	Italian city destroyed in AD 79 by the eruption of the volcano Vesuvius
Pompey (Pompeius)	106-48 BC; Roman statesman and soldier
Porsena, Lars	Etruscan king who attacked Rome
Poseidon	god of the sea (called Neptune by the Romans)
Praxitiles	Greek sculptor; fl. 400 BC
Priam	king of Troy at the time of the siege of Troy
Priapus	god of fertility and gardens
Procrustes	the legendary 'Stretcher'; he would lay victims on a bed, and if they were too short for it stretch their limbs, and if they were too tall he would cut them short
Prometheus	god of fire, subject of many myths; he stole fire from Zeus and was chained to a pillar where an eagle eternally tore at his liver
Proteus	legendary old man of the sea; if he was seized he would change into many different forms, but if held firmly enough he would prophesy the future
Psyche	personification of the human soul
Ptolemy	name given to many kings of Egypt
Pygmalion	king of Cyprus; he fell in love with an ivory statue which he had fashioned; Aphrodite brought her to life and they married
Pyrrhus	Greek general who invaded Italy in 280 and 279 BC, but his victories were so costly to him that they were virtually defeats, hence the expression 'Pyrrhic victory'

Pythagoras	fl. 540-510 BC; Greek philosopher famous for his mathematical and religious teachings
Quintilian	c. AD 40-100; great Roman rhetorician
Regulus	Roman statesman and soldier of the 3rd century BC
Rhea	ancient Greek goddess of nature
Romulus	traditional founder of Rome, with his brother Remus
Rubicon	small Italian river, famous because by crossing it with his army Caesar declared war on the Roman republic
Salamis	Greek island off which the Greeks defeated the fleet of the Persian Xerxes in 480 BC
Salus	Roman goddess personifying health and prosperity
Sappho	Greek lyric poetess
Saturn	Roman god of agriculture
Satyrs	demons of mountain forests and streams
Scylla	along with *Charybdis*, mythical sea monsters which devoured sailors and ships
Selene	(called *Luna* by the Romans) goddess of the moon
Seneca	Roman rhetorician of the 1st century BC
Sibyl	name given to various prophetesses in Greek legend
Silenus	one of the male Naiads
Silvanus	god of the countryside, fields, small farmhouses, etc.
Simonides	Greek poet; fl. 660 BC
Sirens	sea-nymphs whose singing lured sailors to their doom
Sisyphus	wicked ruler punished in the after-life by having to roll a rock eternally uphill
Socrates	469-399 BC; great Greek philosopher
Solon	c. 638-558 BC; great Greek lawmaker
Sophocles	495-406 BC; Greek tragic poet
Spartacus	leader of a slave rebellion in 73-71 BC
Spes	personification of hope
Sphinx	female monster in Greek legend; in Egypt, the huge figure of part lion, part human
Strabo	Roman geographer, of the 1st century BC
Styx	main river in the underworld
Tacitus	Roman historian of the 1st century AD
Talos	nephew of Daedalus; credited with the invention of the saw, the chisel, compasses, etc.

Tantalus	son of Zeus, father of Pelops. As a punishment for telling the secrets of Zeus, he was placed in a lake in the underworld with a terrible thirst, but every time he tried to drink the water receded.
Tarquin	kingly family in early Roman history
Terminus	Roman god of frontiers and boundaries
Terpander	fl. 700-650 BC; father of Greek music
Thales	fl. 636-540 BC; Ionic philosopher
Themis	in Homer, the personification of lawful order, custom, justice, and the goddess who convened the assembly of the gods
Themistocles	fl. 520-460 BC; Athenian statesman
Theocritus	Greek poet whose *Idyls* described the ordinary life of peasants
Theophrastus	fl. 300-278 BC; Greek philosopher
Theseus	great legendary hero who slew the Minotaur, carried off the queen of the Amazons, etc.
Thespis	father of Greek tragedy
Thetus	goddess of the sea and mother of Achilles; she could assume any shape she chose
Thisbe	sweetheart of *Pyramus*. As their parents did not approve, they met secretly. Once, at the tomb of Ninus, Thisbe was frightened off by a lioness and left her garment among the remains of an ox killed by the beast. When Pyramus arrived he thought Thisbe had been killed and he committed suicide. Thisbe returned, found his body, and killed herself.
Thucydides	fl. 450-440 BC; Athenian statesman
Tiberius	Roman emperor, AD 14-37
Timon	Athenian misanthrope (hero of Shakespeare's play, *Timon of Athens*)
Tiresias	blind soothsayer of Greek legends
Titans	twelve sons and daughters of Uranus and Gaea; among them were Oceanus, Phoebe, Hyperion and Themis
Triton	son of Poseidon; he lived in a golden palace at the bottom of the sea. His lower body was that of a fish. He would ride over the sea on a seahorse and blow a shell-trumpet.
Troy (or *Ilium*)	city ruled by Priam and besieged by the Greeks in the war described in Homer's *Iliad*
Ulixes	another name for *Ulysses* or *Odysseus*
Uranus	husband of Gaea

Vandals	German peoples who invaded Spain in AD 409 and sacked Rome in AD 455
Venti	four winds — Boreas (North), Eurus (East), Notus (South), and Zephyrus (West)
Venus	Roman goddess of love
Virgil	70-19 BC; Roman poet, author of the *Aeneid*, the *Eclogues*, the *Georgics*, etc.
Vespasian	Roman emperor, AD 70-79
Vesuvius	volcanic mountain in Campania, Italy
Xanthippe	wife of Socrates
Xenocrates	396-314 BC; Greek philosopher
Xenophon	Greek general in the wars against the Persians in the 4th century BC
Xerxes	king of Persia 485-465 BC; he invaded Greece with a huge army, but was defeated at the battle of Salamis
Zeno	founder of the Stoic school of philosophy
Zenobia	queen of Palmyra *c.* AD 260
Zephyrus	West wind
Zeus	king of the gods (called *Jupiter* by the Romans)

SPORTS AND GAMES

Angling   The sport of fishing. There are three types of angling: *game fishing* (for salmon, trout and large salt-water fish), *sea fishing*, and *coarse fishing* (for 'inferior fish' such as bream, pike, roach).

Archery   The shooting of arrows at targets. *Target archery* involves shooting at static targets at measured distances. *Field archery* involves shooting at targets placed at varying points and distances.

Athletics Competitive running, jumping, throwing, etc. *Track events* include sprinting, middle-distance and long-distance running, hurdling over obstacles, steeplechasing, etc. *Field events* include the high jump, the long jump, the pole vault and throwing the shot, hammer, discus and javelin. *All-round events* are a combination of various track and field events. *Marathon running* requires a run of 26 miles 385 yards. *Race walking* is a less popular sport.

Badminton	Striking a shuttlecock (made with feathers) across a net with a racket. A game of old English origin, first played in its modern form at Badminton, the home of the Duke of Beaufort. Badminton is now a favourite indoor sport in Britain, USA, Asia, Scandinavia, etc.
Baseball	A game based on striking a ball around a field with the use of a bat. Developed from the old English game of rounders. Baseball is now played mainly in the USA and Japan, and to a lesser extent in Australia.
Basketball	A five-a-side game played in a gymnasium, requiring the dropping of a round ball through a net basket placed at either end of the court. Immensely popular throughout the world. Basketball was invented in the USA in 1891 and remains a favourite sport in America.
Billiard Table Games	*Billiards* in the modern form developed in England towards the end of the 18th century. It is played on a table about 12 feet by 6 feet with three balls, the object being to strike one ball with a cue (length between 3 feet and 4 feet 10 inches) to score by 'potting' a ball into pockets around the table or by 'cannons' which result from the cue ball touching the other two. In *Snooker* the cue ball is struck to pot 21 coloured balls, 15 of which are red and the others black, pink, blue, brown, green and yellow. *Pool* is a variation of snooker using 15 coloured and numbered balls and a white cue ball. Pool is an American game but is increasingly popular in Britain, partly because it requires a smaller table.
Bowls	Played on a lawn (or 'rink'), the game requires the rolling of wooden balls towards a small white ball, or 'jack', aiming to finish nearest to the jack.
Bowling	Ten-pin bowling is played in an indoor 'alley'. The object is to roll a ball down a wooden 'lane' to knock down 10 skittles or 'pins'.
Boules	A French game similar to bowls, but using metal balls which are thrown, not rolled, at a metal jack.
Boxing	A man-to-man fighting sport. Boxing is a world-wide spectator sport. The modern version is based on rules drawn up by the Marquess of Queensberry in 1867. In *professional*

boxing the contestants wear regulation sized gloves and fight for a prescribed number of 'rounds' in a ring between 14 and 20 feet square.

Canoeing

Participants row small slim boats and undertake various activities in water. *Competitive canoeing* was begun in the 1860s by a Scottish sportsman, John MacGregor. In the 1930s *slalom racing* was developed in Austria. Canoeing began as an Olympic sport in 1936.

Cricket

An old-established English sport now played in Australia, the West Indies, India, Pakistan, New Zealand and other former or present members of the British Commonwealth. With 11 players on each of two teams, the game is played in a field containing a pitch 22 yards in length. At each end of the pitch stands a wicket consisting of three stumps 28 inches high. Two batsmen defend these wickets and aim to score runs by striking a leather ball which is bowled by players of the opposing team. A run is scored when the two batsmen cross and reach their ground at the opposite wicket. There is an elaborate set of rules governing the game, and a high degree of skill is needed by all the players. A game may last one, two, three or five days. *International Test Matches* are played annually in the major cricketing countries.

Croquet

A game played on a lawn. Two or four players compete by striking balls with a mallet to run through hoops.

Curling

Played on ice, the game consists of sliding stones towards a target circle. Originating in Scotland, curling is now increasingly popular in Canada, the USA, Scandinavia and other European countries.

Cycling

A sport taking various forms. *Road racing* involves cycling from stage to stage along roads. *Track racing* includes sprints, pursuiting, time trial and motor paced races. *Sprints* are contests of speed timed over the last 200 metres, the first period being occupied by the riders jockeying for position against one another. *Pursuiting* requires the riders to chase one another over a set distance (from 3000 metres). In *time trial* racing the riders leave the starting post at different times and the winner is the rider who completes the set distance in the fastest time. In *motor paced* races the cyclist is partnered by a motor-cycle. A world-wide sport, cycling is now included in the Olympics.

Darts	A game which comprises throwing darts at a target board. Darts is now vastly popular in Britain (where it features regularly on TV) and is increasingly played in other countries. It is closely associated with public houses.
Equestrian Sports	*Show jumping* is a new sport, involving horse-jumping over a variety of fences. This is increasing as a spectator attraction (often on TV) in Britain, Germany, France and the USA. *Horse trials* are a series of events held over three days, often referred to as *eventing*. *Dressage* is the art of riding a horse through a sequence of movements.
Fencing	A sword-play sport using a foil, épée or sabre. An old sport developed particularly in France and Germany, fencing became an Olympic sport in 1936.
Football	*Association Football*, or *Soccer*, is an 11-a-side sport in which a round ball is kicked towards goals erected on a pitch which varies in size between 50 × 100 yards and 100 × 130 yards. Probably the most popular spectator sport throughout the world, soccer is played in almost every country. *American Football*, which is played almost exclusively in the USA, is played between teams of 11 players with an oval-shaped ball. *Canadian Football* is very similar but is played by 12-a-side teams. *Australian Rules Football* is played on a large oval field with 18 players in each of two teams. *Gaelic Football* uses a round ball and has 15 players a side. *Rugby Union* is played in Britain, France, Australia, New Zealand, South Africa, Japan and other countries. 15-a-side teams compete by passing an oval ball, as in American and other forms of football. *Rugby League* is a version of this game popular in the English midlands and in Australia. It is played by 13-a-side teams.
Gliding	Flying a light unpowered aircraft by using air currents.
Golf	Invented in Scotland, golf is played over a stretch of countryside specially landscaped to provide smooth-grassed fairways, patches of rough grassland, sand-filled hazards and smooth flat greens. Any number of players can compete, usually in twos or foursomes. It is essentially a simple game consisting of hitting a small ball with a club until it can be putted into a hole in the green; but it requires a very high level of skill and in its professional and international forms it has

become one of the most popular spectator sports in many countries. In Britain, the USA, Australia, Japan and other developed countries, golf has become a favourite amateur pastime.

Gymnastics

Particularly popular in the USSR, East Germany, Rumania and Japan, gymnastics comprises exercises on apparatus such as parallel bars, rings, horse, beam, etc. and on mats. The sport was included in the first modern Olympics in 1896.

Handball Games

Indoor Handball is played 7-a-side on a court varying in size from 38 × 18 metres to 44 × 22 metres with goals at either end. Players score goals by throwing a round ball into the opposing goal. There are three forms of *wall handball: soft-ball four-wall, soft-ball one-wall,* and *hard-ball four-wall* (played in Ireland). *Eton Fives, Winchester Fives* and *Rugby Fives* are variations played in England.

Hang Gliding

Gliding by means of a wing stretched over a light framework, from which the pilot hangs in a harness.

Hockey

A field game comprising 11-a-side teams hitting a ball with sticks towards opposing goals. The rules are similar to those of soccer. Now an Olympic sport, hockey is popular in Britain, India, Pakistan, Australia and other countries formerly associated with the British Commonwealth. *Hurling* is a variation played in Ireland, and *Shinty* is a Scottish variant.

Horse Riding

Known as 'the sport of kings', horse racing is pursued in Britain, the USA, France, Australia and many other countries. *Steeplechasing* requires horses to jump fences. *Harness Racing* involves horse-and-vehicle events.

Ice Hockey

Popular in Canada, USA and Britain, ice hockey is played 6-a-side by skaters, in specially constructed ice-rinks. Players aim at striking a 'puck' with sticks into their opponents' goal.

Judo

A form of wrestling originating in Japan. The sport was included in the Olympics in 1964.

Karate

A form of unarmed combat which originated in Japan and is now popular throughout Europe.

Lacrosse

Played in Britain, the USA, and Australia, this is a 10-a-side game requiring the movement of a rubber ball with a '*crosse*' (stick with a net at the end).

Netball	A 7-a-side game played mainly by women. It comprises passing a soccer-type ball towards a basket, as in basketball.
Polo	A horse-riders' game developed by the British in India. Two teams of four players strike a hard white ball with mallets towards goalposts.
Shooting	*Clay Pigeon Shooting* requires competitors to shoot at saucer-shaped discs propelled into the air. *Skeet* is a variant invented in the USA in 1932. *Full-bore Target* shooting and other forms consist of shooting at static targets. Various forms have been included in the Olympic games for many years.
Skiing	Travelling on skis on snow, this is now an Olympic sport. *Downhill skiing* is a time-measured dash down a specially designed slope. The *slalom* involves weaving around poles set at intervals in the snow. Skiing is immensely popular in Germany, Austria, Italy, France and the USA. In Britain it is becoming popular due to the building of dry nylon slopes.
Speedway	A form of motor-cycle racing, this is a spectator sport which attracts a following in the USA, Britain and Scandinavia.
Squash	Played by striking a ball against a wall in a specially built court, this is a fast and exciting participant sport, increasingly popular in Britain and the USA.
Surfing	An increasingly popular sport in warm coastal areas, this is riding a surfboard along waves in the sea. *Windsurfing* involves a similar board equipped with a sail.
Swimming	Included since the 1896 Olympic Games, this is a sport popular throughout the world. Competitive forms are the *breaststroke*, the *crawl*, the *backstroke* and the *butterfly stroke*.
Table Tennis	This game evolved from 'ping pong', a parlour game. Played by two or four competitors at a special table, it consists of striking a small white celluloid ball over a net, with round bats.
Tennis	Now a world-wide professional sport and amateur pastime, the game was developed in England in the 19th century. Two or four players strike a ball with a racket across a net, and score points in accordance with a long-established scheme of scoring. Tennis can be played on grass, on hard-surfaced courts or indoor courts.

Trampolining   A form of acrobatics performed by jumping on a
                tightly-sprung bed.

Volleyball   Developed in the USA, this is a 6-a-side game involving
                hitting a ball over a net.

Water Polo   An 11-a-side game requiring the passing of a ball towards
                goals set at each end of the pool.

Water Skiing   Travelling on skis over water, on the sea or a lake.

Weightlifting   An Olympic sport since 1920, this is the competitive lifting of
                heavy bars of various weights.

Wrestling   A man-to-man contest requiring each competitor to 'throw'
                his opponent. It was included in the first modern Olympics in
                1896, and is now a popular professional spectator sport in
                Britain.

Yacht Racing   An old-established pursuit for sailors, involving many classes
                of sail boat. Yachting can be a very costly pursuit requiring
                expensive boats and crews with great experience and skill,
                but it can also be an inexpensive sport for amateurs using
                comparatively cheaply-made craft.

THE WORLD'S COUNTRIES, CAPITALS & CURRENCIES

CONTINENT	COUNTRY	POPULATION (millions)	CAPITAL CITY	CURRENCY
Africa	Algeria	17.3	Algiers	dinar/centimes
	Angola	6.4	Luanda	kwanza/iweis
	Benin	3.2	Porto Novo	franc
	Botswana	0.7	Gabarone	pula/thebe
	Burundi	3.9	Bujumbura	franc
	Cameroun	6.5	Yaoundé	franc
	Cape Verde Islands (Atlantic)	0.3	Sao Vicente	Cape Verde escudo
	Central African Empire	1.8	Bangui	franc

CONTINENT	COUNTRY	POPULATION (millions)	CAPITAL CITY	CURRENCY
Africa	Chad	4.1	N'Djamena	franc
	Comoro Islands (Indian Ocean)	0.3	Moroni	franc
	Congo	1.4	Bangui	franc
	Djibouti	0.1	Djibouti	franc
	Egypt	38.1	Cairo	pound/piastres
	Equatorial Guinea	0.3	Bata	ekuele
	Ethiopia	28.6	Addis Ababa	dollar
	Gabon	0.5	Libreville	franc
	Gambia	0.5	Banjul	dalasi/bututs
	Ghana	10.1	Accra	cedi/pesewas
	Guinea	4.5	Conakry	syli
	Guinea-Bissau	0.5	Bissau	franc
	Ivory Coast	6.8	Abidjan	franc
	Kenya	15	Nairobi	shilling/cents
	Lesotho	1.1	Maseru	rand/cents
	Liberia	1.6	Monrovia	dollar/cents
	Libya	2.5	Tripoli	dinar/dirhams
	Malagasy Republic	7.7	Antananarivo	franc
	Malawi	6	Lilongwe	kwacha/tambala
	Mali	5.8	Bamako	franc
	Mauritania	1.3	Nouakchott	ouguiya/khoums
	Mauritius (Indian Ocean)	0.9	Port Louis	rupee/cents
	Mozambique	9.3	Maputo	metical
	Namibia	0.9	Windhoek	rand
	Niger	4.7	Niamey	franc
	Nigeria	94	Lagos	naira/kobo
	Reunion (Indian Ocean)	0.5	St Denis	franc (French)
	Rwanda	4.4	Kigali	franc
	St Helena (Atlantic)	small	Jamestown	St Helena pound
	Sao Tomé e Principe (Atlantic)	0.1	Sao Tomé	dobra
	Senegal	4.5	Dakar	franc
	Seychelles (Indian Ocean)	0.06	Victoria	Seychelles rupee

CONTINENT	COUNTRY	POPULATION (millions)	CAPITAL CITY	CURRENCY
Africa	Sierra Leone	3.1	Freetown	leone/cents
	Somali			
	Republic	3.2	Mogadishu	shilling/cents
	South Africa	26.7	Pretoria	rand/cents
	Sudan	18.2	Khartoum	pound/piastres
	Swaziland	0.5	Mbabane	lilangeni/cents
	Tanzania	15.6	Dodoma	shilling/cents
	Togo	2.3	Lomé	franc
	Tunisia	5.9	Tunis	dinar/millimes
	Uganda	11.9	Kampala	shilling/cents
	Upper Volta			
	(Bourkina Fasso)	6.2	Ouagadougou	franc
	Zaire	25.6	Kinshasa	zaire/makuta
	Zambia	5.1	Lusaka	kwacha
	Zimbabwe	6.5	Harare	dollar/cents
North	Antigua	0.07	St John's	dollar/cents
America	Bahamas, The	0.2	Nassau	dollar/cents
(including	Barbados	0.2	Bridgetown	dollar/cents
Central	Belize	0.1	Belmopan	dollar/cents
America,	Bermuda	0.06	Hamilton	dollar/cents
Caribbean)	British Virgin			
	Islands	0.01	Road Town	dollar/cents
	Canada	23.1	Ottawa	dollar/cents
	Cayman			
	Islands	0.01	Georgetown	dollar/cents
	Costa Rica	2	San José	colón/centimos
	Cuba	9.7	Havana	peso/centavos
	Dominica	0.08	Roseau	dollar/cents
	Dominican			
	Republic	5.6	Santo Domingo	peso/centavos
	El Salvador	4.5	San Salvador	colón/centavos
	Grenada	0.1	St George's	dollar/cents
	Guadeloupe	0.4	Pointe-à-Pitre	franc/centimes
	Guatemala	6.8	Guatemala City	quetzal/centavos
	Haiti	6.0	Port-au-Prince	gourde/centimes
	Honduras	3.5	Tegucigalpa	lempira/centavos
	Jamaica	2.2	Kingston	dollar/cents
	Martinique	0.3	Fort-de-France	franc/centimes
	Mexico	62.3	Mexico City	peso/centavos

CONTINENT	COUNTRY	POPULATION (millions)	CAPITAL CITY	CURRENCY
North America (including Central America, Caribbean)	Montserrat	0.01	Plymouth	dollar/cents
	Netherlands Antilles	0.2	Willemstad	guilder/cents
	Nicaragua	2.7	Managua	cordoba/centavos
	Panama	1.7	Panama City	balboa/cents
	Puerto Rico	3.2	San Juan	dollar/cents
	St Kitts, Nevis and Anguilla	0.07	Basseterre	dollar/cents
	St Lucia	0.1	Castries	dollar/cents
	St Vincent	0.1	Kingstown	dollar/cents
	Trinidad and Tobago	1.1	Port-of-Spain	dollar/cents
	Turks and Caicos Islands	small	Grand Turk	dollar/cents
	United States of America	215.3	Washington	dollar/cents
South America	Argentina	25.7	Buenos Aires	peso/centavos
	Bolivia	5.8	La Paz	peso/centavos
	Brazil	110.2	Brasilia	cruzeiro/centavos
	Chile	10.8	Santiago	new peso/old escudos
	Colombia	23	Bogotá	peso/centavos
	Ecuador	6.9	Quito	sucre/centavos
	Falkland Islands	small	Stanley	pound/pence
	Guiana, French	0.05	Cayenne	franc
	Guyana	0.8	Georgetown	dollar/cents
	Paraguay	2.6	Asuncion	guarani/centimos
	Peru	16	Lima	sol/centavos
	Surinam	0.4	Paramaribo	guilder/cents
	Uruguay	2.8	Montevideo	peso/centésimos
	Venezuela	12.3	Caracas	bolivar/centimos
Asia	Afghanistan	19.5	Kabul	afghani/puls
	Bahrain	0.2	Manama	dinar/fils
	Bangladesh	76.1	Dakar	taka/paise
	Bhutan	1.2	Timphu	ngultrum

CONTINENT	COUNTRY	POPULATION (millions)	CAPITAL CITY	CURRENCY
Asia	Brunei	0.18	Bhandar Seri Begawan	dollar/sen
	Burma	31.2	Rangoon	kyat/pyas
	China	1000	Peking	yuan/fen
	Hong Kong	4.4	Victoria	Hong Kong dollar
	India	620.7	New Delhi	rupee/paise
	Indonesia	135.4	Djakarta	rupiah/sen
	Iran	34.1	Tehrán	rial/dinars
	Iraq	11.4	Baghdád	dinar/fils
	Israel	3.5	Jerusalem	pound/agorot
	Japan	112.3	Tokyo	yen
	Jordan	2.8	Amman	dinar/fils
	Kampuchea	8.3	Phnom Penh	riel/sen
	Korea, North	16.3	Pyongyang	won/jun
	Korea, South	34.8	Seoul	won/jun
	Kuwait	1.1	Kuwait City	dinar/fils
	Laos	3.4	Ventiane	kip/ats
	Lebanon	2.7	Beirut	pound/piastres
	Malaysia	12.4	Kuala Lumpur	dollar/cents
	Maldives	0.1	Malé	rupee/laris
	Mongolia	1.5	Ulan Bator	tugrik/mongö
	Nepal	12.9	Katmandu	rupee/pice
	Oman	0.8	Muscat	rial/baiza
	Pakistan	72.5	Islamabad	rupee/paise
	Philippines	44	Manila	peso/centavos
	Qatar	0.1	Doha	riyal/dirhams
	Saudi Arabia	6.4	Riyadh	riyal/qursh
	Singapore	2.5	Singapore	dollar/cents
	Sri Lanka	14	Colombo	rupee/cents
	Syria	7.6	Damascus	pound/piastres
	Taiwan	16.3	Taipei	yuan/fen
	Thailand	43.3	Bangkok	baht/satangs
	Turkey	40.2	Ankara	lira/kurus
	Union of Soviet Socialist Republics	257	Moscow	rouble/copecks
	United Arab Emirates	0.2	Abu Dhabi	dirham/fils
	Vietnam	46.4	Hanoi	dong/xu
	Yemen Arab Republic	6.9	San'a	riyal/bogaches
	Yemen PDR	1.7	Aden	dinar/fils

CONTINENT	COUNTRY	POPULATION (millions)	CAPITAL CITY	CURRENCY
Europe	Albania	2.5	Tiranë	lek/qindarka
	Andorra	0.03	Andorra	franc (French) & peseta (Spanish)
	Austria	7.5	Vienna	schilling/groschen
	Belgium	9.8	Brussels	franc/centimes
	Bulgaria	8.8	Sofia	lev/stotinki
	Cyprus	0.7	Nicosia	pound/mils
	Czechoslovakia	14.9	Prague	koruna/haleru
	Denmark	5.1	Copenhagen	krone/öre
	Faroe Islands	0.04	Thorshavn	krone
	Finland	4.7	Helsinki	markka/penniä
	France	53.1	Paris	franc/centimes
	Germany, Democratic Republic	16.8	Berlin	mark/pfennings
	Germany, Federal Republic	62.1	Bonn	mark/pfennings
	Greece	9	Athens	drachma/lepta
	Greenland	0.05	Godthaals	krone
	Hungary	10.6	Budapest	forint/fillér
	Iceland	0.2	Reykjavik	krona/aurar
	Ireland	3.1	Dublin	pound/pence
	Italy	56.3	Rome	lira
	Liechtenstein	0.02	Vaduz	franc (Swiss)
	Luxembourg	0.4	Luxembourg	franc/centimes
	Malta	0.3	Valletta	pound/cents
	Monaco	0.02	Monte Carlo	franc (French)
	Netherlands	13.8	The Hague	guilder/cents
	Norway	4	Oslo	krone/öre
	Poland	34.4	Warsaw	zloty/groszy
	Portugal	8.5	Lisbon	escudo/centavos
	Rumania	21.5	Bucharest	leu/bani
	Spain	36	Madrid	peseta/centimos
	Sweden	8.2	Stockholm	krona/öre
	Switzerland	6.5	Bern	franc/centimes
	Turkey	40.2	Ankara	lira/kurus
	United Kingdom	56.1	London	pound/pence
	Yugoslavia	21.5	Belgrade	dinar/paras

CONTINENT	COUNTRY	POPULATION (millions)	CAPITAL CITY	CURRENCY
Oceania	Australia	13.8	Canberra	dollar/cents
(Austral-	Fiji	0.6	Suva	dollar/cents
asia and	Gilbert Islands	0.07	Tarawa	Australian dollar
Pacific)	Guam	0.1	Agana	dollar/cents
	Nauru	small	Nauru	dollar/cents
	New Caledonia	0.1	Noumea	franc
	New Hebrides	small	Vila	franc
	New Zealand	3.2	Wellington	dollar/cents
	Papua New Guinea	2.8	Port Moresby	dollar
	Pitcairn Islands	small	—	pound & New Zealand dollar
	Solomon Islands	0.2	Honiara	dollar/cents
	Tonga	0.1	Nuku'alofa	pa'anga/seniti
	Tuvalu	small	—	Australian dollar
	Western Samoa	0.1	Apia	tala/sene

12 FURTHER REFERENCES

The following have proved useful in the establishment of lists for this book, and are recommended for further reference:

A Communicative Grammar of English ..... G. LEECH and J. SVARTVIK (Longman 1975)

A Dictionary of Literary Terms .... J. A. CUDDON (Penguin Books 1982)

A Pocket Guide to Written English .... M. TEMPLE (John Murray 1978)

A Study of English .... W. A. GATHERER (Heinemann Educational Books 1980)

Beyond the Dictionary in English .... V. KAY and P. STREVENS (Cassell 1978)

British and American English .... P. STREVENS (Cassell 1978)

Business Dictionary .... B. McKENNA and A. M. FLEMING (Collins 1974)

Common Mistakes in English .... T. J. FITIKIDES (Longman 1963)

Dictionary of Abbreviations .... N. MARSHALL (Collins 1980)

Dictionary of Biography .... ed. J. MALLORY (Collins 1971)

Dictionary of Computers .... A. CHANDOR (Penguin Books 1977)

Dictionary of English Idioms .... (Longman 1979)

Dictionary of Management .... D. FRENCH and H. SAWARD (Pan Books 1977)

Dictionary of Science .... E. B. UVAROV, D. R. CHAPMAN, A. ISAACS (Penguin Books 1979)

Encyclopedia of Sport .... N. BARRETT (Purnell Books 1974)

English in Use .... G. M. SPANKIE (Nelson 1975)

Everyman's Dictionary of Literary Biography D. C. BROWNING (J. M. Dent & Sons 1982)

Everyman's Factfinder .... ed. M. W. DEMPSEY (J. M. Dent & Sons 1982)

Oxford Companion to English Literature .... ed. P. HARVEY (Oxford 1958)

Payton's Proper Names .... G. PAYTON (Frederick Warne 1969)

Pocket Science Dictionary .... (Longman 1982)

Smaller Slang Dictionary .... E. PARTRIDGE (Routledge & Kegan Paul 1964)

The New Penguin World Atlas .... ed. P. HALL (Penguin Books 1979)

Webster's Thesaurus .... (Merriam 1976)

INDEX